Dracula
the Novel & the Legend

Books by Clive Leatherdale

Literary Criticism
   Dracula: The Novel and the Legend
     A Study of Bram Stoker's Gothic Masterpiece (Desert Island Books)
   The Origins of Dracula
     The Background to Bram Stoker's Gothic Masterpiece (William Kimber)

Travel
   The Virgin Whore – and Other Chinese Characters
     Travels & Traumas (Desert Island Books)
   To Dream of Pigs
     Travels in South and North Korea (Desert Island Books)

International Relations
   Britain and Saudi Arabia 1925-1939: The Imperial Oasis (Frank Cass)

Sport
   England's Quest for the World Cup – A Complete Record (Methuen)
   Scotland's Quest for the World Cup – A Complete Record (John Donald)
   The Aberdeen Football Companion (John Donald)

Education
   So You Want to Teach English to Foreigners (Abacus Press)

DRACULA

THE NOVEL & THE LEGEND

A Study of Bram Stoker's Gothic Masterpiece

(revised edition)

CLIVE LEATHERDALE

**DESERT ISLAND
BOOKS**

First published 1985 by The Aquarian Press

This revised edition published
in 1993 by
DESERT ISLAND BOOKS
31 George Street, Brighton, East Sussex BN2 1RH

British Library Cataloguing-in-Publication Data.
A catalogue record for this book is available from
the British library.

ISBN 1-874287-04-X

Set in 11 pt Times
Printed and bound by Antony Rowe Ltd, Chippenham, Wiltshire

Contents

Acknowledgments

1993 is a fitting year to publish this revised edition of *Dracula: the Novel & the Legend*, for it marks the centenary of the evil Count's demise. Bram Stoker tells us that 1893 was the fateful year that Dracula brought his pestilence to England.

I was helped by many in writing the first edition of this book. Bruce Wightman and Bernard Davies, co-founders of the Dracula Society, welcomed me among its ranks and made available to me the Society's archive material. Leslie Shepard guided me around Stoker's Dublin, and Richard Dalby also gave useful information.

Dr Paul Dukes, now Professor of History, and Dr Robert Lawson-Peebles, both of the University of Aberdeen, keenly followed my progress. Julia Kruk of the Dracula Society and Pauline Huntington read and challenged every word I wrote.

The kindly staff of the Rosenbach Museum and Library, Philadelphia, permitted me to consult Bram Stoker's working notes in their delightful reading room. The people of Transylvania fuelled the imagination by being themselves.

I was encouraged by the book's reception to write *The Origins of Dracula* (1987). We are now advised of the dawning of a new age of Gothic consciousness. It therefore gives me much personal satisfaction to present this revised edition to those who share my fascination with the vampire king. My thanks to Julia Johnson.

Needless to say, I owe a continuing debt to Bram Stoker for providing the sternest challenge to the imagination and the intellect. I hope I have done him justice. If I have not, the responsibility lies solely with me.

Clive Leatherdale

Enquiries to the Dracula Society may be made to:
 The Secretary
 The Dracula Society
 36 Ellison House
 100 Wellington Street
 LONDON SE18 6QF

Introduction

If he were alive today, Bram Stoker would be an unhappy though undeniably rich man. He would be rich because his novel *Dracula* has never been out of print since it was first published in 1897. There are those who claim it to be the second highest selling book of all time, outstripped only by the Bible.[1] *Dracula* has been translated into numerous languages, and the image of 'the Count' is familiar the world over. He is part of the landscape of a universal culture: the black cape, the dripping fangs, the scream of terror ...

Bram Stoker would be unhappy because the creation of his pen has been overtaken and habitually trivialized by the creation of the cinema, which has escaped the censure of his furious intervention. A regular answer to the question 'Have you read Dracula?' is 'No, but I saw the film.' The consequence of the cinema's prurient debasement of Stoker's novel and complete domination of the public Dracula image is that while 'Dracula' has become a household name, his creator remains a household nobody. One of the world's best-known books was written by one of its least-known authors. As an object of serious critical study the novel has been, until quite recently, almost totally ignored. If the book is like the films, it is asked, what could it hold of serious interest? As one critic has commented: 'Only a few years ago, to write about Dracula meant being taken for an eccentric loafer, and one's main worry was to prove that one's work was legitimate.'[2]

It remains the case that serious examination of supernatural fiction frequently sidesteps *Dracula*. The wholesale dismissal of the novel borders on the extraordinary. It is akin to discarding Plato from the study of Western philosophy, for *Dracula* is almost *the* Gothic novel *par excellence*, and has given rise to arguably the most potent literary myth of the twentieth century. A N Wilson, in his introduction to the Oxford University Press edition of *Dracula*, decries Stoker as an author, yet still concedes that 'with *Dracula* he composed, indeed, one of the World's Classics'.[3]

An outline of the novel is easily told. A young solicitor, Jonathan Harker, travels to a remote castle in Transylvania to finalize arrangements with a local nobleman, Count Dracula, for the purchase of an estate near London. While Harker is left behind, imprisoned, Dracula journeys to England by sea, landing at Whitby where he encounters his first victim in beautiful, privileged Lucy Westenra. To Dracula's ultimate misfortune, she is well connected. She has three suitors: Arthur Holmwood, Quincey Morris and Dr Seward, the last of whom summons the services of his old master, Professor Van Helsing, in a futile attempt to treat Lucy's malaise. Perchance, her best friend, Mina, is the wife of Jonathan Harker. Abetted by Renfield, one of the inmates at Dr Seward's lunatic asylum, Dracula 'visits' Mina. Shortly afterwards he is nearly cornered in Piccadilly and flees the country for the sanctuary of his castle, to where, in the climax of the novel, he is pursued.

If that were all there is to *Dracula* then, indeed, it would not demand closer attention. But it is not all. First there is the question of 'authenticity' – Stoker's known researches into folklore, the occult and much else. Wilson remarks: 'It would seem likely that he did some – but very little – research for his fantasy'.[4] To read such a statement in a prestigious edition of *Dracula* over a decade after the discovery in a Philadelphia repository of three packages of Stoker's surviving working notes, detailing over a period of six years many of his researches for his novel-to-be, requires some forbearance. Whatever *Dracula*'s shortcomings, allegations of lack of research on Stoker's part cannot be sustained.

Equally worthy of attention is the breadth of vision that *Dracula* attains. It can be read on many levels. Like all 'classics', every fresh reading unearths new insights, new puzzles. With little in the way of previous full-length interpretations to build upon, the present book has many functions to fulfil in seeking to explore

Dracula. The analysis that follows falls into three sections. First, the ground is prepared by exploring the notion of 'vampires', and their place in European folklore and literature; surveying the life and works of Bram Stoker; and examining what can be deduced about the origins of *Dracula*. Second, turning to the novel itself, each of Stoker's major characters will be put under the microscope. This is intended to clarify what type of creature *Dracula* was, and outline the functions of the novel's mortal cast. Third, we shall embark upon five alternative readings of the novel – allegories that transcend the basic ingredients of vampire, victims, and avengers. *Dracula* can be read as an instrument of sexual repression; it yields readily to Freudian psychoanalysis; it is a testament to the perceived arbitrary power of Christ; it pays homage to occult and literary myths in the shape of the Tarot and the Holy Grail; and it opens a window on the social and political tensions operating in late Victorian Britain. The novel also provides ready-made myths for twentieth-century consumption: *Dracula* has been turned into a manifesto for Marxist economic theory and provides a dark analogue of the Cold War.

At the very least, one aspiration of the present book is to awaken interest in a novel for too long unjustly ignored and contemptuously pushed aside. *Dracula* is not lacking in fertile imagination, complexity of plot or an unsurpassed capacity to send a chill down the spine. In cultural terms it deserves to be treated as a major work of fiction, for *Dracula* possesses that rarest of attributes – an invitation to be read and re-read, each time disclosing fresh glimpses of insight and further layers of meaning and symbolism.

---

[1] This claim is found in several sources, among them Grigore Nandris, 'The Historical Dracula': The Theme of his Legend in the Western and in the Eastern Literatures of Europe'. p.369. The claim is, of course, impossible to substantiate.

[2] Franco Moretti, *Signs Taken for Wonders: Essays in the Sociology of Literary Forms*, pp.15-16.

[3] A N Wilson (introduction), *Dracula* (Oxford University Press, 1983), p.x.

[4] ibid.

1

The Vampire

In all the darkest pages of the malign supernatural there is no more horrible tradition than that of the vampire, a pariah even among demons. Foul are his ravages; gruesome and seemingly barbaric are the ancient and approved methods by which folk must rid themselves of this hideous pest.

Montague Summers,
The Vampire: His Kith and Kin, p.ix.

The modern imagination does not afford much respect to the notion of the vampire. Over-exposure to the cult of the horror cinema, and the commercial exploitation of a tried and tested money spinner, has filled our collective consciousness with a sensationalist pastiche of blood, fangs, black cloaks, and sharpened stakes. The word 'vampire' may invite a laugh or a smirk, where in previous centuries it instilled terror.

Few societies in the past were without their own version of the vampire. Its gradual disappearance from the active superstitions around the world is attributable to many factors. Science has much to answer for, not least for the invention of the electric light, which pierces the shadows of the deepest recesses and denies the shapes of our imaginings their hiding places. Night has lost its mysteries, its secrets, its fears. Were science to have lagged in its headlong rush to annihilate our fantasies, no doubt we should still acknowledge the realm of the vampire, for its intellectual foundations are by no means illogical or incoherent. The concept of the vampire is founded upon two precepts: the belief in life after death, and the magical power of blood.

The biological and mystical significance of blood was recognized by the earliest human communities. They knew nothing of viruses or bacteria, or other organisms which can debilitate or kill, but one cause of death was easily ascertained, for it depended on no more than simple observation. From injuries sustained in battle or by accident, through the torn flesh seeped a strange, mysterious, bright red fluid. Lose enough of it and you died. No other bodily fluid was endowed with such power.

The sight of blood was the sight of death, and therein lies the basic emotion it evokes – fear. Human strength and health reside within blood. It is the elixir of life, the child's first nourishment in the mother's womb. From awareness that blood was essential to life, it was but a short step to the belief that it was synonymous with life. The 'soul' of a living creature lay within its veins. Blood was not only life, it was soul – and therefore an object of magic and taboo. A perverse logic then intervened. If emission of blood weakens and destroys, it surely followed that consumption of that magic ichor could restore, rejuvenate, bring back life. If blood was life, then absorbing blood was absorbing life – and soul.

This 'logical' deduction resulted in widely comparable patterns of human behaviour. Blood came to form the basis of medical care. As their scientific nature was unknown, diseases were presumed to be the consequence of a sinful life and the displeasure of the gods. This necessitated the spilling of the sufferer's bad blood, both as cure and repentance. The curative 'bleeding' of patients survives to the twentieth century in societies that would resent the label 'primitive'. Since antiquity, crude blood transfusions from the healthy to the sick have been performed, and an ancient prescribed remedy for leprosy was to bathe in blood. Warriors in battle would drink the warm blood of the slain, not only as a gesture of domination and possession, but in the belief that the victim's strength and courage would pass into the victor. Blood could also act as fertilizer and be sprinkled over crops; it was endowed with cosmetic properties and would be generously smeared over the skin; and it would be ceremonially mingled between comrades, even today, in the practice of 'blood brothers'.

Preoccupation with this magic substance provides the first prerequisite for belief in vampirism. The second is 'death', as fear-provoking as blood. Its force is irresistible. Death always wins, for no one can fend it off indefinitely. It claims its victims indiscriminately. Throughout history unseen aggressive forces

14

have been held responsible for all deaths, the violent and the calm. Dying could only be the product of a ruthless assailant, seen or unseen, who managed to overpower the unwilling victim.[1]

Moreover, the land of the dead seemed to be a place apart. It was governed by its own customs and laws of nature, which the living could not penetrate, but to which they were inexorably drawn in the fullness of time. It was a source of apprehension that the world of the dead far outnumbered the world of the living, because should its inhabitants for any reason rise in anger, then the consequences for the living would be dire indeed.

These instinctive fears presuppose a world of the living dead. The concept of nothingness, that death nullifies both spiritual and physical existence, has been throughout most human societies inconceivable. In the wake of death a corpse remains, but what of the spirit, the 'soul' that once inhabited it – where does it go?

The usual explanation was that death was a passage into another world, populated by spirits rather than bodies, but which was otherwise not dissimilar to life here on earth – a kingdom in the sky. In other words, death was not 'death' at all, but a new form of 'life'. Dying in this world was a prerequisite and a guarantee of being born in the next.

Man has always been morbidly preoccupied with the deceased. As the 'dead' were in fact 'alive', inhabiting a spiritual netherworld, elaborate rituals evolved to assist communication between the terrestrial and the celestial. For this purpose, blood performed an integral function. Being indispensable for life, it seemed reasonable that the 'living' spirits were also in need. Without sources of their own, it was up to man to provide it. Blood became the bridge between two disparate universes.

To facilitate this communication, and to guard against the displeasure of the departed, who might seek retribution for wrongs inflicted in life, the practice of blood sacrifices proliferated. This might take the form of mourners lacerating themselves at funerals, or involve animal or human sacrifices. Whatever the form, the purposeful spillage of blood fulfilled two functions. It served as a libation for the spirits, providing them with the blood they craved for vitality, youthfulness and power. It also propitiated them, removing any temptation to visit harm on the living. By offering the dead what they wanted, it was hoped to forestall the threat of them returning to take it by force.

It was not only blood that the spirits were thought to covet. Earthly possessions were also in demand for use in the hereafter, instanced by the widespread practice of burying such items as food, armour, jewellery, and household utensils along with the corpse. The dead had physical needs, too – witness the custom of providing a 'woman' for a deceased male. A lifelike female carving, excessively proportioned, would be entombed alongside the corpse to help remove the death trauma.[2] In sum, cosseting the dead by such means would nourish, appease, and distract, all to the calculated advantage of the living.

Already the constituents of vampirism are apparent. The common belief that the dead can sustain life by imbibing the blood of the living is itself an expression of the vampiric process. Donations of blood through the deliberate and controlled medium of sacrifice were both prudent and necessary, whereas the prospect of losing it unwillingly and uncontrollably through perverse activity on the part of the spirit world could induce terror and hysteria. The human imagination was more than equipped to fantasize on this threat and rationalize all manner of blood-sucking spiritual demons.

The universality of these two laws of nature – the rejuvenating power of blood and the presumption of life after death – meant that the product of their combination (the vampire) was equally universal. Legends of the dead returning to drink human blood have been found in nearly every culture where records have survived. Vampires, to borrow a phrase, have appeared almost everywhere that men have bled.[3] Stoker explains this in *Dracula* through his sage, Van Helsing:

> For, let me tell you, he [the vampire] is known everywhere that men have been. In old Greece, in old Rome, he flourish [sic] in Germany all over, in France, in India, even in the Chersonese; and in China ... He have [sic] follow the wake of the berserker Icelander, the devil-begotten Hun, the Slav, the Saxon, the Magyar (D18:285-86).*
>
> * (References to *Dracula* provide the chapter number, followed by the page number of the 1979 Penguin edition, reprinted in 1984.)

Tracing the geography and chronology of vampires is a hazardous undertaking, given the exaggeration and distortion that is an inevitable accompaniment of folklore. Nonetheless, perhaps the most ancient sources of vampire belief stem from the Orient.[4] In Asia, Chinese tales spoke of blood-sucking creatures that were green, covered with mould, and which had a propensity to glow in the dark. The Melanesian *talamaur* was known as the soul of the dead, which preyed on the ebbing vitality of the dying. In India, vampire lore is largely dissipated by the influence of Brahman- and Buddhist-inspired asceticism and vegetarianism. These, together with the practice of corpse disposal through cremation, effectively removed the foundations of the belief. Notwithstanding, Kali is revered as a blood-sucking mother goddess of disease, war, and death, and Siva is identified with ghoulish (flesh-eating) propensities. The mythical *rakskasas*, moreover, were protean phantoms, changing shape at will; the *hant-pare* would cling leech-like to the open wound of an injured person; while the *vetala* resembled an old hag and would seek the blood of sleeping women – for some reason preferring them drunk or insane.

The most spectacular of Asian vampires was the Malaysian *penanggalen*. Had he known of its existence, it might have buttressed Charles Darwin in his theory of natural selection. As the only apparatus indispensable to a vampire is a mouth and a stomach, the *penanggalen* consisted of just a head, stomach, and dangling entrails. It would soar through the air to pursue its preferred victims: babies or women in labour.

Africa is similarly rich in the diversity of its vampire species. The Ashanti's *asambosam*, for example, likes to suck blood through the thumbs of the sleeping. It is readily identifiable, having in place of feet a pair of books to stand on. Kenya's blood preoccupation was demonstrated in the oath-taking ceremonies of Mau Mau tribesmen in the early 1950s. These involved the drinking of sheep's blood – if none of murdered Europeans was available.[5]

Nor are the Americas immune from vampire superstition. In parts of the West Indies the local vampire answers to the name of *loogaroo* (from the French expression for werewolf – *loup garou*). It comes in the guise of an old woman who, in a pact with the devil, sheds her skin and changes into a blob of light in order to draw blood, which is then conveyed to her patron. For their part, Brazilians refer to a *jaracara*, which resembles a snake and enjoys a penchant for either the blood or the milk of breast-feeding mothers – milk, like blood, being a life-supporting fluid. Wherever vampires stalk, they seem able to appear in animal form: as cats in Japan, pigs in Serbia, snakes elsewhere. Creatures that can fly by night are particularly suspect: butterflies, owls, and bats.

The vampire concept was not confined to the imaginings of far-flung peoples. It is with the European tradition that this book is primarily concerned. The classical civilizations of Europe developed their own, more sophisticated, manifestations of vampiric activity, as revealed in Plato's dialogue *Phaedo*.[6] His *Republic*, furthermore, relates an incident of a slain warrior whose body refused to decompose. It returned to life just as it was about to be cast to the flames and proceeded to speak of its time spent in the 'other world'.[7] Homer's *Odyssey* recalls how Odysseus offered the blood of a slaughtered sheep to ghosts weakened through lack of nourishment.[8] The literature of ancient Greece and Rome provides encounters with so-called 'lamias', precursors of vampires, ill-defined serpentine spectres emanating from corpses who would divest the living, especially children, of their vitality. By the Middle Ages, this tradition had acquired distinctly sexual overtones: the succubus would seduce young men in their sleep and withdraw their vital fluids at the moment of climax. The male version, the incubus, associated with the devil and impregnated suitable female victims, such as witches.

It is at this point that the European vampire of folklore begins to crystallize. The preceding gallery is composed of phantoms of the spirit world. They manifest an ethereal existence. Two changes are needed for the successful metamorphosis into the true European vampire: first, the acquisition of corporeal structure; second, the development of sexual predilections, as hinted at in the lamia/succubus tradition. To appreciate these advances in human fantasy it is necessary to return once more to the psychology operating between the living and the dead.

Given that the deceased are inhabiting an unknown spiritual kingdom, the possibility of their return evokes complex psychological responses. Usually they are those of terror. Let the dead remain where they are! On other occasions, especially in the case of severed close emotional ties, the opposite can occur, producing a desperate yearning to be reunited with the dead. The bereaved may cherish the thought of their loved ones returning, as instanced by Orpheus' frantic attempts to bring back Eurydice from the Underworld. The desired passage may, however, be in the opposite direction: the living partner may seek reunion in death, for then there can be no more parting sorrow. A loving embrace in death spells exclusive possession for eternity.[9]

Inherent in grief is the idea of projecting emotions on to the deceased. The living do not forget the dead: nor, therefore can the dead forget the living. Those left behind do not wish to be forgotten by the dead. They may not envisage themselves, when the time comes, lying peacefully in their graves. They may feel compelled to return, whether driven by love, hate, guilt, conscience, revenge, or whatever. The dead, themselves, it is assumed, must surely think likewise. Love, in particular, is bound up with the European vampire. The separation of lovers, of husbands and wives, of parents and children, is the essence of its manifestation. From this springs several consequences: firstly, vampirism frequently entails a sexual aspect; secondly, it centres around a family unit, for it is relatives and loved ones who are most at risk; and thirdly, it produces conflicting emotional responses of attraction and repulsion – the yearning for a departed loved one, mixed with terror of contact with the dead. Initial desire may soon be replaced by loathing, for the vampire does not rejoin the living in life, but draws them back into death. It conforms to a perverse cyclical order: it kills, then recreates; it destroys, then preserves.[10]

The other important modification to the spectral vampires of antiquity is the wrapping of the European variety in flesh and bone. They are not ghosts, but actual corpses on the move. To illustrate, let us skim through the spectrum of man's relationship with the dead. At one end are to be found bizarre but otherwise earthly attachments. These include cannibalistic consumption of human remains (necrophagy), mutilation of corpses (necro-sadism), and copulation with a corpse (necrophilia). Likewise, the witch is very much alive despite her powers of communication with the spirit world. The vampire's cousin, the werewolf, is similarly human despite his susceptibility to the moon. He has the capacity, whether through vengeance of the gods, diabolic possession, or undiagnosed mania, to transform into a wolf, or behave accordingly.[11] In south-east Europe there is held to be a link between lycanthropy (werewolfism) and vampirism: a werewolf in life transforms into a vampire on death.

At the other extreme, ghosts, ghouls,[12] phantoms, and the vampiric spirits of Asia, Africa, the Americas, and classical Europe are manifestly dead. They exist as a spiritual presence but do not possess corporeal substance. In European folklore, however, because of the belief that the deceased were resting impatiently in their graves, waiting to walk among the living, a corollary evolved to the effect that dead bodies would not automatically decompose. The dead would clearly need their bodies if they were to rise again. Consequently, the European vampire on the life-death spectrum is usually, and uniquely, described as being situated 'in between'. It is both; it is neither. Physical death, from which no mortal can escape, has taken place, but not the normal accompaniment of death, bodily dissolution. The body dies in the natural sense, but then is resurrected as a risen dead. Demonic spirits reanimate it, and it lives a twilight existence of its own beyond the land of the living but not yet in the land of the dead: living in death. Put another way, the European vampire is a kind of amphibious entity with equal access to two opposed worlds.[13] The vampire, then, occupies three-dimensional space, and having a real body, it needs real blood.

The fusion of these characteristics gave rise to the vampire of central and eastern Europe, which is documented from around the fifteenth century onwards. The term 'vampire' stems from the Magyar *vampir* and Slavic derivatives: *vapir* in Bulgaria, *upuir* in Russia.[14] The etymology is confused, but seems traceable to 'blood-sucker' or 'blood-drunkenness'. Pseudonyms abound, notably 'undead' and *nosferat* (plural: *nosferatu* – plague carriers). There exist local variations. Parts of Romania feared the *strigoi*; the Germans have a species known as *nachzehrer*, which unaccountably kept its left eye open in its grave and clasped the thumb of one hand with the other; the Greek *vrykolakas* was both vampire and werewolf, being recognizable from its puffed-up, parchment-like skin which reverberated like a drum when struck. The Wallachian *murony* was another vampire-werewolf cross-breed; while the Bulgarians talked of a creature having just one nostril, a boneless frame, and fungoid flesh. Whatever the nuances, European communities had little difficulty in accepting the philosophical dimensions of vampires. After all, they had had a proven demonstration of man's capacity to die, to be buried, and to rise again with special powers to visit the living – Christ himself. Had he not promised to resurrect the dead and offer eternal life? Even today the words 'Rest in Peace' contain dark allusions. Is there a suggestion that the corpse might not rest, but walk?

Central and eastern Europe can rightly claim to be the Pandora's Box of vampirism. This Eurocentric tradition retained the blood/death facets central to all such demons, but took on one further aspect, giving the European vampire its distinctive stamp. The Continental model of the undead was conceived, then proliferated under the guidance and doctrine of the Christian Church. It is from this tradition that Stoker's *Dracula* draws its inspiration.

---

[1]   Ernest Jones, 'On the Vampire', in Christopher Frayling (ed.), *The Vampyre: Lord Ruthven to Count Dracula*, p.315.

[2]   Ornella Volta, *The Vampire*, p.10.

[3]   Leonard Wolf, *A Dream of Dracula*, p.125.

[4]   Devendra Varma (introduction), *Varney the Vampire*, Vol 1, pp.xiv, xviii.

[5]   Anthony Masters, *The Natural History of the Vampire*, p.48.

[6]   Plato, *Phaedo*, 77E.

[7]   Varma, op. cit., p.xiii.

[8]   Homer, *Odyssey*, X-XI.

[9]   Jones, op. cit., p.317.

[10] Varma, op. cit., p.xiv.

11 Montague Summers, *The Vampire: His Kith and Kin*, p.165.
12 The distinction between ghouls and vampires might require clarification. A ghoul is a corpse that devours other corpses, though it has no special taste for blood. Ghouls are robotic, under external control, whereas vampires move and direct themselves.
13 Volta, op. cit., p.80.
14 Summers, op. cit., p.18.

2

The Vampire in Christian Europe

It has indeed lately come to Our ears that ... many persons of both sexes ... have abandoned themselves to devils, incubi and succubi.

> Pope Innocent VIII, Papal Bull 1484; Introduction to
> *Malleus Maleficarum* (the Witch Hammer).

It is the height of folly to attempt to deny that such bodies are not infrequently found in their graves incorrupt, and that by use of them the Devil, if God permits, devises most horrible complots and schemes to the hurt and harm of mankind.

> Jacob Sprenger and Heinrich Kramer,
> *Malleus Maleficarum*.

The source of the Christian influence on the vampire superstition in the Middle Ages and post-Renaissance Europe is impeccable – the Bible itself. Not only does it celebrate a corpse rising from the tomb, but the Old and New Testaments persistently speak of blood. There exists much controversy over these references. In the Old Testament, for example, blood is an expression of violence and death, intimately bound up with the notion of sacrifice. Equally, one finds expressions like 'the blood is the life'. In the New Testament, St John's Gospel exhorts us to drink Christ's blood as a means of absolving our sins and becoming closer to God. Here, the regenerative power of blood could hardly be more explicit:

Who so eateth my flesh and drinketh my blood hath eternal life; and I will raise him up at the last day. For my flesh is meat indeed, and my blood is drink indeed. He that eateth my flesh and drinketh my blood dwelleth in me and I in him.[1]

The Latin Church's celebration of Holy Communion, the Eucharist, operates from the belief that the taking of bread and wine – re-enacting the Last Supper – partakes of a mystical conversion. The bread and wine are not *symbolic* of Christ's flesh and blood: they *are* Christ's flesh and blood. Absorbing Christ's uncorrupted blood amounts to a regenerative transfusion. The conversion process is explained through the obscure notion of transubstantiation.

The early Church Fathers faced a dilemma: they needed to stress the primordial link between blood and life inherent in the Eucharist, while simultaneously discouraging too literal an interpretation. In this, they could point to ample warnings against blood-letting and blood-drinking carried by the Old Testament[2] and later by St Paul.

These aims are largely countermanded in the Middle Ages. Transubstantiation seemed to the sceptical to be on a par with ancestor worship and sacrifice. Worse, being asked to consume the *actual* flesh and blood of Christ was surely tantamount to cannibalism. Rather than resort to abstruse theology, the Christian essence was more easily explained to would-be converts in terms already familiar through pagan superstitions. The Christian grip on medieval Europe was so tenuous that pagan observances were necessarily tolerated at first, then adapted to advantage. Transubstantiation was taught in the language of vampirism. As the devil's objective was to drain the blood of sinners and commandeer their spirits, so the righteous could taste Christ's blood as a means of sharing his Holiness.

The Eucharist was not the only means of reinforcing belief in the mystical properties of blood. The cult of the Virgin Mary encouraged charlatans to prescribe uncorrupted virgins' blood as an antidote for every conceivable malady.[3] Throughout much of medieval Europe maidens were much sought after, not so much for their sexual favours as for their 'innocent' blood.

But it needed more than the Christian preoccupation with blood for the spectre of the vampire to come to haunt half a continent. It needed the proselytizing zeal which accompanied political and territorial expansion. Between the fifteenth and eighteenth centuries central and eastern Europe was the battleground of

Christian and Turk. Within the imperial struggle a spiritual war was waged. The Western (Roman) Church, the Eastern (Orthodox) Church, and the Ottoman Moslems formed a fluctuating triumvirate battling for the minds of men.

In this context it is hardly surprising that excesses were committed, spiritual as well as physical. Much could be achieved by trading on fear of the devil. Both the Roman and Orthodox Churches preyed on the credulity of the populace, exploiting ignorance and hysteria to retain the faithful, and threatening eternal damnation for the slightest heresy. The vampire was ready-made for this purpose. Taken from its pagan origins and updated with Church embellishments, vampirism was the fate that awaited for errors of prescribed belief. In effect, the two competing pillars of the Christian Establishment took advantage of a closed system. They specified the vampire menace, thereby sanctioning its existence, then claimed a self-imposed monopoly on vampire counter-measures.

On the Roman side, threatened from all quarters, within and without, the 1490s heralded one of the most notorious publications ever to receive the papal seal. Compiled by two Dominicans, the *Malleus Maleficarum* fulfilled the demand of Pope Innocent VIII for a systematic investigation into the activities of witches, incubi and succubi. For two centuries this volume became a principal authority in Rome's battle against satanic influences. Nowadays it is difficult to find formal Catholic acknowledgment even of its existence.

When discussing the European vampire, it is helpful to distinguish between its pagan superstitious origins, which lay down their own, often conflicting, criteria for the undead, and distinctively Christian crimes and indiscretions. These fused with the pagan base to provide a new genus of vampires: a pagan-Christian alloy. Corroboration of the existence of these vampires is, regrettably, somewhat sketchy.[4] The area in focus broadly corresponds to what, prior to the end of the Cold War, was referred to as behind the Iron Curtain.

As a rule of thumb, the pre-medieval heritage failed to distinguish between the innocent and the guilty when recruiting for the undead. Persons were cast as vampires through no fault of their own, by being stillborn, or drowning, or by meeting their deaths violently. The vampire taint could be hereditary. Victims of unavenged murders were at risk, for they supposedly could not rest in their graves until they had quenched their thirst from the blood of their assailants. Relatives of victims who did not, or could not, dutifully track down the culprits would likewise be punished for their failure.[5]

Encounters with certain animals could lead to vampirism: for example, eating the flesh of a sheep killed by a wolf, or allowing a cat or other animal to pass over one's grave. This demonstrated lack of respect for the place of burial.[6] For safety's sake it was common to keep animals indoors until after a funeral. Paternal curses could allegedly induce vampirism in the child, and the same fate awaited a pregnant woman who neglected to put salt on her food. Her laxity would seal the baby's future, as would receiving the 'evil eye', unless some antidote were effected.[7]

Omens elsewhere regarded as favourable are reversed in some Balkan states. According to Gaelic mythology, a seventh son is held to possess healing powers. Not so in south-east Europe, where a seventh child was particularly suspect and would grow a little tail to warn of its presence.[8] Similarly, a baby born with a caul (a membrane from the amniotic sac enveloping the head) is held to be lucky in many cultures outside the Balkans. This region harboured particular fears of the stillborn, illegitimate child of illegitimate parents.

Equally vulnerable to the taint of vampirism were those unfortunate enough to be deformed, or the victims of particular nervous disorders. The hare-lipped were automatic candidates for would-be werewolves or vampires. So were those afflicted with a cleft palate, for they had an involuntary drawing-up of the upper lip. Given the significance of the vampire's teeth, a child born with any was an obvious suspect. Persons with unsightly birthmarks were believed to have the curse. In regions where brown eyes predominated, those with blue eyes were suspect, and *vice versa*. Physical disorders producing vampirism included epilepsy and chorea (St Vitus' dance), whose unaccountable convulsions were put down to demoniacal possession.

By these means communities strove to induce con
anybody 'odd' was likely to be held responsible for w
misfortunes arose. In the hands of the Church, a range o
religious-based offences was laid down as leading to a vampiric
afterlife. To the jumbled fears of the peasants were added sharply
defined transgressions, each carrying the curse of the undead.
These included crimes such as murder, theft, dabbling in black
magic, and perjury. But the bulk of the Church's energies were
directed at emphasizing the fate that awaited the excommunicated
and the suicide.

Excommunication was the Church's ultimate weapon for those
bent on sacrilegious practice: the withdrawal of all spiritual
privileges, coupled with lasting damnation beyond the grave. The
act of excommunication could not annul the earlier baptism. The
victim remained within the Christian fold but was henceforth
spiritually exiled until such time as his misdeeds were absolved.
Anyone upbaptized or apostate, and thereby immune to excommunication, was also scheduled to become a vampire. In view of
the frequency of excommunication in early modern Europe, the
Church felt it advantageous to instil into wrongdoers the fate of
those denied proper burial rites. The devil would gain admittance
to those deprived of Christ's protection and resurrect them as
undead.

Vampire allegories illuminated the implications of excommunication, as they had illuminated the Eucharist.[9] No leap in the
imagination was required to picture those lying condemned in
their graves returning as vampires. Word spread that the corpses
of excommunicants inadvertently buried in consecrated ground
had been mysteriously thrown up and dumped by the side of their
graves. These beliefs were encouraged by the Greek Orthodox
Church, which declared that excommunicants and other heretics
would not decompose in their unhallowed graves.[10] The devil, it
was explained, would intervene to preserve excommunicants from
dissolution. This would prevent the release of the soul, damning it
inside the corpse and enabling it to walk as a vampire.[11]

By accounting for the non-dissolution of vampire corpses, the
Greek Church, in effect, awarded to itself power over the body as
well as the soul. But it did more than that. The doctrine clashed

with one of the most cherished precepts of the Roman Church. The Latin tradition held that the non-decomposition of a corpse was an exclusive sign of sanctity. For the Greek Church to attribute the suspension of bodily dissolution to earthly wickedness and diabolic intervention prompted doctrinal confusion in both Churches. Catholic wisdom came to explain vampirism within the doctrine of purgatory: the undead did not inhabit hell, but a place of temporal punishment. The Greek Church resolved its own paradox by the application of cosmetic criteria. The uncorrupted bodies of saints could be recognized by their fragrant smell and purity of complexion, whereas the flesh of the damned would be black, bloated, and mephitic. In the event, the distinction remained largely hypothetical, because when the bodies of known excommunicants were disinterred they were found, invariably, not to be black, bloated, and mephitic, but simply rotted away. This, in turn, warranted the fresh theological explanation that such a corpse was already damned in hell with no possibility of absolution for the soul.

The second misdemeanour liable to be repaid by vampirism was the taking of one's own life. In other cultures at other times suicide has been regarded either with indifference or respect. This is not the case in the eyes of the Christian Church, where such action is taken to flout God's arbitration on matters of life and death. As man is not responsible for his own birth he does not possess the right to determine his death. God is the sole author of life, master over everything: therefore suicide is a blasphemous act usurping His omnipotence – to the point of denying His existence.

To assist in the campaign against suicides, the spectre of the undead provided a happy twist of fate. The Church recruited the public terror of vampires, which it had instilled in the first place, by declaring that suicides would not attain their objective. They would not find everlasting peace and oblivion. Their fate would be everlasting life as a vampire. The penalty for suicide would be immortality.

Irrespective of their association with vampirism, suicides have over the centuries been subjected to specific provisions, such as burying them at crossroads. This served the double precaution of reminding the restless spirit of the sign of the cross which lay above the grave, while confusing the risen suicide in his wanderings. With four paths from which to choose, he would not know which to take. For good measure the suicide could also be staked down in his grave to immobilize him and prevent his soul from travelling abroad. Despite these precautions sensible travellers kept clear of crossroads after nightfall. Aside from wandering suicides, they were likely to encounter witches' sabbats and creaking gallows.

Fear of suicides is endemic in British folklore. The Scots held that the corpse of a suicide would not crumble until nature had taken its course. There are records in England of the graves of suicides being aligned north-south, rather than with the head in the west facing east, as prescribed for proper Christian burial. Not until 1823 did Parliament abrogate the law permitting the transfixing of suspect suicides, and not until 1882 was it possible for the corpse of a suicide to be buried with whatever rites could be arranged.[12]

Aside from excommunicants and suicides, many other hapless persons were accused of vampirism on grounds as spurious as those in pagan cultures. Dates in the Christian calendar came to assume an ominous significance. Babies unwise enough to be born at Christmas were doomed, presumably because their parents had been engaged in base, earthly pleasures at the time of divine conception by the Virgin Mary. In Greece, such infants were referred to as *callicantzaros*. To guard against their later transformation it was known for them to have their feet and nails singed.[13] The period known as Epiphany (the twelve days following Christmas) was a period when the forces of evil were widely held to prevail. The Easter child was likewise at risk.

St Andrew's Eve and St George's Eve were dates when the powers of goodness were reputed to be at their lowest. St George was the patron saint of England and protector of other regions, including Bavaria, Venice, and Constantinople. He was also the divine protector of cattle and horses. His protective shield against phantom predators was weakest upon his 'Eve', when the powers of vampires and evil spirits were correspondingly at their peak.

Within the Greek Orthodox tradition, Saturday was the most effective day to go vampire-hunting. The day following the crucifixion was believed to be sacred to the Virgin Mary, who had clung to her faith during her darkest hour. Vampires were allegedly confined to their resting places on that day and were unable to escape if discovered.[14] Witches, too, shunned that particular day and were unable to hold their sabbat. It was supposed that persons born on a Saturday had a special ability to detect ghouls and ghosts, and were immune to the vampire.

Other persons eligible to become undead through Christian-based superstition were those with red hair (as was possessed by Cain and Judas[15]) and the sexually promiscuous. Witches enjoying carnal intercourse with the devil would undoubtedly produce vampire offspring. Most terrifying of all, vampirism was said to be contagious. Those who died as a result of a vampire attack would themselves transform into the undead. The 'dormant' vampires in life would become 'active' vampires in death. In other words, they would not 'die' at all: the husk of the body would be taken up to serve the devil, recruited as an energumen. All in all, the list of qualifying procedures was sufficiently wide as to include almost anybody.

But what of the vampire itself? What does it look like; how does it behave; and what powers are at its command? The undead are commonly associated with poorer communities, and their appearance and behaviour reflects their social origins. The notion of tall, handsome aristocrats inhabiting cliff-top castles is the product of the literary imagination, not folklore. Vampires are more usually depicted as lean, gaunt, hollow-eyed, and with scabs on their arms and legs. Their skin is dry and of extraordinary pallor, save after consumption of blood, when the countenance turns fresh and ruddy and the mouth will be slobbered with blood. The eyes glow red with perdition, and as the life functions are not arrested the nails will be long and crooked, the hair long, unkempt and matted, but the skin will feel icy to the touch. The lips will be red and blubbery, and may be involuntarily drawn back. In which case they should reveal gleaming white teeth and extended canines – yet another association with the werewolf.[16] Only in repose after 'feasting' is the vampire other than emaciated, for the trunk then swells up in obese repletion. Some locations pursue the animalistic imagery further, speculating that the original dead skin of the vampire slowly peels away to reveal fresh skin and nails underneath.

Their thirst for blood is unquenchable, yet some districts hold that vampires can take normal food and will drink the blood of sheep and cattle in addition to that of humans. Their nauseous panting and drooling of saliva is lycanthropic, as is the downy hair to be found in the centres of the palms. The entire creature reeks of excrement and arrested decay. Despite their physical lack of condition, vampires are reputed to possess great strength and can run like the wind. Obliged to commute to and from their graves wearing no more than a burial shroud torn, blood-stained and covered with grime, it cannot be wondered at that they present a grisly, and ghostly, spectacle to any who catch sight of one.

Perhaps the most formidable aspect of the vampire's armoury is transmutation, the ability to change shape into a wolf, into phosphorescent specks, or even dissipate into mist, through which the dematerialized essence of the vampire may drain blood from all it envelops. The modern association with the vampire bat stems from literature and the cinema, not with Continental folklore. The vampire bat is not native to Europe, and was only discovered in South America in the seventeenth century. Its links with the human vampire were not forged until the arrival of nineteenth-century vampire literature. As the bat was named after the vampire, and not *vice versa*, the vampire could not add bat-like attributes to its repertoire, save in the imagination of horror writers and film makers.

Like others in the devil's army, the undead are nocturnal, loathing the sun but invigorated by the moon. A full moon could revive and energize the vampire, whereas the sun could destroy it, or deprive it of its supernatural powers till dusk. It was commonly supposed that in daylight the vampire must retain whatever shape it held at the moment of sunrise. The vampire's sensory powers are basically ocular: they may induce hypnosis in potential victims, and can see in the dark – with appropriate control over wolves and other creatures of the night.

31

One Christian legacy is the devil's inability to conduct commerce with unwilling clients. The undead cannot therefore enter a dwelling unless invited in upon their first visit. This is not much of a deterrent: the vampire's relatives may welcome the return of the departed loved one. If not, they can be hypnotized in order to effect entry. The vampire also shrewdly arrives in the early hours, when psychological resistance is at its lowest.

The alert villager could determine the identity of any visitor by the handy positioning of mirrors. It is a deeply ingrained folk-belief that a reflection in a mirror or in a pond (nowadays on camera film) is that of the person's soul. In keeping with other evil spirits, vampires have no soul, so fail to cast a reflection. Upon a household bereavement, mirrors were customarily turned to face the wall, lest the deceased caught a glimpse of his soul and sought to be reunited with it, or else contaminated the reflection of the living.[17]

In the hands of the Church, the vampire's sexual aspect was magnified, threatening unwanted immortality for the immoral and licentious. The physical hallmarks of the vampire – sallow, lean, hairy, smelly – are typical of the Church's conception of the promiscuous. The sexual connection was all the more pertinent in view of the usual target for the vampire attack. Contrary to literary and cinematic corruption of the myth, the vampire's motive was not the recruitment of other vampires, but the search for analeptic nourishment through blood. Nevertheless, the fact that vampire assaults occurred at night, and that the selected victim was often the spouse or lover, gave the whole business a sexual, not to say necrophilic, undertone. The sexual aspect is enhanced by the preferred regions from which to suck. A predilection for the neck is frequently mentioned. Sucking blood from the external jugular vein invites associations with the sado-sexual aspect of the love-bite.

Having identified the vampire, there now arose the matter of precaution. What could be done for the protection of self, family, and homestead? Pagan superstitions in this respect are encyclopaedic. Many pay tribute to man's ingenuity. When burying a likely vampire, care would be taken to dig deeper than was customary, so that the corpse would experience difficulty in reaching the surface. Sensibly, the body would be interred face down, so that on awakening it would unwittingly scrabble downwards into the bowels of the earth. Thorns placed at strategic places, around the coffin or in the home, were helpful in ensnaring any active vampire. By piling stones over a grave it was hoped to obstruct any surfacing demon, and therein possibly lies the origin of cairns and tombstones.[18]

Regional precautions included a Polish bread-like concoction from flour mixed with blood from a destroyed vampire. Immunity was assured if you ate the bread. In Wallachia, rubbing one's body with the lard of a pig killed on St Ignatius's day was efficacious. The assumption that the vampire lacks intelligence was illustrated by scattering grain or millet along the road and around the home. The vampire is easily distracted, and out of curiosity or some other misunderstood motive will stop to count each grain. Preoccupied in this manner it would still be counting at sunrise.

A variation on the above was to sprinkle seeds on the empty grave. The replete creature would feel compelled to count the seeds, whereupon it would be surprised and neutralized by the rising sun. The bloated Greek *vrykolakas*, which had a penchant for squatting on victims to squeeze the life out of them, was prone to an equally nonsensical habit. Visiting its intended victim, it would wait outside and call his or her name. But it could not hail more than once. Consequently, Greek peasants refused to answer a surprise knock at their door – unless reassured by its repetition.[19]

Plants and herbs have long been considered potent against malevolent spirits. Pride of place goes to garlic, to which have been ascribed medicinal and insecticidal properties. Garlic is famed for its smell, significant in that demons are supposedly repelled by odours stronger than their own.[20] For the purpose in hand, garlic would be applied to the vampire's grave or likely victim's home, smearing it around windows and doors, leaving it in vases, or garlanding it around the necks of the occupants.

Belief in the powers of garlic, onions, and other strong smelling substances alludes to a primitive homoeopathic protection against demonic threats. Symbols of purity or holiness were held to have the same effect. Against nocturnal foes the colour 'white' was highly valued. White eyes would be painted on a black dog, and the animal despatched to meet any unwelcome night visitor. Water is another pure, 'holy' element. Vampires are unable to cross running water, further evidence of the lunar influence, except at the ebb and flow of the tide. The salt water of the sea provides a compound repellent, for salt is yet another sign of purity. Deportation of vampires to tiny islands in the Mediterranean was therefore to be commended, except that growing numbers of vampire colonies would haunt passing sailors with their wailing.

The view of the Church was that the most effective insurance against the undead was piety: daily attendance at mass, devout communions, regular recitation of the Rosary, and veneration of holy relics.[21] These religious observances were more usually supplemented by attributing sacred qualities to various plants and trees. The wild rose has enjoyed mystic associations since antiquity, but in Byzantine Europe it came to be used to repel unholy spirits. Mountain ash, hawthorn, buckthorn, and black-thorn were likewise benignly endowed. Primitive magic posits an association between sharp, erect, blood-letting prickles of thorn and fertility-bestowing phallic symbols.[22] This survives today in several modern languages – in English through a slang term for the male organ. As applied to vampires, it is said that scratches from sacred thorns will destroy them – presumably a harkback to the image of Christ's crown of thorns.

The Church, however, had a store of potent symbolism of its own. The cross, or crucifix, was not only an affront to the Turks. It could likewise ward off the undead. Eucharistic particles and holy water were believed to be capable of searing the flesh, like acid. They could also sterilize the vampire's tomb. The custom persisted in Greece of placing a crumb of consecrated bread on the lips of the undead.[23] This may relate to the ritual of placing a coin in the mouth of the deceased – the 'Ferry Man's Coin' – designed as passage money, bribery to avoid being landed in hell.

Despite all precautions, the vampire on occasions would break through. and general safeguards had to give way to stronger measures. Undiagnosed sickness, unexplained deaths, failed crops, missing children or animals – all were liable to be put down to a vampire. Symptoms associated with loss of blood – anaemia, emaciation, languor, loss of appetite – especially following bereavement, were sure evidence of vampire visitation.

This vampire glossary may be vague, but it includes one incontrovertible factor: despite physical death, the vampire's body resists decomposition. Hence, find a corpse stubbornly intact, and (presuming it was not earmarked for sainthood) here lay an undead. Consequently, at times of local consternation graves would be opened on the slightest pretext. Under the guidance of the Greek Church, bodies were in any event disinterred periodically to gauge the rate of dissolution. Once a corpse had proved its innocence by leaving only the bones, these would be cleansed by relatives and reburied with due solemnity. This practice unknowingly encouraged happy endings, for re-exposing a corpse to fresh air accelerates decomposition. Non-Christian China carried the idea one stage further, refusing to bury potential vampires until they were well on the way to decay.

Vampire detection and disposal commanded strict ceremonies and rituals. If no obvious suspect came to mind, it was necessary to determine his resting place. As horses are supposedly capable of detecting the presence of evil, a boy would be mounted on an all-black or all-white virginal colt and led around a burial site. Sooner or later the horse would baulk at a grave. Popular belief insisted that a vampire slept beneath. Horses were useful because the vampire left few clues to his presence. Villagers did not waste time, for example, searching for piles of fresh earth or a lidless coffin. The vampire had the power of dematerialization, and could come and go by means of small holes of finger's breadth.[24] Such holes would be assiduously searched for.

Methods of vampire disposal (you could not 'kill' a vampire since it was already dead) may be divided into the pagan and the Christian. Both traditions concurred that special techniques were required. Pagan measures retained a strong local individuality. Those parts of Serbia that believed its undead to be invisible recommended employing a 'dhampire'.[25] The dhampire contradicts the notion of inherited vampirism, for the dhampire is the vampire's son. In effect, he turns Queen's evidence, for he is believed to have inside knowledge of his father's pestilential activities, and in return for a fat fee could be called upon to exorcise him. The feat would be performed through an elaborate display of nose-blowing and wrestling with an invisible foe (his father). After a suitable lapse of time, emphasizing the strength of his opponent, the exhausted dhampire would announce the destruction of his dad, and of course nobody could prove otherwise.

Other regions, haunted by visible vampires, were more direct. In Dalmatia, the leg muscles and tendons of suspects were severed, to impede escape. The same result was achieved in Finland by nailing down the vampire, or snapping its spine, and other places reported tying the toes and thumbs together.[26] Bulgarians advocated stealing up on a bloated vampire and pricking it with a pin to enable its noisome gases to escape.

According to Christian tradition, the ritualistic element is no less compulsory. A chance destruction of any wandering vampire would lack credibility – and witnesses to the Church's awesome power. A priest must be summoned, for only he comprehended the power of Satan and enjoyed access to the necessary implements of counter-vampirism.

Once located and the coffin opened, the tell-tale signs of vampirism should be apparent. The creature should display a ruddy complexion, with the mouth and nails clotted with blood. It might even be floating on a reservoir of blood. If the flesh is punctured with a pin, blood should gush as from a burst balloon. The eyes will be open, glazed, and malefic. If the vampire has gone hungry or thirsty, the burial shroud will show signs of having been eaten, and perhaps also the limbs.

Shortly after dawn is propitious for destroying a vampire, for it will be heavy and torpid after its banquet. Three methods of destruction are prescribed: impalement, cremation, and decapitation. Impalement with a sharpened stake, properly known as 'transfixion', should be performed with a single blow through the heart or navel. Strange to say, transfixion does not achieve its effect in the way imagined. Piercing the heart may be fatal to humans, but this overlooks the immunity of the vampire. The creature must be impaled with one stroke, for repetition resuscitates the vampire, who could reputedly pull out the stake himself.[27]

The usual purpose of transfixion is to immobilize, to impale the vampire to the coffin floor. Writers and film makers would depart from folklore in having the hero hammer away till he drops from exhaustion, and also in showing the vampire 'killed' in consequence. Another cinematic distortion is the vampire's writhing, screaming and foaming at the mouth. These tantrums are not the death-agony of the folkloric vampire: they are purposeful and contrived.[28] Should the staker keep a steady hand, the vampire is doomed, but should his concentration falter, or his eyes meet that hypnotic, malevolent stare, then the tables are instantly turned, and the would-be exorcist becomes the next undead. It is for this reason that the need to transfix at the first attempt is paramount. Finding the wretched beast is straightforward compared with the nerves of steel needed to dispose of it.

The Christian connection found its way into the specifications of wood used for the stake – aspen, maple, ash, oak, whatever the local belief regarding the wood used for the Cross. Proper transfixion enabled the priest to effect victory by decapitation or cremation, unless the corpse had been 'dead' for many years, in which case it would crumble into dust. In theory, cremation was the safest procedure, provided that every scrap of flesh and bone was incinerated, and any spiders, lice, or worms trying to scuttle from the flames were tossed back in. The ashes would then be scattered to the winds or into a river.

The difficulty with cremating suspect vampires – despite its undoubted efficiency – was that it ran counter to the approval of the Church. A cremated corpse destroyed the body which Christ was pledged to resurrect at the Day of Judgment. Moreover, cremation seemed to imitate heathen practices. To the Orthodox tradition, in particular, consuming with fire a body which had received the last rites and been sprinkled with holy oil smacked of sacrilege.

Decapitation achieved the same effects as cremation, but with fewer drawbacks. The vampire's head would be removed, not by any handy blade, but by a sexton's spade. The body would then be hacked to pieces in the manner of notorious criminals or political offenders. The value of decapitation was that it destroyed the physical intactness of any creature that wished to rise again.[29] To be absolutely sure, the heart could be removed, treated with oil or vinegar, and then shredded. Holy water poured over the now-empty grave should finally spell defeat for the vampire.

Other methods noted in Christian climes include silver bullets (silver being a pure metal) properly blessed by a priest. The vampire must be 'shot' away from moonlight, which would otherwise resuscitate it with enhanced malevolence. Bulgarians were ingenious enough to lure the undead into a huge bottle, which would then be plugged with an equally huge cork decorated with holy images. The masterminding 'bottler' would be handsomely rewarded, and the whole – bottle and contents – tossed on to a blazing pyre.[30] This particular tale would seem to be rooted in the Oriental belief that evil spirits can be enclosed in glass vessels, and is a classic instance of hybrid pagan-Christian folklore.

How is one to explain this gallery of incredible happenings? Inaccurate diagnosis of death was a cardinal factor. Even today, in the face of the controversy surrounding brain- versus tissue-death, there is dispute as to the precise moment of death. There is no irrefutable test to confirm the moment of expiry. Cataleptic trances, for example, may be accompanied by a rapid slowing of the body mechanism, producing a condition which even to the trained medical eye can seem indistinguishable from death. The limbs may become rigid, and the skin cold to the touch. Pronouncements of death, even in 'advanced' societies, are on occasions premature. The only incontrovertible proof was, and is, dissolution. In Bram Stoker's time this was openly acknowledged: in 1885 the *British Medical Journal* confirmed: 'It is true that hardly any one sign of death, short of putrefaction, can be relied upon as infallible.'[31] To the superstitious, logic would dictate that as decomposition was the only sure sign of death, so non-decomposition must be proof of the undead.

This fundamental diagnostic difficulty has, upon a moment's thought, an unpalatable consequence. Throughout history premature burials have been commonplace. The lucky would not have regained consciousness: others would, only to succumb to asphyxia or starvation. A very few would have broken out of their confinement, for burial arrangements were frequently haphazard – fragile coffins and shallow graves. Communal burial grounds were not commonplace in continental Europe. The dead would be buried almost anywhere: on hills, in caves, in woods, in fields, in proximity to other graves or in isolation, either singly or in family groups.[32] Needless to say, any dishevelled, hysterical, blood-stained, mud-smeared, white-shrouded figure that did somehow escape from its grave would try to locate its loved ones, inducing panic in anyone it encountered, and unleashing a vampire mania.

Bodies easily buried could easily be disinterred. And they were – whether in the search for vampires or loot. The age-old custom of taking personal valuables to the grave encouraged a reciprocal profession of grave robbing. Sometimes the theft would be of jewellery, sometimes of the corpse itself. These could fetch handy sums from no-questions-asked anatomy schools unable to procure adequate supplies from legitimate sources. The infamous Burke and Hare, convicted in Edinburgh in the 1820s, are the most celebrated British practitioners of the body-trade. In Europe, the discovery of a rifled grave, empty or with the corpse disturbed in the thieving of personal effects, had only one explanation – the vampire, for the corpse must surely have moved itself.

The rate of bodily decomposition is not constant. Soil conditions can vary the speed, dry soils tending to preserve, as does freezing. Differing causes of death likewise affect the rate of dissolution, and through not being exposed to air once the vital functions had ceased, a body interred alive would take longer to decompose.

Rare diseases were at one time equated with vampirism. Albinos possess the requisite pallor and photophobia. A disorder known as porphyria results in the teeth, hair and nails glowing fluorescently. Sufferers are super-sensitive to sunlight, and the disease can be hereditary. With iron-deficiency porphyria, the body cannot metabolize iron, and must take it in digestible form, such as drinking blood. For persons with this disorder, garlic is not recommended. Garlic activates the functions that break down old blood cells, thereby removing the iron that the body needs.[33]

In the case of pernicious anaemia, the body may shrivel up and produce a physical craving for blood. Tuberculosis could result in recognizable vampire symptoms: weight loss and fatigue, not to mention coughing and spitting blood in advanced cases. TB may be conveyed by a carrier who is himself immune – an obvious vampire candidate should his or her identity be disclosed. Cholera dehydrates the body and produces a physical wasting, and cancer has comparable manifestations. The advanced symptoms of rabies may include spasms, convulsions, difficulty in breathing, together with terror of water.

Above all, there was the plague, whose epidemics were silent, invisible, and inexplicable. The Great Plague which decimated London in 1665-66 is now known to have been caused by rats and fleas. At the time, it was widely attributed to heavenly punishment for earthly sins. On the Continent, only a vampire onslaught could account for the massive loss of life inflicted by periodic epidemics. For reasons of hygiene, victims were disposed of with unseemly haste. Doctors and undertakers were too few to cope: many of the afflicted were buried alive in graves hastily dug and shallow.

Continental vampire-itis peaked in the 1720s and 30s. The Ottoman star was on the wane, its troops and administrators pushed inexorably back through the Balkans. Habsburg Catholicism, the ascendant military and religious force, stepped into the vacuum. Conflict continued, ecclesiastical rather than territorial, between Roman Catholicism and Muscovite Orthodoxy. Much of Europe – Poland, the Ukraine, western Russia, Slav and Balkan states – reverberated to the clash between Christian East and West. Each side denied that the dead would find eternal peace in the unhallowed soil of the other.[34] The watershed of this conflict was identified as an area of modern Romania known as Transylvania. Originally Greek Orthodox, its peasant communities found themselves threatened by Islam and Catholicism. They became the terrified and helpless victims of a religious maelstrom. The tentacles of this struggle and its resultant psychosis spread far and wide until much of central and eastern Europe was seething with vampire paranoia.

Excommunications multiplied and popular superstition manipulated to serve the goal of true belief.

The seriousness of this epidemic can be gauged from the response of German academia. The intellectual climate had entered the rational era of the Enlightenment. Learned treatises spilled off the presses between 1728 and 1734, many from the prestigious universities of Leipzig, Jena, and Nuremberg. Each tried to account, in theological, psychological, medical, or philosophical terms, for the sensationalist vampire stories reaching them from the East. Belief in God was taken for granted, and philosophical speculation could not easily avoid that premise. The vampire seemed self-evidently a diabolic creature permitted by God. As everlasting life awaited the pure and holy, it seemed natural that this longing would be parodied by the devil.[35] Much of the debate, in other words, took place against the framework of the devil's challenge to God's earthly order.

Not surprisingly, the questions asked were couched in metaphysical language. Were vampires actual risen corpses, or merely souls not yet freed from earthly bondage? Did the spiritual element of the vampire emanate from its former, living existence? Or was it animated by the devil, who directed an evil spirit to take possession of the body once the soul of the owner had departed? What unknown forces lay behind the supernatural powers of the undead? If the body of the vampire was spectral, how, and by what means could it suck blood and engage in coitus with the living? Similarly, how could a three-dimensional body, dead or otherwise, pass to and from the grave without disturbing the earth in between? In sum, could a corporeal substance possess astral dimensions?

Among the speculative conclusions was the idea that an undead dematerialized to escape its grave. Alternatively, a double was somehow created by the vampire, independent of the corpse that remained buried. Such notions raised profound theological disquiet, for if vampires were endowed with such talents, it implied that Satan enjoyed comparable powers to those of Christ.

What needs to be appreciated is that popular superstition, ecclesiastical practice, and the most learned minds of the eighteenth-century all fuelled the vampire myth. The spreading psychosis found no remedy from physicians, so quacks added to the hysteria with their anti-vampire ointments and talismans.[36] East central Europe was no stranger to wars or epidemics, successive waves of Black Death, smallpox, and pestilence having savaged the region in previous generations. Only later was it noticed that most vampire reports stemmed from those lands where Catholic Hungarians and Orthodox Serbs and Wallachs intermingled; where the peasant population was most exposed to the dire threats of the rival faith.

The multiplying persecution of alleged vampires was instrumental in turning popular superstition into an actual hysterical epidemic. Local communities took the law into their own hands, digging up the graves of suspected vampires, until Rome, angered by the 'heresies' preached by the Orthodox schismatics, established an effective legal framework for official vampire trials.[37] These trials did not set out to establish the nature of vampirism or its causes, far less the guilt or innocence of the accused. They restricted themselves to the Catholic precept that, as vampires depended for their existence on the devil, it was God's will that they should be destroyed. God permitted Satan to tempt mankind with evil, thereby justifying a resolute Christian campaign to eradicate the undead.

That Britain was not party to the vampire craze was due not to a lesser capacity for superstition, but to the effects of the Reformation. Part of the Catholic explanation of vampirism concerned the doctrine of purgatory. The Protestant challenge denied the existence of purgatory, and therefore insisted that beings returning from the grave could not be the spirits of the departed. In time, Rome would amend its association between the undead and purgatory. But Protestant clerics, needing an alternative explanation for the vampire phenomenon, subsumed it under the category of 'witchcraft'.[38] Consequently, while central and eastern (Catholic or Orthodox) Europe suffered from vampires, north-western (Protestant) Europe suffered its witches. This results in the different colour of demonology found in different parts of Christendom. Ireland aside, Britain was virtually bereft of indigenous vampire lore. When the eighteenth century invasion arrived, it came not through folklore but through literature.

1   John 6:54-56
2   Genesis, 9:4; Leviticus 17:10-14, 19:28; Deuteronomy 12:16, 23.
3   Gabriel Ronay, *The Dracula Myth*, p.10.
4   The searcher after vampire folklore has few reliable sources. The doyen is Montague Summers, who builds on the work of earlier Catholic scholars such as Dom Augustin Calmet. Summers' problems are twofold: he does not know fact from heresay; and he believes passionately in the existence of vampires.
     Nonetheless, few other investigators are as thorough. Other works such as Masters, Garden, and Wright offer little that cannot be found in Summers.
5   Montague Summers, *The Vampire: His Kith and Kin*, pp.140-41.
6   Ernest Jones, 'On the Vampire', in Frayling, p.322.
7   See A Murgoci, 'The Evil Eye in Roumania, and its Antidotes'.
8   Montague Summers, *The Vampire in Europe*, p.302.
9   Ronay, p.10.
10   Felix J Oinas, 'Heretics as Vampires and Demons in Russia', pp.437, 40.
11   Summers, *The Vampire: His Kith and Kin*, p.95.
12   ibid., pp.153-54.
13   Jones, p.321.
14   Summers, op. cit., pp.31-33.
15   ibid., pp.182-83.
16   ibid., p.179.
17   Ornella Volta, *The Vampire*, pp.12, 83.
18   Dudley Wright, *Vampires and Vampirism*, p.13.
19   Summers, op. cit., p.30.
20   Bernard Davies, 'Mountain Greenery', The Dracula Journals, No 1, p.10.
21   Anthony Masters, *The Natural History of the Vampire*, p.180.
22   Davies, pp.12-13.
23   Summers, op. cit., pp.165-66.
24   ibid., pp.194-95.
25   Masters, p.107.
26   Summers, op. cit., p.202.
27   ibid., p.204.
28   Summers, *The Vampire in Europe*, p.311.
29   Volta, p.129.
30   Wright, p.107.
31   *British Medical Journal*, 31 October 1885, p.841.
32   Summers, *The Vampire in Europe*, p.284.

33   Lionel Milgrom, 'Vampires, Plants, and Crazy Kings', p.13.
34   Ronay, p.16.
35   Summers, *The Vampire: His Kith and Kin*, p.56.
36   Ronay, p.24.
37   ibid., p.27.
38   ibid., p.11.

3

The Vampire in Literature

Her beautifully rounded limbs quivered with the agony of her soul. The glassy, horrible eyes of the figure ran over that angelic form with a hideous satisfaction – horrible profanation. He drags her head to the bed's edge. He forces it back by the long hair still entwined in his grasp. With a plunge he seizes her neck in his fang-like teeth – a gush of blood and a hideous sucking noise follows. The girl has swooned, and the vampire is at his hideous repast!

Varney the Vampire; or, the Feast of Blood, Vol 1, p.4.

The vampire epidemic that swept across much of the Continent in the second quarter of the eighteenth century was ready-made to excite German academia rather than her writers and artists. The haughty atmosphere of the Enlightenment viewed vampirism as a phenomenon to be analysed, not romanticized. The plethora of explanatory dissertations streaming from German universities were, in time, translated and worked their way across the English Channel. As early as the 1730s the term 'vampire' had made its debut in English writing. While the Age of Reason lasted, these startling revelations of walking corpses found little enthusiastic reception in the higher literary circles of Britain or the Continent. Not till the later decades of the century did Gothic and Romantic sentiments became fashionable, when, as part of the great mystery of love, life, death, and the supernatural, the vampire became something of a vogue. It would take a century for the transformation to be complete, but the folkloric vampire of central and eastern Europe eventually metamorphosed into the British-built vampire of Romantic literature. Purported fact would live on and derive nourishment as fiction, as a post-Enlightenment literary phenomenon.

Abetted by the earlier labours of their academic countrymen, it was the poets of Germany who first realized the potential of the vampire, and who transported the undead from Church-dominated superstition into the respectable channels of verse. Ossenfelder's *The Vampire* (1748), Bürger's *Lenore* (1773), and Goethe's *The Bride of Corinth* (1797) announced the new medium for the vampire tale.[1] *Lenore* was clearly known to Bram Stoker, who would include in *Dracula* (D1:20) its vivid phrase *'Denn die Todten reiten schnell'* (For the dead travel fast). In *The Bride of Corinth*, Goethe demonstrates his knowledge of Greek vampire lore when he fuses the quest for love and blood. A young woman returns from the grave to seek her lover:

> From my grave to wander I am forced,
>> Still to seek the God's long sever'd link,
> Still to love the bridegroom I have lost,
>> And the lifeblood of his heart to drink.

In Britain, Samuel Taylor Coleridge's *The Rime of the Ancient Mariner* (1797) comes close to the vampire essence with these lines:

> Her lips were red, her looks were free,
> Her locks were yellow as gold:
> Her skin was white as leprosy,
> The Nightmare Life-in-Death was she,
> Who thicks man's blood with cold.
>> (Part III, lines 190-94)

But credit for the unambiguous arrival of the vampire into English verse goes to Robert Southey's Gothic epic *Thalaba the Destroyer* (1797), which was published complete with explanatory notes for bewildered readers:

> 'Yea, strike her!' cried a voice, whose tones
>> Flow'd with such a sudden healing through his soul,
>> As when the desert shower
>> From death deliver'd him;
> But obedient to that well-known voice,
>> His eye was seeking it,

When Moath, firm of heart,
Perform'd the bidding: through the vampire corpse
    He thrust his lance; it fell,
    And howling with the wound,
    Its fiendish tenant fled.
A sapphire light fell on them,
And garmented with glory, in their sight
    Oneiza's spirit blood.

(Book 8, Stanza II)

The following year Southey's *The Old Woman of Berkeley* ranged widely over lamias, ghosts, and witches, providing a sound base for the explosion of the literary vampire that arrived in the second decade of the new century. John Stagg's grisly *The Vampyre* (1810) emphasized the blood and gore aspect of the undead:

The choir then burst the funeral dome
    Where Sigismund was lately laid,
And found him, tho' within the tomb,
    Still warm as life, and undecay'd.
With blood his visage was distain'd,
    Ensanguin'd were his frightful eyes,
Each sign of former life remain'd,
    Save that all motionless he lies.

By this time, the great Romantic poets were able to discern the potential of the vampire for their own creative purposes. By 1820 many had experimented with the vampire motif. Some made use of the male vampire as an instrument of domination; others worked with the she-vampire/lamia tradition to project female seduction. Among the latter is Sir Walter Scott's *Rokeby*:

For like the bat of Indian brakes,
Her pinions from the womb she makes,
And soothing thus the dreamer's pains,
She drinks the life-blood from his veins.

Coleridge told of the she-vampire *Christabel*; Shelley explored the male version in *The Cenci*; while Keats' prolific output of

47

vampire poems – *The Eve of St Agnes*, *Lamia*, and above all *La Belle Dame sans Merci* – alternated the sex of the undead. In *To Fanny Brawne* Keats uses vampiric language to illustrate the power of love:

> This living hand, now warm and capable
> Of earnest grasping, would, if it were cold,
> And in the icy silence of the tomb,
> So haunt thy days and chill thy dreaming nights
> That thou wouldst wish thine own heart dry of blood
> So in my veins red life might stream again,
> And thou be conscience-calm'd – see here it is.
> I hold it towards you.

Most influential of all was Byron, himself steeped in folklore. His curse of *The Giaour* spells out the terror of the vampire – prince of phantoms:

> But first on earth, as Vampyre sent,
> Thy corpse shall from its tomb be rent;
> Then ghastly haunt thy native place,
> And suck the blood of all thy race;
> There from thy daughter, sister, wife,
> At midnight drain the stream of life;
> Yet loathe the banquet, which perforce
> Must feed thy livid living corse,
> Thy victims, ere they yet expire,
> Shall know the demon for their sire ...
>
> ... Yet with thine own best blood shall drip
> Thy gnashing tooth, and haggard lip;
> Then stalking to thy sullen grave
> Go – and with Ghouls and Afrits rave,
> Till these in horror shrink away
> From spectre more accursed than they.

What will already be clear from these extracts is that the vampire has radically changed its image – from the pestilential outgrowth of superstition to a vehicle for artistic expression. If the vampire of folklore is difficult to define, such an amorphous concept in the hands of poets and writers could only dilute the substance of vampirism still further, as they freely adapted folklore for their own ends. Romantics were not interested in the undead as such. In their hands, vampires ceased to be 'the end', and became the 'means', the catalyst. The creatures now depicted bore little resemblance to the foamy-mouthed, walking corpses of Slavonic legend. Vampire imagery in Romantic literature is employed not to frighten, but to entertain and enlighten.

The Gothic and Romantic epochs were well-served by durable and adaptable myths. Among these are the Wandering Jew, Don Juan, and the Seeker After Forbidden Knowledge. But the vampire myth could be uniquely harnessed to illustrate one consequence of human emotional entanglement; when one partner gains vitality by draining that of the other. Literary vampirism is frequently an expression of energy transfer, psychological as much as intravenous. The central theme becomes love, not blood, and the nocturnal visits prompted by earthly rather than spiritual intent. Vestigial supernatural elements may be reduced to a dead lover returning to pursue the source of his or her unrequited affections. As for the flexibility with which the myth became endowed, this has been well essayed by Twitchell:

In the works of such artists as Coleridge, Byron, Shelley, Keats, Emily and Charlotte Brontë, Stoker, Wilde, Poe and Lawrence the vampire was variously used to personify the force of maternal attraction/repulsion (Coleridge's Christabel), incest (Byron's Manfred), oppressive paternalism (Shelley's Cenci), adolescent love (Keats' Porphyro), avaricious love (Poe's Morella and Berenice), the struggle for power (E. Brontë's Heathcliff), sexual suppression (C. Brontë's Bertha Rochester), homosexual attraction (Le Fanu's Carmilla), repressed sexuality (Stoker's Dracula), female domination (D. H. Lawrence's Brangwen women), and, most Romantic of all, the artist himself exchanging energy with aspects of his art (Coleridge's Ancient Mariner, Poe's artist in *The Oval Portrait*, Wordsworth's Leech Gatherer, Wilde's Dorian Gray, and the narrator of James's *The Sacred Fount*).[2]

This utilization of metaphorical vampirism to serve social, emotional and erotic purposes often distances the central character from outright vampirism. The energy transfer performed may be psychological, not vampiric. Even where the author is guarded in this respect, the vampire association may be obvious. In other instances greater scope for expression was encouraged by minimizing vampiric features – to the point of being unconscious of their presence.

With the greatest poets of the age turning their minds to the vampire, it was only a matter of time before it appeared in English prose. Whereas it is not possible to cite with precision its first entry into poetry, there is no comparable difficulty in dating its advent into prose. Before the nineteenth century no discernible vampire motif appeared in an English short story or novel, though Matthew Lewis's *The Monk* (1796) has a bleeding nun appear in blood-stained habit to drink the blood from the hero with a long, cold kiss. On the Continent, an obsession with spilled blood was evidenced by the Marquis de Sade's *Justine* (1796). *Justine*, however, was devoid of supernatural presence, which could not be said of Johann Ludwig Tieck's *Wake Not the Dead* (c.1800).

Both *Dracula* and *Frankenstein* emerged from the same seed. In 1816 Lord Byron was at the peak of his fame and, on account of his indiscretions, of his notoriety. Making news for the wrong reasons he left London for Geneva in the company of a young physician and travelling companion, John Polidori, there to rendezvous with fellow poet Percy Shelley and his young wife-to-be, Mary. A horror-writing contest was decided upon, but it was neither Byron nor Shelley who provided a new direction for English literature. It was Mary who came up with *Frankenstein*, while Polidori developed a rough outline scribbled by Byron to complete a short, twenty-page tale of his own. It was published in 1819 under the title *The Vampyre*, and became with hindsight one of the most influential works of the century.

The Vampyre's initial impact was almost entirely due to the association with Byron – a coincidence happily encouraged by the publishers – and despite repeated disavowals his lordship was long credited with authorship. Goethe added to the mischief, describing it as Byron's best work,[3] so that *The Vampyre* won for itself a readership that spanned western Europe, leaving Polidori to be pilloried for plagiarism.

Not only was *The Vampyre* the first work of its kind in English prose, but its leading character, Lord Ruthven, embodied many of the characteristics of the literary vampire that shape the genre to the present day. Ruthven is an aristocrat, world-weary, coldly evil, aloof, cunning, and irresistible to innocent women, whom he willingly corrupts. In short, he is a stereotypical, misanthropic, moody, nocturnal libertine – a classic Byronic hero with super-natural trappings. By casting Ruthven as a nobleman, Polidori invests him with greater literary potential: the vampire becomes more mobile, his erotic qualities are enhanced, and he is able to exercise *droit de seigneur* over his victims. Part of the tale is sited in Greece, authentic vampire country, to provide local colour. The 'blood' aspect of vampirism is played down – Ruthven acts more as a psychological sponge – but the impact and originality of the story were such that it was translated and adapted for the Paris stage within a year of publication. In time, it would appear in comic operas and vaudeville.[4]

Polidori may not have thought of his tale in vampire terms – to him it was a further variation on the Gothic villain – but it opened up new possibilities for the fictional vampire. Bram Stoker's *Dracula* would, in time, stand as the apotheosis of the tradition inaugurated by Lord Ruthven, but in the meantime the vampire motif explored fresh avenues. The lamia-esque *femme fatale*, as instanced in *Christabel* and *La Belle Dame sans Merci*, broke out of its poetic confines on both sides of the Atlantic. Theophile Gautier's little French tale *La Morte Amoreuse* (1836) tells of a priest carnally seduced by a she-vampire, who is ultimately destroyed by holy water. From the United States, Edgar Allen Poe wove vampire elements into many of his short stories, without identifying the vampire for what it was. He explored the ways in which lovers – one of whom is usually dead – might 'suffocate' each other outside prescribed vampire conventions. Poe's stories are full of women dead but alive: Berenice, Morella, Ligeia, Madeleine Usher. In an innovative twist in 'The Oval Portrait', the artist paints a portrait of his wife, but as colour is added to the picture it is drained from her. When the portrait is complete and lifelike, his wife is dead. The energy exchange has taken place not between people, but between a person and her image.

Other notable vampire tales appeared during the mid-nineteenth century. Alexander Dumas' (père) *The Pale Faced Lady*, with its setting in the Carpathian mountains; *The Vampire of Kring*; and contributions by Hoffman, Baudelaire, and Alexis Tolstoy. The year 1847 was climactic in the evolution of the literary vampire. The adaptation of Continental superstition was by now infiltrating literature of all kinds. Both Charlotte and Emily Brontë took advantage. In *Jane Eyre*, Bertha Rochester's promiscuity is portrayed as so abhorrent that she is described by Charlotte Brontë as like 'that foul German spectre – the Vampyre'. As for Heathcliff in Emily's *Wuthering Heights*, his nocturnal wanderings, bloodless hue, refusal to eat, and his ability to drain the vitality of others are suggestive in themselves. But in the concluding chapter the question is explicitly asked: 'Is he a ghoul or a vampire?' and Brontë includes the following passage: 'I tried to close his eyes: to extinguish, if possible, that frightful, life-like gaze of exultation before any one else beheld it. They would not shut: they seemed to sneer at my attempts: and his parted lips and sharp white teeth sneered too!' (Chapter 34). Brontë does not *say* that Heathcliff is a vampire, but her readers in the 1840s, more so than today, knew enough of the legend to draw their own conclusions.

Mention of *Jane Eyre* and *Wuthering Heights* illustrates how rarefied and pervasive the original vampire motif had become. Neither sister was writing about, or was especially interested in, vampires *per se*, yet they reveal themselves familiar with its use as social metaphor. The greater significance of 1847, however, lies not with the Brontës but with a contribution from the other end of the literary spectrum. By the middle of the century literacy was increasing. Steam presses and assembly-line publishing techniques were already churning out 'penny dreadfuls' – blood-thirsty, proletarian pot-boilers, tales of murder, lurid romance, and other sensationalist happenings laced with sexual innuendo. It was from these developments that *Varney the Vampire; or, the Feast of Blood* first appeared.

Polidori had told his tale in some twenty pages: the author of *Varney* – James Malcolm Rymer or Thomas Pecket Prest (the authorship is disputed)[5] – needed 868 double-columned pages divided into 220 chapters. The tale was reissued in 1853 in penny parts. With *Varney* there is no pretence at literary art; just a rattling story repeated in its essentials time and again. Set in the 1730s, the exploits of Sir Francis Varney mark him as the principal literary precursor of Count Dracula. Those ingredients in *Varney* later employed by Bram Stoker include: the maidens' sexual initiation and ambiguous responses; the vampire's roots in central Europe; the quasi-medical-scientific methods of vampire disposal; and the Keystone-Cops-style hunt for the vampire.[6] Varney also includes sleep-walking victims and a villain in black cloak who climbs down castle walls and arrives in Britain aboard a shipwrecked vessel during a tempest.

After *Varney* there seemed no other avenue for the fictional vampire to explore. The genre seemed exhausted, both as a literary metaphor and as a scaremonger in its own right. But there remains to be considered one further mainstream vampire work pre-dating *Dracula*. Its author, like Stoker, was an Irishman. Among the five tales comprising *In a Glass Darkly* (1872) by Joseph Sheridan Le Fanu, appeared the novelette *Carmilla* – credited by many aficionados as the finest of all vampire tales. Despite its late year of publication, *Carmilla* is soundly Gothic, punctuated with evening mists, full moons, black stagecoaches, and central European locations.

Unlike *Varney*, *Carmilla* is a tasteful, sensuous work. What is unprecedented is that Carmilla is a lesbian. The feminine perspective of both vampire and victim serves to heighten the sexual quality of the vampire act, which is described in greater erotic detail than in any previous example of the genre.

> Sometimes after an hour of apathy, my strange and beautiful companion would take my hand and hold it with a fond pressure, renewed again and again; blushing softly, gazing in my face with languid and burning eyes, and breathing so fast that her dress rose and fell with the tumultuous respiration. It was like the ardour of a lover; it embarrassed me; it was hateful and yet overpowering; and with gloating eyes she drew me to her, and her hot lips travelled along my cheek in kisses; and she would whisper, almost in sobs, 'You are mine, you *shall* be mine, and you and I are one for ever'. (*Carmilla*, Chapter 4).

Carmilla, moreover, is no supernatural fiend or disguised Gothic villain, but a complex, self-motivated personality. The female vampire would become a popular acquisition for film-makers, who would link Carmilla with the real-life Hungarian mass-murderess Elizabeth Bathory to create a new sub-cult of the species.

The dying years of the nineteenth century witnessed an Indian summer for the Gothic novel. Stevenson's *Dr Jekyll and Mr Hyde* (1886) and Oscar Wilde's *Picture of Dorian Gray* (1891) are – along with *Dracula* – perhaps the most striking examples of this unexpected burst of symbolic energy.[7] The vampire motif once again began to sprout in unexpected directions. H G Wells' *The Flowering of the Strange Orchid* deals with vampire plants; Conan Doyle's *The Parasite* delves into psychic sponges; and Jules Verne's *Carpathian Castle* presents evil scientists posing as vampires.[8] Guy de Maupassant's *The Horla*, vividly tells of the anguish of a vampire assault from the perspective of the victim.

Dracula would be the next, and last, great vampire work. It will be useful to enumerate the changes spanning a century which transformed the vampire of folklore into the vampire of literature. The one is real and to be feared; the other fictional and to enlighten. In literature, the undead are commonly from the ranks of nobility. They are able to travel far and wide to plague great cities, where they find shelter in their anonymity. Whereas the folkloric vampire restricts itself to its family, and is not bound to visit the opposite sex, the literary vampire usually has no family and may attack whom it pleases where it pleases. Its affairs are nevertheless in the main heterosexual.

With regard to age, the vampire of superstition will not be long dead, yet will be zombie-like, thick-headed, dim-witted. This contrasts with his fictional counterpart, who – though dead for centuries – has used his time profitably to become learned and adroit. The sexual element is latent in folklore, magnified in fiction, and embellished by the corruption of innocents. The god-devil conflict is to the forefront in literature, which might also express pity for the vampire, in keeping with the tradition of Faust and the Wandering Jew. The vampire of folklore may have acquired its condition from countless causes. The origins of its literary cousins are either left undisclosed, or result from some pact with the devil. Finally, the vampire of literature possesses formidable powers. Like the villain in modern crime thrillers, the vampire must not be caught too easily. The destruction of the literary vampire usually borrows from folklore.[9]

This wealth of folkloric and literary antecedents was assimilated by Bram Stoker. *Dracula* fuses the tradition of the Byronic hero/Gothic villain with that of the *femme fatale*, and overlays the whole with a topping of folklore. Stoker ignores the popular device of siting his tale in a remote land in a bygone age, and brings his all-powerful Count to contemporary England – to the crowded streets of London in the 1890s. The late Victorian upsurge in tales of the supernatural helped him construct a character more evil than Carmilla and more substantial than Varney. As Leonard Wolf has said: 'There is nothing in Varney, nothing at all, that is capable of sounding anything like the chords of dark understanding that reverberate in page after page of Stoker's *Dracula*.'[10] With that in mind, it is time to take a closer look at Bram Stoker – the man who wrote *Dracula*.

---

1   James Twitchell, *The Living Dead: A Study of the Vampire in Romantic Literature*, p.33.
2   ibid., pp.4-5.
3   Christopher Frayling (ed.), *The Vampyre: Lord Ruthven to Count Dracula*, p.15.
4   M M Carlson, 'What Stoker Saw: an Introduction to the History of the Literary Vampire', p.27.
5   For many years it was accepted that Prest was the author. Some scholars indicate that *Varney* might have had multiple authors (Twitchell, p.123). Current opinion favours Rymer as the author.
6   Frayling, pp.42-43.
7   See David Punter, *The Literature of Terror*, p.239.
8   Frayling, p.64.
9   Carlson, pp.30-31.
10 Leonard Wolf, *A Dream of Dracula*, p.170.

4

The Life and Works of Bram Stoker

In my babyhood I used, I understand to be, often at the point of death. Certainly till I was about seven years old I never knew what it was to stand upright ... This early weakness, however, passed away in time and I grew into a strong boy and in time enlarged into the biggest member of my family ... I was physically immensely strong.

Bram Stoker, writing of himself in
Personal Reminiscences of Henry Irving, Vol 1, pp.31-32.

Close acquaintance with Bram Stoker is regrettably not possible. His immortal creation lives on but the author remains elusive. Even with the arrival of two biographies, nothing but the basics of Stoker's life have been revealed. It is known what he did, but not who he was. The principal source on Stoker is a two-volume biography he wrote about the actor Henry Irving, with whom he spent nearly thirty years of his life, in which Stoker indulges in plenty of personal reminiscences of himself.[1] Most of his personal papers have failed to survive, so that this major work provides the mainstay of his own biographers – Harry Ludlam and Daniel Farson (Stoker's grand-nephew).[2] Neither biographer could do more than offer tantalizing glimpses into the personality who created arguably the most enduring figure of Victorian fiction. To supplement these biographies and unwitting autobiography, there exist the voluminous writings of Bram Stoker, though caution should be exercised when attributing characteristics of an author's fiction to the author himself.

Bram Stoker was born on 8 November 1847 at 15 The Crescent, Clontarf, just north of Dublin. Ireland was then an integral part of the United Kingdom, though nationalist sentiment was on the rise, as evidenced by the activities of such organizations as the 'Young Ireland' group. His father was Abraham, by all accounts devoid of ambition, content to fend for his growing family while a civil servant in Dublin Castle. Abraham was forty-eight years old when Bram was born, the third of seven children born inside ten years – William, Matilda, Abraham junior (Bram), Tom, Richard, Margaret, and George.

Bram's mother, Charlotte, eighteen years younger than her husband, was a handsome, strong minded woman who, if she could see no ambition in her husband, was determined to invest it in her sons. Three – William, Richard, and George – would enter the medical profession. William would become an eminent surgeon and be knighted in 1895. As for her daughters, Charlotte 'did not care tuppence'.[3] So far as the responsibilities of rearing a large family permitted, Charlotte was an ardent social reformer and visitor to the workhouses. Perhaps surprisingly in view of her reported attitude to her daughters, she was active in promoting women's rights. She was also Irish to the core, reared on Gaelic mythology and folk tales.

For the infant Abraham, named after his father and reputedly the closest to him of his sons, the first years of life were taken up with simple survival. He was bed-ridden for his first seven years. The nature of this disorder has never been established, nor even hinted at with any confidence. In view of his complete recovery and the athletic feats which followed, it is possible that the malady had its roots in his mind rather than his body.

Being bed-ridden, Bram had plenty of time to absorb Irish myths and legends from his mother. He turned to books at an early age, availing himself of his father's well-stocked collection. When fully recovered, he attended a private school run by a Reverend Woods, and by the age of sixteen he was already a compulsive scribbler. He was admitted to Trinity College, Dublin, where the once retiring introvert was introduced to the cut and thrust of university life. He blossomed into an effective debater, held the most prestigious student offices, and acquired many sporting honours. The one-time infant invalid was capped at football and became marathon walking champion.

His personality at university developed into that recognizable in him in adulthood. 'Hearty' and 'stalwart' is how Farson describes him, very much a man's man, and chivalrous towards women.[4] He was active in the literary and dramatic activities of Trinity and was not deterred by controversy. He took up cudgels on behalf of the controversial American poet, Walt Whitman, and wrote long, passionately supportive letters across the Atlantic.

Now a burly six footer and sporting a lush, reddish beard, Stoker graduated with honours in science (pure mathematics). Bram followed his father into the civil service as a junior clerk in Dublin Castle. This was hardly a suitable outlet for his energy or his ambitions, and his spare time was productively filled. To alleviate his parents' mounting financial difficulties he provided private tuition. He continued his studies, gaining a Master of Arts and being elected to the office of Auditor of the Historical Society – the equivalent of President of the Union at Oxbridge. Such high office, together with the acquired social graces, gave Stoker access to the Dublin social élite. Among his acquaintances were Sir William and Lady Wilde (parents of Oscar). Both were authorities on Irish folklore, and Sir William was a noted Egyptologist.[5] Bram's visits to him would help sow the seeds of one of his later novels, *The Jewel of Seven Stars*.

Bram inherited from his father a deep interest in the theatre. Lack of theatrical coverage in the Dublin press resulted in his taking on the responsibilities of unpaid drama critic for the *Dublin Evening Mail*. He also found time to develop his short-story writing. The efforts of an unknown author in finding a publisher were as confidence-sapping then as now, but the breakthrough came in 1872 when *The London Society* published 'The Crystal Cup', a dream fantasy climaxing with the evil king 'pallid with the hue of Death'.[6]

Stoker next set himself to being a part-time newspaper editor. *The Halfpenny Press* could not build up sufficient circulation, however, and after four months he resigned the editorship.[7] Yet failure in one venture was countered by another writing success. Le Fanu's sophisticated vampire tale *Carmilla* appeared in the Dublin University Magazine. It was met with critical acclaim and made a deep impression on Stoker. He wrote more short stories, one of which was far from the light fantasy of his first. The four-part serialization of 'The Chain of Destiny', appearing in *The*

Shamrock in 1875, was full of nightmares and curses, and introduced the 'phantom of the fiend'.[8]

In the meantime, Bram's father had retired. Under financial pressure he had taken his wife and daughters to the Continent, where the cost of living was easier to bear. Abraham senior continued to fret about Bram's restlessness, counselling against his moving to London to try his hand at full-time authorship. He also disparaged Bram's idea of applying for the post of Dublin city treasurer on the grounds that 'none but an advanced Liberal or a Roman Catholic would be elected'.[9]

This remark hints at the political and religious tensions operating in nineteenth-century Ireland, it being implied that the Stoker family were neither advanced Liberal nor Roman Catholic. It is known they were of Protestant faith, living in a land of Catholics. Trinity College was at that time still a Protestant university. The Stoker's political affiliations, however, are less clear. It is true that the Dublin Castle elect to which father and son aspired were steadfastly Tory,[10] but if Bram was at one time a Tory he became a Liberal later in life (joining the National Liberal Club). Stoker was a political thinker: his inaugural address as Auditor of the Trinity Historical Society had spoken of 'the necessity for political honesty' and a plea for some kind of United Nations.[11] Though written many years later, his memoirs of Henry Irving are peppered with his own political views, among them his support for Gladstone's attempts to introduce Home Rule – the failure of which would eventually split the Liberal Party. Stoker described himself as a 'philosophical Home-Ruler',[12] though he was opposed to the extra-Parliamentary activities being addressed by certain Irish agitators.

Stoker senior died in 1876 in Naples, with the knowledge that his son's security had not yet been tossed to the wind; but within months Bram experienced a chance encounter that would transform his life. It was in his Trinity days that Stoker, a regular theatre-goer to Dublin's only sizable auditorium, the Theatre Royal, first set eyes on a rising actor destined to become the Olivier of his day. In this respect it was fortunate that Dublin could attract the major touring players. The young actor was Henry Irving, playing Captain Absolute in *The Rivals*. Stoker was then nineteen, Irving ten years older. The star-struck student was enraptured by the burgeoning talent before him.

Now, ten years later, on a further trip to Dublin, Irving played the lead role in *Hamlet*. Stoker was overwhelmed and conveyed his feelings to the Dublin public through his theatre column. The actor was impressed, inviting the critic backstage. During the course of several meetings a bond, personal and professional, was forged between the two men. Stoker was among a select group privy to a private recitation of Thomas Hood's *The Dream of Eugene Aram*, at the conclusion of which Irving slumped from the emotional effort, leaving Stoker shell-shocked by the performance: 'Here was incarnate power, incarnate passion ... Irving's genius floated in blazing triumph.' Stoker described his own reaction in a striking piece of autobiography:

> I burst out into something like a violent fit of hysterics. Let me say, not in my own vindication, but to bring new tribute to Irving's splendid power, that I was no hysterical subject. I was no green youth; no weak individual, yielding to a superior emotional force. I was as men go a strong man, strong in many ways.[13]

Describing their mutual admiration, Stoker wrote: 'Soul had looked into soul. From that hour began a friendship as profound, as close, as lasting, as can be between two men.' The pair met regularly over the next two years, Stoker enjoying Irving's unique talents, the actor benefiting from Stoker's astute criticism. Meanwhile, Stoker had been promoted at work to become an Inspector of Petty Sessions, removing him from the monotony of a desk-bound job and enabling him to tour the Dublin courts. The clerical muddles his visits unearthed prompted him to commence work on a weighty tome which was finally published in 1879. It was Stoker's first full-length book, and bore the unlikely and unromantic title *The Duties of Clerks of Petty Sessions in Ireland*. 'Dry as dust' Stoker would later call it,[14] but it became a standard reference work in its field.

Stoker also found time to woo his future wife. Nineteen-year-old Dublin beauty Florence Balcombe was already sufficiently eligible to number Oscar Wilde among her ex-suitors.[15] She and

Bram planned to marry in 1879 but the date was brought forward at short notice. Henry Irving had taken control of his own theatre company – the London Lyceum – but was dissatisfied with the incumbent management. He had already appointed a new stage manager, Harry Loveday, and in December 1878 approached Stoker to look after the business side of the new venture. Bram needed no second invitation to resign his lengthy stint in the civil service, forfeit his pension, move to London with his new wife, and assume the duties of Acting Manager of the Lyceum Theatre.

Had he lived to see it, Abraham senior would not have approved, and Charlotte was livid. The acting 'profession' was widely disparaged in those days as socially disadvantageous. When Bram had earlier written of his attachment to a certain actress, his father had replied that he did not think that actors and actresses 'are altogether desirable acquaintances to those not connected with their own profession (if I may call it) ... Under all the circumstances I believe such acquaintanceship is better avoided'. Now, upon sacrificing his security to throw in his lot with Irving, Charlotte scolded her son for becoming a 'minstrel to a strolling player'.[16]

Stoker's reputation, not to say his prosperity, was thereafter inextricably linked to the fortunes of Henry Irving. The actor was nothing if not controversial. Aside from his autocratic and egotistical temperament, the principle of an actor owning his own theatre rankled the critics, among them George Bernard Shaw. Irving, they sniped, ensured that the talents of the Lyceum's supporting cast were transparently inferior to his own.[17]

For the moment, the newly-weds set up home in fashionable Cheyne Walk in Chelsea. Within a year Florence gave birth to Noel, their only child. The succeeding years were probably the most fulfilling of Stoker's life as, without any previous business experience, he threw himself into his new challenge. Such were his responsibilities – controlling a full-time staff in excess of a hundred, grappling with the accounts of a new enterprise, and protecting Irving from those eager to exploit his acquaintance – that all thoughts of further writing were temporarily eclipsed.

Proximity to Henry Irving meant for Stoker access to London's rich and famous. Theatreland was the hub of high society, with the Lyceum the most glittering of venues for the capital's well-to-do. Stoker could count among his neighbours the artist James McNeil Whistler and the novelist George Eliot. He would eventually be introduced to no fewer than four American Presidents, as well as merit an entry in his own right in *Who's Who*.

Stoker had only been in London a couple of years when the publishing firm of Sampson Low expressed interest in a collection of 'weirdies' – stories that Stoker had written over the years and which were gathering dust instead of royalties. As he had no time for writing, this unexpected outlet for some of his past efforts brought the power of his literary imagination to general notice. *Under the Sunset*, as the anthology was called when published in 1881, was a far cry from *The Duties of Clerks*.

Bram Stoker was hardly the first author to perceive a market for children's stories. Lewis Carroll, for example, had done well with his Alice adventures and *The Hunting of the Snark*. But Stoker's tales were altogether more scary. Liberally scattered with lurid illustrations from William Fitzgerald and W V Cockburn, the book was a sequence of allegories about a mysterious land, far away – a land 'under the sunset'.

Though each constituent tale is self-contained, they reflect the same motifs: familial love; the division of the world into good and evil; the horrendous punishments meted out to those who sin; the inevitable triumph of good; and the mysterious boundary between life and death. The oppressive moralizing that pervades them was common to many nineteenth-century fairy tales. Even their gratuitous cruelty was not out of keeping with the mainstream of the genre. It is frequently forgotten how gruesome are the conclusions of a number of popular fairy tales: Cinderella's stepsisters rendered blind and crippled; and Snow White's stepmother being forced to dance to her death in red-hot slippers.[18]

Nonetheless, the overall package was a triumph of imagination, and at that level was well-received by the critics. 'Charming', said *Punch*.[19] 'Delicate and forceful allegories', agreed the *Daily Telegraph*, while others noted the book's 'dreamy beauty of style' and its 'remarkable purity and grace'. The *Spectator* noted:

'*Under the Sunset* may be tried with the grown-up world with perfect success. To its intellectual and critical perception, the literal charm of the stories ... will commend themselves highly.'[20] On the question of suitability for infants, however, there were sterner reservations:

> The judicious mother may prefer to omit some of the ... dismal doings which might banish sleep from the children's pillows ... A terribly grim picture ... might haunt any little one's imagination for many a night; while the words ... are ... decidedly 'creepy'.
>
> We can quite believe that this sort of picture may have a kind of fascination for young readers, but we very much doubt whether it is well to subject them to it, and could therefore wish that these lurid passages had been expunged from a book which in many respects is very pleasing.[21]

At the very least, Bram Stoker's fiction had been acclaimed. Only lack of opportunity prevented any sequel, as Stoker revelled in the world of theatre management and hob-nobbed with the stars.

In 1882 an oft-discussed incident took place, whose details may have warped with the years. Whilst travelling down the Thames on a steamboat, a man jumped overboard. Stoker leapt after him, and despite struggling against a strong tide and the man's suicidal intent, managed to haul him aboard. Efforts at resuscitation failed, whereupon Stoker carried the body back to his Chelsea home. He laid it out in the dining room, in front of a horrified Florence, until such time as a doctor arrived to pronounce death.[22] For his bravery, Stoker was praised at the inquest and in time awarded the Bronze Medal of the Royal Humane Society. Displaying a corpse at home, however, appears to have done little for an already deteriorating marriage. His nocturnal existence – much of his work at the Lyceum was done in the early hours following curtain fall – and his natural preference for male company, meant that his wife and son saw little of him.

The evidence is hazy, but there is more than a suggestion of estrangement after the first happy months. Certainly the couple were to be separated for long stretches, as when Irving took his company on a six-month tour of North America. For a British theatre company to cross the Atlantic complete with scenery and equipment was at the time unprecedented. In addition to the major east coast cities, the company performed in Chicago, St Louis and Cincinnati, as well as Toronto, Canada. Irving was famous in America even before he arrived, and so successful was the tour that it would be repeated regularly over the next twenty years. A second tour left England in September 1884, just five months after returning from the first, and this time it would result in another Bram Stoker publication.

The United States made a profound impression on Irving's acting manager, who was painfully aware of British ignorance of all things American. There existed at the time no balanced instructive source of general information for a British public contemptuously prejudiced against her ex-colony. Stoker set to work, and on his return to Britain delivered a lecture to the London Institution entitled 'A Glimpse of America', which was published the following year.

Stoker extolled almost everything to do with the United States, be it her constitution, her education system, her fire-fighting service, her workmen, good manners, hospitality, practical spirit, sense of humour, or tolerance. He admired American fire-fighters for exhibiting that 'calm coolness that marks the brave'.[23] Against this, his professed admiration for America's lack of class consciousness must be treated lightly, for it is abundantly clear from his reminiscences and his later fiction that Stoker was highly class conscious. To all intents, he was a model, upright Victorian gentleman, imbued with all the prejudices of his station – a station granted by God. During one of Irving's visits to Dublin the two men came upon an organized street fight. Stoker later wrote: 'We saw the gathering crowd and joined them. They did not know either of us, but they saw we were gentlemen, strangers to themselves, and with the universal courtesy of their race put us in the front ...'

Elsewhere his language bordered on the extreme: 'An individual who is not in any way distinguishable from his fellows is but a poor creature after all and is not held of much account by anybody.'[24] He reserved his most ferocious tirade for America's tramps and criminal elements: 'The criminal classes are the same the world over, only they would molest a woman ... tramps and other excretions of civilization ... a percentage of incurable drones ... they form a dangerous element.'[25] Towards the end of his life Stoker proposed his own solution to the American tramp problem: to 'brand' them, preferably about the ears, so that they might be readily identified, sent to a labour colony, and taught the virtues of hard work to which he had ascribed all his life.[26]

Even with her occasional blemishes, America was still a land of which Stoker was proud, and he concludes his glimpse in positive fashion. It was a 'joy that England's first born child has arrived at so noble a stature ... We have not, all the world through, so strong an ally, so close a friend ... America has got over her childhood. Our history is their history, they are bound to us, and we to them'.[27] Praise for Stoker's little book came from many, including the explorer Henry Morton Stanley, who carried it on one of his African expeditions and confessed that it contained more information about America than any other book.[28]

A Glimpse of America illustrated more than Stoker's contempt for society's misfits and outcasts. It also revealed his views on women. He praised the American 'high regard with which women are held ... and the deferential and protective spirit afforded to them'[29] – such as inviting them to jump queues. On one occasion, when a fire broke out on stage, one of the audience bolted for the exits. He was seized by the throat and hurled to the floor by Stoker, who then sent him back to his seat with his ears ringing: 'It is cowards like you who cause death to helpless women.'[30]

A more detailed look at Stoker's attitude towards women will be postponed, though the following remark made of actress Ellen Terry (whose beauty is commented upon in *Dracula*) is typical: 'Doubtless she has her faults. She is a woman; and perfection must not be expected even in the finishing work of creation.'[31] To Stoker, women were hopelessly dependent upon the valour of strong men. Following a storm at sea he wrote: 'In such cases the only real comfort a poor woman can have is to hold on to a man. I happen to be a big one, and therefore of extra desirability in such cases of stress.'[32] Evidently, any woman who was not a cowering wreck was not truly a woman.

In the company of men, Stoker was quick to appreciate strength of character. During his early trips to America he fulfilled a

Trinity ambition by being introduced to the ageing poet Walt Whitman: 'I found him [Whitman] all that I had ever dreamed of, or wished for in him: large-minded, broad-viewed, tolerant to the last degree, incarnate sympathy, understanding with an insight that seemed more than human ... A man amongst men.'[33] His reminiscences of Irving are likewise saturated with hero-worship, nowhere permitting his subject to be criticized, let alone ridiculed. Stoker viewed his employer with a mixture of worship and fear: it is not stretching the point to suggest that he was, at heart, married to Irving, not Florence.

Stoker's idealized, guileless appreciation of strong men can be detected all through his memoirs. So can his preoccupation with striking facial features, especially the mouth and teeth. Of Lord Tennyson, who became a close acquaintance (receiving a signed copy of *Dracula*), he noted: 'Tennyson had at times that lifting of the upper lip which shows the canine tooth.' And Sir Richard Burton, the intrepid Oriental explorer/scholar, he described in the following remarkable language: 'The man riveted my attention. He was dark, and forceful, and masterful, and ruthless. I have never seen so iron a countenance ... Burton's face seemed to lengthen when he laughed; the upper lip rising instinctively and showing the right canine tooth ... As he spoke the upper lip rose and his canine tooth showed its full length like the gleam of a dagger.'[34] Evidently, Stoker would have little difficulty when he turned to describing vampires.

By 1888, having completed his first ten years with Irving and undertaken three tours of the United States, Stoker was ready to widen his horizons. He already enjoyed a strong legal background, both from his years in Dublin Castle and from handling the legal affairs of the Lyceum. He now found the necessary hours to study for the Bar, being called to the Inner Temple in 1890. He also made time to write his first romantic novel. Set in Ireland and full of Irish brogue and customs, *The Snake's Pass* (1890) concerns a wealthy young Englishman who finds himself caught up in the bogs while on a quest for lost gold. As with Stoker's writings to date, *The Snake's Pass* was applauded by the critics, even drawing praise from Tennyson and Gladstone[35] – a frequent Lyceum visitor. As if to confirm Stoker's arrival as a major Irish novelist, an episode from the book called 'The Gombeen Man' (an Irish money lender) would in time win a place in an anthology of classic works from Irish authors and poets.[36]

Enjoying the flush of recognition, Stoker was already making notes for a massive vampire novel, but these notes were progressing slowly, and did not impede the output of other works. These works were much influenced by a holiday he took in 1893 in Cruden Bay, situated between Aberdeen and Peterhead on the Buchan coastline of north-east Scotland. Cruden Bay is a picturesque inlet surrounded by cliffs upon which stands Slains Castle, inhabited since the thirteenth century by the Earls of Errol.[37] Stretching across the mouth of the bay lies the skares reef, one of the most merciless destroyers of ships anywhere on the British coastline. The visual effect of the area on Stoker must have been profound, for he would return, alone, every summer, occupying rooms at the Kilmarnock Arms Hotel, until eventually taking a small summer cottage in the hamlet of Whinnyfold on the southern lip of the bay.

Stoker soon churned out a succession of novels and short stories, many set in, or inspired by, Cruden Bay. 'The Man from Shorrox's' (1894) was a droll tale about a sales traveller asked to share a bed in an inn with a corpse. 'Crooken Sands' (1894), set in a thinly disguised Cruden Bay, tells of a London merchant on holiday who kits himself out in highland regalia and casts eyes on his own image being sucked down under quicksand. Two other stories dating from the same period were yet more horrific. 'The Burial of the Rats', set among the garbage heaps of a Paris suburb, and 'The Squaw', a euphemistically named iron torture chamber which claims its victim through the wiles of a black cat, showed the direction in which Stoker's literary talents would most profit.

The short novel *The Watter's Mou'* (Buchan dialect for 'The Water's Mouth') (1894) centred around a gorge running into the North Sea just north of Cruden Bay. This romance features the lovers Maggie and Sailor Willie, who find themselves involved in smuggling and shipwrecks, but it earned indifferent reviews on account of its excessive melodrama and 'stagey' writing.[38] No sooner was it published than its successor appeared. *The*

Shoulder of Shasta (1895) was another torrid romance, written in the wake of the Lyceum's performances in California during the 1893-94 tour. It concerns a frail, city girl's love for Grizzly Dick, a husky mountain man living on Shasta, an extinct volcano in northern California. This time the critics were merciless: *The Athenaeum* castigated the book for its lack of maturity, haste, poor humour, weakness of plot, and lack of characterization.[39] Nothing Stoker had written had been so maligned. An author of acknowledged potential was in danger of ridicule.

He was, in any case, deep into the writing of *Dracula*, which was published by Constable in June 1897. The novel was sufficiently broad in panorama to please, or displease, a wide cross-section of the 1890s reading public. Many critics have concurred that had *Dracula* been written at the beginning, not the end, of the nineteenth century its impact would have been far greater. It was less likely to succeed in an intellectual climate of scientific rationalism and scepticism. Moreover, *Dracula* was not set, as with mainstream Gothic romance, in a far-off land in a far-off time. The monster was here, now, a vampire stalking the streets of late-Victorian London.

Critical response was mixed. The *Daily Mail* compared it favourably with Mrs Radcliffe's *The Mysteries of Udolpho*, Mary Shelley's *Frankenstein*, Emily Brontë's *Wuthering Heights*, and Poe's *The Fall of the House of Usher*. The *Pall Mall Gazette* thought it 'excellent', and *The Lady* admitted that the book was so fascinating that it was impossible to put down.[40] Other reviewers were more equivocal. *The Bookman* conceded:

A summary of the book would shock and disgust, but we must own that, though here and there in the course of the tale we hurried over things with repulsion, we read nearly the whole with rapt attention. It is something of a triumph for the writer that neither the improbability, nor the unnecessary number of hideous incidents recounted of the man-vampire are long foremost in the reader's mind, but that the interest of the danger, of the complications, of the pursuit of the villain, of human skill and courage pitted against inhuman wrong and superhuman strength, rises always to the top.[41]

Punch, too, saw flaws as well as virtues:

It is a pity that Mr. BRAM STOKER was not content to employ such supernatural anti-vampire receipts as his wildest imagination might have invented without rashly venturing on a domain where angels fear to tread. But for this, [the reviewer] could have unreservedly recommended so ingenious a romance to all who enjoy the very weirdest of weird tales.[42]

Other reviewers found few redeeming features. *The Athenaeum* once again emerged with guns blazing. *Dracula* it assessed as being highly sensational, but the novel was 'wanting in the constructive art as well as in the higher literary sense. It reads at times like a mere series of grotesquely incredible events ... he merely commands an array of crude statements of incredible actions.' Even the summary was grudgingly given: 'his object, assuming it to be ghastliness, is fairly well fulfilled.'[43]

The most glowing tribute came from Stoker's mother: 'It is splendid, a thousand miles beyond anything you have written before, and I feel certain will place you very high in the writers of the day ... No book since Mrs Shelley's "Frankenstein" or indeed any other at all has come near yours in originality, or terror – Poe is nowhere. I have read much but I have never met a book like it at all. In its terrible excitement it should make a widespread reputation and much money for you.'[44] In the event, it did neither.

Stoker's final book in this intensely creative phase reverted to the slush sentimentality to which he was regrettably prone, a tear-jerker full of romance, honour, and the unquestioning acceptance of fragile womanhood. *Miss Betty* (1898) – dedicated to his wife – is today deservedly forgotten. Stoker wrote nothing else in his next years, responsibility for which lies with a series of setbacks for Henry Irving's theatre company. Stoker's *Dracula*, his crowning work of fiction, coincided with the beginning of the Lyceum's slide. In 1895, as the novel was taking shape, Stoker's elder, surgeon brother, William, was knighted, and so too was Henry Irving – the first actor to be so decorated. This honour brought tribute to the entire acting profession, establishing the precedent that would later ennoble Laurence Olivier.

Ironically, troubles then escalated for Henry Irving. He slipped down some stairs, injured his leg, and was compelled to close the theatre for some weeks. In 1898 disaster struck, when the Lyceum storehouse was consumed by fire, destroying scenery and stage props. The entire repertory equipment of the company was lost. Insurance cover had been reduced to a fraction of the loss. Coming on top of a recent drop in audience figures, and the emergence of flourishing rival theatre companies, the fire reduced the Lyceum's finances to disarray. Before the year was out Irving succumbed to pneumonia and pleurisy. Against Stoker's advice, the management of the Lyceum was sold to a syndicate which soon collapsed. By this time, Stoker's own trusted position was becoming precarious. Irving hired a press agent, without consulting Stoker, and a working relationship of twenty years was superseded by a perceptible rift between actor and manager.[45]

There are many indications that Stoker jealously guarded against intrusion into his relationship with Irving. As for Stoker's responsibility for the Lyceum's fortunes, Irving's own biographers are either dismissive or scathing. Austin Brereton, the press agent in question, barely gives Stoker a mention. The actor's grandson, Laurence, offered this damning assessment. Stoker, he wrote, was:

> inflated with literary and athletic pretensions [and] worshipped Irving with all the sentimental idolatry of which an Irishman is capable, revelling in the patronage which, as Irving's manager, was at his disposal, and in the opportunities which this position gave him to rub shoulders with the great ... This weakness and his emotional impetuosity handicapped him in dealing with Irving's business affairs in a forthright and sensible manner ... Stoker, well-intentioned, vain, impulsive, and inclined to blarneying flattery was perhaps the only man who could have held his position as Irving's manager for so many years; from him Irving got the service he deserved, but at a cost which was no less fatal because it was not immediately apparent.[46]

In 1900 Stoker's mother died in Dublin. As his stories once more began to roll, it was to Cruden Bay that he turned for inspiration. *The Mystery of the Sea* (1902) features Gaelic runes, ancient manuscripts in cryptic writing, hidden treasures, secret agents, castles with hidden passageways, shipwrecks on the

Cruden skares, and even a futuristic naval gun battle. As always, there was the predictable romance, blushing damsels wilting in the face of male valour.

By the time *Mystery* was published the Lyceum syndicate had folded and Irving had become an actor without a theatre, having to turn to provincial tours and periods in other London auditoriums. Stoker's next novel, *The Jewel of Seven Stars* (1903), was indebted to those discussions on Egyptology with Sir William Wilde held way back in Stoker's Dublin days. As with *Dracula*, in *The Jewel* Stoker brought a foreign-based tale to England. It deals with mummies, witchcraft, and an Egyptian queen intending to resurrect herself five thousand years after her death. Later editions would contain a less traumatic climax, at the publisher's request.[47]

The grand old Lyceum reopened as a music hall, and as if to bow to the changing cultural patterns of British life, Irving, now in his late sixties, embarked upon a two-year grand tour of retirement, taking in Britain and North America. The scheduled farewell was never completed. Irving collapsed and died at Bradford in October 1905, and his remains were laid to rest in Westminster Abbey. Bram Stoker, approaching his fifty-eighth birthday, was now without a regular income. Without the direction provided by Irving, he was also rudderless. He made an attempt to look after the business interests of an American opera singer, but the venture collapsed, as did a proposed lecture tour. His pen would now provide his sole revenue for the rest of his days. The earlier torrent of books had been partly inspired by Cruden Bay: his final rush of publications would be prompted by sheer survival.

The Man (1905) was actually written before Irving's death, and in the light of higher things promised in *The Jewel* was an unwelcome return to naïve romance. There followed his two volumes of *Personal Reminiscences of Henry Irving* (1906), a catalogue of impressions and incidents spanning their long relationship. It is not a biography as such, for there is no attempt at a detached appraisal, just unabashed adulation of his subject.

Bram Stoker was still sufficiently involved in high society to be invited to the wedding of Winston Churchill in 1906, but his health was failing fast. He had a stroke following Irving's death, suffered from Bright's disease, and was losing his sight. Poor health, coupled with financial insecurity, made his final years less than happy ones. Of the novels to come, *Lady Athlyne* and the theatrical tales in *Snowbound* (both 1908) were rushed, hack works that could not raise his fallen literary reputation. He then turned his hand to a final work of non-fiction. In *Famous Impostors* (1910), Stoker rambles through the great impersonators, hoaxers, and swindlers of history. In so doing he demonstrates his familiarity with the great myths of romantic literature: he includes a chapter on the Wandering Jew, together with others on the practitioners of magic, witchcraft, and clairvoyancy.

For an author inextricably associated with literary terror, it should be remembered that only four of his final tally of eighteen books were novels on the supernatural. To *Dracula* and *The Jewel of Seven Stars* were added in his final years *The Lady of the Shroud* (1909) and *The Lair of the White Worm* (1911). *The Lady of the Shroud* deals with an apparent she-vampire who turns out to be playing at deception. It is perhaps most intriguing for its conclusion, which contains a prophetic air battle, just months after the Wright brothers had made their inaugural flight. *The Lair of the White Worm* would be Stoker's last and most disturbing novel, based on the ancient English legend that giant serpents/worms once dominated the landscape. He resurrected one such worm, gave it human, feminine form, and housed it in a slimy, subterranean cave.

The White Worm was riddled with sexual hallucinations and was clearly the work of a man sick in mind if not in body. Nonetheless, it gave insight into its author's vivid imagination, and for that, if nothing else, the book was charitably received by reviewers. But Stoker, the one-time athletics champion, was now bed-ridden as in his infancy. He died on 20 April 1912 at 26 St George's Square, London. He was sixty-four, and *Dracula* was by then in its ninth edition. Stoker was cremated at Golders Green, north London. It was somehow typical of the man that his death, as his life, should be overshadowed. Just five days previously the *Titanic* had sunk. In the shocked and numbed aftermath no one paid much attention to the deceased theatre manager and part-time author, particularly as he chose to die on the opening day of the American enquiry into the disaster. Only one obituary appeared, in *The Times*. In those days Stoker was still principally associated with Irving, though *The Times* conceded that 'he was the master of a particularly lurid and creepy kind of fiction'.[48]

One more volume of Stoker's fiction remained to be published, posthumously. He had died while sifting through piles of his earlier short stories in the hope of assembling a suitable anthology. This task was completed by his widow, and the compendium was released in 1914. It was named after one particular tale: a short, self-contained incident entitled 'Dracula's Guest'. As for Stoker, he would be consigned to historical oblivion. Even though his creation, *Dracula*, is familiar throughout the world, it is still difficult to find any general encyclopaedia with an entry under 'Bram Stoker'.

Bram Stoker – civil servant, drama critic, theatre manager, barrister, author – was inescapably a man of his time, a Victorian gentleman for whom good manners, proper decorum, and a chivalrous attitude towards women were prime forces in character development. Even so, those of his writings which touch on questions of morality reveal a certain prickliness and brittleness. He may have been the owner of a strong physique, but he does not come over as a strong character. There are numerous indications of how his life was shaped by others stronger than he: his mother, Henry Irving, and the countless celebrities of whom he wrote like an awe-struck adolescent. If subjectivity be permitted, then examination of his eyes in the few surviving photographs suggest a vulnerability, a far-off frightened look. This adds to the complexity of the man, known to be bluff and hearty in male company, and who obviously did not lack physical courage.

With so little incontrovertible evidence pertaining to his life, it is inevitable that half-truths, rumour and gossip should circulate to fill the gaps. Stoker's death certificate reads 'Locomotor Ataxy 6 months Granular Contracted Kidney. Exhaustion'.[49] In his biography of Stoker, Farson equates these words unequivocally with tertiary syphilis. If confirmed, such a revelation could transform the moral perspective on Stoker's life. It is said that he and Florence did not enjoy a close marriage, that she became frigid after the birth of their son, and that he had to seek satisfaction elsewhere. Farson does not blanch over Stoker's reputation as a womanizer.[50] If that was the case, Stoker would have found no shortage of opportunity. Work for the Lyceum took him to all the fleshpots of Europe and North America, and even in Victorian Britain there would have been the equivalent of the modern 'groupie', impressionable girls offering Stoker physical favours in return for access to their stage idol.

This is not to say that he took advantage of them. Farson's assertion is far from proven. The brief words on the death certificate, while consistent with syphilis, do not rule out alternative causes of death – though the vagueness of the wording was typical of that used to refer to sexually transmitted diseases. Syphilis was at that time virtually unmentionable, particularly for the respectable middle classes, for it brought dishonour upon the family of the afflicted.

Leaving aside Bram Stoker the man, there remains the question of assessing Bram Stoker the author. No one would claim that he was a 'great' writer. He was an author of extremes, veering from sentimental romances which make the modern reader squirm, to exploration of supernatural themes which were always on a higher plane. It should not be overlooked that Stoker was a part-time writer – save in his last years when he was already terminally ill – who crammed in his books in whatever spare minutes he could find. He had little time to eradicate the haste so often apparent in his works. However, a writer ought not to be judged on style alone. In Stoker's case, his principal literary attribute was a quite exceptional imagination, and in *Dracula* this vision was harnessed to immense power of presentation.

How does one assess an athlete who never rises above the second rate, but then unexpectedly shatters the world record, only to succumb to mediocrity again? Such is the difficulty in assessing Bram Stoker, a hack writer who in one solitary work wrote as if inspired. It is now time to examine how *Dracula* came to be written.

1   Bram Stoker, *Personal Reminiscences of Henry Irving* (hereafter:
    (*Reminiscences*).
2   Harry Ludlam, *A Biography of Bram Stoker: Creator of Dracula.*
    This biography was first published under the confusing title *A
    Biography of Dracula: The Life Story of Bram Stoker.*
    Daniel Farson, *The Man who Wrote Dracula: A Biography of
    Bram Stoker.* Both biographies are deficient in not providing
    sources for information presented, hampering further research.
    Phyllis A Roth's *Bram Stoker* is a thorough guide to Stoker's
    literary output, while Richard Dalby's *Bram Stoker: A
    Bibliography of First Editions* demonstrates that many reprints
    of Stoker's novels are abridgments of the originals.
3   Ludlam, p.14.
4   Farson, p.19.
5   ibid., p.39.
6   *The London Society*, Vol 22, No 129.
7   Farson, p.25.
8   *The Shamrock*, Vol 12, Nos 446-49.
9   Farson, p.26.
10 Peter Denman, 'Le Fanu and Stoker: A Probable Connection',
    p.153.
11 Ludlam, p.27.
12 *Reminiscences*, Vol 2, p.31.
13 ibid., Vol 1, p.31.
14 Ludlam, p.63.
15 Farson, p.38.
16 ibid., pp.26, 42.
17 ibid., p.45.
18 Douglas Oliver Street, 'Bram Stoker's "Under the Sunset", with
    Introductory Biographical and Critical Material' pp.xci-xcii.
19 *Punch*, 3 December 1881.
20 *Spectator*, 12 November 1881.
21 *The Academy*, 10 December 1881.
22 Ludlam, p.72.
23 *A Glimpse of America*, p.22.
24 *Reminiscences* Vol 1, p.51; Vol 2, p.6.
25 *A Glimpse of America*, pp.14, 23.
26 *North American Review*, Vol 190, November 1909.
27 *A Glimpse of America*, p.42.
28 Farson, p.78.
29 *A Glimpse of America*, p.23.

30 *Reminiscences*, Vol 2, p.274.
31 ibid., p.199.
32 ibid., p.290.
33 ibid., pp.100-1.
34 ibid., Vol 1, pp.200, 350, 355, 359.
35 ibid., Vol 2, p.29; Ludlam, p.88.
36 Ludlam, p.169.
37 Slain's Castle ceased to be inhabited in the 1920s.
38 See *The Athenaeum*, 23 February 1895.
39 ibid., 16 November 1895.
40 See Ludlam, pp.120-21.
41 *The Bookman*, August 1897.
42 *Punch*, 26 June 1897.
43 *The Athenaeum*, 26 June 1897.
44 Ludlam, p.122.
45 Farson, p.192.
46 Laurence Irving, *Henry Irving: The Actor and his World*, p.453.
47 Ludlam, pp.143-44; Dalby, p.43.
48 *The Times*, 22 April 1912.
49 Farson, p.233.
50 ibid., pp.212, 214.

5

The Origins of *Dracula*

Having some time at my disposal when in London, I had visited the British Museum, and made search among the books and maps in the library regarding Transylvania; it had struck me that some foreknowledge of the country could hardly fail to have some importance in dealing with a noble of that country. I find that the district he named is in the extreme east of the country, just on the borders of three states, Transylvania, Moldavia, and Bukovina, in the midst of the Carpathian mountains; one of the wildest and least known portions of Europe.

Jonathan Harker's Journal,
Dracula 1:9-10.

In view of the paucity of information on Bram Stoker's life, a satisfactory account of how and why *Dracula* came to be written is still lacking. The present author has tried to fill some of these gaps with *The Origins of Dracula*. The more speculative literary and psychological influences on Stoker will be postponed for later discussion. Here we are concerned with surveying more obvious factors, his background, acquaintances, and known researches.

Stoker had the entire Gaelic tradition of folklore to call upon, for Ireland is among the most superstition-ridden lands of Europe. Its geographical position on the western extremity of the continent has given it a unique heritage. Because Ireland escaped conquest by the Romans, the classical imprint so evident in the mythology found elsewhere in Europe is absent; yet, like the ripple effect on a pond, those Continental myths that did filter through continued to circulate long after their disappearance from their points of origin. These European influences merged with the indigenous Irish folk tradition, and the consequent richness and diversity of Gaelic superstition has inspired many Irish authors.

In Stoker's case, he had availed himself of the fund of folk tales collected by Sir William and Lady Wilde, both of whom published anthologies on Irish folklore.[1] His mother also provided an early stimulus for Stoker's fiction, and her graphic account of the 1832 Sligo cholera epidemic[2] (instancing premature burial and the deadly suspicion of strangers) had directly inspired one of his fairy tales. 'The Invisible Giant', from *Under the Sunset*, told of a young girl who sees in the sky beyond the city 'a vast shadowy Form, with its arms raised. It was shrouded in a great misty robe that covered it, fading away into air so that she could only see the face and the grim, spectral hands ... the face was as that of a strong man, pitiless, yet without malice; and ... the eyes were blind'.[3] A second tale from the collection can likewise be seen to anticipate *Dracula*. 'The Castle of the King' relates a young poet's quest to find his beloved, who has apparently died in a strange castle. This quest is obstructed by various horrors, until the hero finally arrives at the castle – huge, dead, and shrouded in mist.[4]

Although from a Protestant family, Stoker's homeland was, and is, overwhelmingly Catholic. It is a feature of Catholic lands across Europe that they are receptive to belief in vampires. The vampire is almost as entrenched in the folklore of Ireland as on the Continent, though divested of most of its usual macabre manifestations. The 'dearg-due' (the red bloodsucker) of ancient Ireland was reputed to use her beauty to tempt passing men and then suck their blood. Similarly, the 'leanhaun shee' (the fairy mistress) was an eye-catching fairy whose charms were irresistible to men. Energy would be drawn from the ensnared male until he eventually wasted away, or else procured a substitute victim to take his place.[5] Irish fairies were presumed to be bloodless, and their abduction of humans intended to remedy that deficiency.[6]

It is possible to discern in *Dracula* other, non-vampire, elements from Irish folk superstition. The devil, for instance, is in Irish lore traditionally depicted in human guise – as opposed to the grotesque animalistic representations of Europe, or the spirit form familiar to the East. The Irish devil is also able to adopt feminine form and assume the role of temptress, but despite his powers he can nevertheless be outwitted.[7]

Children would often be abducted by the Irish spirit world, with 'changelings' (deformed or senile fairies) left disguised in their place. As with vampires, changelings are said to be vulnerable to fire or water. Any children unbaptized ran an increased risk of abduction by the spirit world.

Some Irish fairies are gregarious. Others are solitary beings, for instance the 'leprechaun' and the 'cluricane' – the latter feared for its cunning and reputed ability to escape capture by becoming invisible. The 'dullahan' is variously conceived as a headless ghost at the reins of a death coach which appears at midnight, or a black coach drawn by headless horses. Whichever guise it takes, the 'dullahan' portends death.[8]

The bitter-sweet, tingling music of seduction with which Stoker arms his vampire ladies might have been suggested by the 'banshee', the indecipherable female wailing which signals an impending death. Stoker's vampires are capable of transformation into phosphorescent specks, like those other Irish omens of death, the 'water sheeries' – the souls of those refused permission to enter either heaven or hell. They frequent churchyards, can appear as dancing flames, and can be repelled with a crucifix.[9] Evil spirits may pass through narrow interstices, and certain plants or herbs – notably the rowan (mountain ash) – protect the bearer against the fairy world.

One clear instance of Irish lore discernible in *Dracula* concerns the climax of the novel. The Count is destroyed on 6 November. In Ireland, the feast of St Martin is celebrated on 11th of that month, and it is the custom for blood to be shed during the nine-day interval following Hallow'een. If St Martin fails to receive his blood sacrifice, the neglectful family can expect ill luck in the year ahead.[10] Dracula's demise, occurring when it does, thereby fulfils the hunters' obligation to St Martin.

As well as his Irish heritage, Stoker was well versed in Gothic/Romantic literature. Among the myths recognizable in *Dracula* are those of Faust and the Wandering Jew – who insulted Christ on his way to Calvary and was condemned to wander the earth till Christ's second coming. Stoker's compatriot, Charles Maturin, had utilized the myth in *Melmoth the Wanderer* (1820). Melmoth was condemned to everlasting life for signing a pact with the devil which had granted him eternal youth. Dracula, however, not only *could* not die, he *would* not die. In this, he resembles Faust. *Dracula* partakes of these myths, together with the Flying Dutchman and the Demon Lover.[11]

Clearly, Stoker drew upon the works of contemporary writers. Stevenson's *Dr Jekyll and Mr Hyde* (1886) reworked the Doppelgänger motif, and Stoker would also utilize the 'split personality' theme. Stevenson, like Stoker, wrapped his tale in late Victorian Britain, and wove detection into the narrative. Neither Dr Jekyll, nor Count Dracula, set out to be evil.

In Oscar Wilde's *The Picture of Dorian Gray* (1891), Dorian, like Jekyll, leads a double life – one respectable, the other cloaked in sin. The core of *Dorian Gray* is the search for immortality: the hero does not age, instead his portrait bears the deterioration owing to his sinful existence. Dorian becomes entranced by blood sacrifice; he preys on the energies of the innocent; and ultimately stabs the artist and the painting to gain release from his torment.[12] Critics have read into *Dorian Gray* just about every Victorian myth – including Faust, Mephistopheles, and Narcissus – and a biographer of Wilde has suggested *Dorian Gray* is 'from one of the sources of the *Dracula* myth'.[13]

One must return to an earlier work for the most profound influence upon *Dracula*. One of the nineteenth century's most popular novels, Wilkie Collins' *The Woman in White* (1860), can be seen imprinted on *Dracula* at two levels. The most obvious is the similar epistolary style. Collins had noticed how, during a court trial, each witness contributed separate pieces of evidence. Each might vary considerably, yet still be directed towards a common goal. Crucially, interest was maintained in the public by this constant switching of point of focus.[14] Collins adapted this courtroom experience to his novel. The omnipresent first or third person narrator was dispensed with, and substituted by a multiplicity of perspective. Stoker made use of the same technique in *Dracula*. This permitted greater authenticity: an individual's account of vampires might be dismissed as fancy, but not the accounts of the entire cast.

Collins' influence, however, goes beyond narrative structure. It extends to the *dramatis personae*.[15] The principal villain of each work is a Count. Each is endowed with personal magnetism and telepathic powers, rendering their victims' reactions ambivalent. Each shares an affinity with the animal world; and is introduced to the reader solely through the impressions of others. Furthermore, both novels witness a young hero embarking on a wild adventure, climaxed by a child becoming heir to the collected testimony. Stoker adapts to his own purposes Collins' scene in which children are attracted to a beautiful lady in a cemetery, and both works feature 'graveyards, insane asylums, dreary mansions, old chapels, zoological gardens, spectral trysts and moonlike nocturnes'.[16]

Relevant works of non-fiction also came to Stoker's notice. In 1890 there appeared Sir George Frazer's *The Golden Bough*, an encyclopaedic excursion through the taboos and superstitions of man: these include a detailed account of the vampire myth. The real world, too, did not escape reports of vampire attack. In the autumn of 1888, in panic-stricken London, the following passage appeared in the *East London Advertiser*:

> It is so impossible to account, on any ordinary hypothesis, for these revolting acts of blood that the mind turns as it were instinctively to some theory of occult force, and the myths of the Dark Ages arise before the imagination. Ghouls, vampires, blood suckers ... take form and seize control of the excited fancy.[17]

This extract confirms the ease with which any unexplained bloodshedding could be laid at the door of vampires. The source of these 'vampire' attacks in Victorian London? – the activities of Jack the Ripper!

Personal contacts provided ideas and stimulation. Stoker's long-time friend Hall Caine – to whom *Dracula* is dedicated (To my dear friend Hommy Beg', Caine's Manx nickname) – was a particular source of supernatural stimulation. Caine was an authority on the folklore of the Isle of Man, and he, Irving, and Stoker whiled away many a night on other-worldly topics. It has been claimed that Stoker was a member of the occult Hermetic Order of the Golden Dawn, whose ranks included W B Yeats. There is no supporting evidence,[18] though Stoker was an acquaintance of J W Brodie-Innes, who invited him to at least one gathering of the 'Sette of Odd Volumes' (a bibliographical society) which debated occult ideas.[19]

Richard Burton was doubtless influential. He and Stoker exchanged tales of myths and legends during their infrequent meetings between 1878 and 1886.[20] It was during their last recorded meeting (when Stoker noted Burton's sharp canine teeth) that conversation turned to the *Arabian Nights*. These had been translated by Burton, and featured their own vampire. Stoker mentions the *Arabian Nights* in *Dracula* (D3:42). Burton also assisted with an anthology of Indian vampire tales – *Vikram and the Vampire* – which he had translated, and which delved into the ancient origins of the undead.

One other of Stoker's known acquaintances is worthy of mention. Among his London neighbours was the celebrated poet and artist Dante Gabriel Rossetti. Elizabeth Siddal, his wife, had died in 1862 from an overdose of laudanum. She was buried in Highgate cemetery along with a volume of poems that her husband had written to her. Seven years later he wanted them back, and friends exhumed the body by firelight one autumn evening in 1869. The corpse was almost perfectly preserved, and Siddal's golden red hair almost filled the coffin.[21] Stoker was deeply impressed by this episode. He would adapt it for one of his short stories, 'The Secret of the Growing Gold', and certain cemetery scenes in *Dracula* would be modelled upon it.

As for more direct incentives for Stoker to write *Dracula*, several commentators have relayed Ludlam's tongue-in-cheek suggestion that in 1895 Stoker had a bad dream following 'a too generous helping of dressed crab at supper'.[22] As an explanation of *Dracula*'s origins this will hardly suffice, principally because Stoker had been at work on the novel for five years before the dream supposedly occurred.

Other commentators have put forward the names of Stoker's mother, father, and wife as figures who found their way into the omnipotent character of the Count. More plausible is Stoker's relationship with the theatre and with Henry Irving. On the subject of dramatic art Stoker was a professional: an astute critic and confidante to the biggest theatrical name of his generation. It can surely be no accident that *Dracula* would eventually achieve success on stage as well as in print. Its first stage production went ahead at the Lyceum within days of publication – a hasty adaptation designed solely to protect the copyright. It is said that Irving was unimpressed: 'Dreadful' was his supposed retort.[23]

Lyceum audiences had come to expect spine-chilling excitement and bloody melodramas. Along with Shakespeare, they were Irving's stock-in-trade. He never fought shy of striking terror into his audiences, and performed all the demonic roles of the supernatural in one form or another. *The Bells* and *Vanderdecken* (based on *The Flying Dutchman*) were standard Lyceum productions. *Faust*, too, was performed on numerous occasions, and Irving's was a powerful rendering of Mephistopheles. It was after researching the background to *Faust* with Irving in Nuremberg that Stoker was moved to write one of his finest short stories, 'The Squaw'.

It is with *Macbeth*, however, that it is necessary to pause. Stoker acknowledged that this was the play that intrigued him most, and that he held profound differences of opinion with his employer over its finer points.[24] Irving had performed the leading part many times before meeting Stoker, but preceding the 1888 production much time was spent debating the nuances of Macbeth's character.

A casual glance shows the resemblance between *Dracula* and *Macbeth*. Both are centred around a lonely, desolate castle, to which an unsuspecting stranger is lured, then 'visited' in his sleep. Both works have as their focus the personification of evil – not earthly, but supernatural evil. Macbeth and Dracula each receive a kind of immortality as a result of their pacts with supernatural forces. This evil is portrayed as more fascinating and more potent than the powers of good arrayed against it, for Macbeth's ultimate downfall, like Dracula's, cannot totally be accounted for by the ingenuity of his enemies. In both cases, their own schemes sow the seeds of their destruction. The contest between good and evil is shown to be unequal. The representatives of good lack mutual trust, undermining their strength. Furthermore, the evil which both works distil is dependent on complicity – the victim must willingly accept the touch of evil/vampirism.

Like Macbeth, Dracula was once a fearless warrior, grown to manhood through the spilled blood of his enemy's armies; a heroic figure for whom the fall from power to perpetrator of evil is a mystery. Both are, as it were, the first victims of the disease which spreads before them, until they are driven remorselessly back to the castle whence they came to have their throats slashed. The 'contagion' in both works is combated by a team of adversaries skilled in medical science. Similarly, what motivates both principal characters is not a thirst for blood (either literally or metaphorically) but power and ambition. Nonetheless, the two works display blood as a central motif, and introduce three weird and evil women in symbolic form. The three witches that open *Macbeth* are reincarnated as vampires near the beginning of *Dracula*.

Two other comparisons deserve mention: first, the respective conclusions. With the death of Macbeth the cry is 'The time is free'. Following Dracula's demise the response is 'The curse has passed away' D27:448).[25] Second, the historical elements of both are abstract rather than factual. The Scotland of *Macbeth* exists in the mind rather than as any geographical entity. The same could be said of Stoker's Transylvania.

In the light of such cross-comparisons it is possible that Stoker wove the vampire theme into the basic *Macbeth* plot with the intention of creating his own novel/play. He doubtless envisaged Irving, with his saturnine appearance and harsh, metallic, hissing voice, in the title role. The set of coincidences is extended when Stoker paid his first visit to Cruden Bay. His were working holidays, some undertaken to explore the atmospheric aspects of *Macbeth*.[26] Certainly the towering – and at that time inhabited – Slains castle, perched high above jagged cliffs, presents one of the most evocative Gothic sights in Britain.

That part of Scotland, furthermore, is a rich repository of pagan beliefs. The local population, with whom Stoker chatted, were among the most superstitious in Britain. That much is clear from his fiction set in Cruden Bay. The Bay is situated near the most easterly point in Scotland, facing out towards the rising sun, and its environs were once known for sun worship and fertility rites. Many remnants of stone circles are still to be seen. Despite opposition from the Church of Scotland (the Kirk), it was in Stoker's day the custom to leave part of the land uncultivated so that wild oats could be harvested by the spirit world. These spirits were presumed to visit the living at certain times of the year, so hallows fires were lit to deter them. Alternatively they were appeased by food offerings, such as goat's milk, or bannocks. It is still known for mistletoe or rowan to be hung above an ailing child in the hope that unwanted 'visitors' would go elsewhere for sustenance.[27]

Buchan funeral customs reflected the locals' fear of demons. They would lock up cats and hens prior to a funeral, in case they were evil spirits in disguise. To prevent the deceased catching a glimpse of his or her old home, and later paying a visit, roundabout routes were taken to the graveyard. As insurance, some portion of the funeral feast would be set aside as a peace offering. Pennies would be placed over the eyes of the dead, salt placed in a box on its chest, mirrors would be covered, and onions laid on window sills. These and other local tales were avidly noted by Stoker. Coincidence or not, following his discovery of Cruden Bay a persistent theme of his fiction would be the return of the dead to haunt the living.

On the question of when *Dracula* came to be conceived, it is now possible to answer with confidence. For many years it had been assumed by Stoker's critics that *Dracula* had been as hastily put together as his other hack productions. It is still popularly believed that he began writing *Dracula* while holidaying at Cruden Bay in August 1895, completing it in the odd moments he found free from Lyceum commitments. Connoisseurs of the novel, however, have long felt that Stoker's meticulous regard for detail in *Dracula* is inconsistent with a 'rush job'. Yet only with the discovery in the 1970s of Stoker's working notes for the novel in a Philadelphia museum[28] has the extent of his researches come to light.

These notes, written in his own hand or typed, and some dated, reveal that *Dracula* was conceived at least as early as 1890. They also confirm the thoroughness with which Stoker went about his research. The year 1890 is significant because it marked the publication of his first full-length novel *The Snake's Pass*. Its favourable reception possibly encouraged Stoker to begin preparing his *magnum opus* there and then, time and opportunity permitting. Far from being a casual yarn, spun from the top of his head and recounted with minimal preparation, *Dracula* would take a further seven years to appear in finished form.

The Philadelphia notes are dated between 1890 and 1896. They were written on anything available, including Lyceum notepaper and even a piece of Philadelphia hotel stationery. It is still not clear when the novel took its final form, for the earliest papers include neither the precise vampire theme, nor the name 'Dracula'. Even so, the first dated note – 8 March 1890 – reveals that the initial chapters had taken recognizable shape in epistolary form, and a week later, on 14 March, the plot is laid down, complete with four sub-books. These are titled: 'To London', 'Tragedy', 'Discovery', and 'Punishment'. Each sub-book comprised seven, later nine, chapters. This quaternary breakdown is suggestive of four acts of a play, and the fact that the finished novel concentrates most of the action in two multi-roomed buildings (one in Transylvania, the other in London), as if inviting a future stage adaptation, suggests that Stoker was alive from the start to *Dracula*'s theatrical prospects. Moreover, the chapter divisions frequently serve no obvious scene-separating function. Many chapters end in mid-scene or mid-conversation, and operate more as curtain calls, providing pauses at regular intervals.

With regard to relevant locations in Britain, almost every place that Dracula stalked, Stoker had preceded him notebook in hand. He had toured Whitby, for example, (scene of the Count's dramatic shipwreck), as early as August 1890, and notes taken then appear almost verbatim in the finished novel. The tombstone inscriptions in the novel are authentic. Stoker had noticed the name 'Swales' on a Whitby grave and lent it to one of his Whitby characters, giving him a dialect in keeping with a glossary of local terminology.[29] He had chatted with the locals, listened to tales of naval tragedies from old sailors, and consulted logbooks and meteorological records. Actual shipwrecks were noted, including that of the Russian schooner *Dimetry* on 24 October 1885, which had crashed through Whitby harbour. In *Dracula*, Stoker's Russian ship, the *Demeter*, does likewise. Other first-hand field researches included a trip to London's Regent's Park Zoo, where Stoker observed the behaviour of certain animals. His notes outline a theory of dreams,[30] while from his surgeon brother, William, Stoker learned the symptoms and treatment of specific head injuries. These he would employ for Dracula's attack on Renfield. One of the latest additions to the notes was a newspaper feature entitled 'Vampires in New England', taken from a copy of *The New York World*, dated 2 February 1896.

Having established the bare bones of his tale, Stoker now needed somewhere to pitch it. It needed to be a truly dreadful place, a fitting haunt for a monstrous Count. His first inclination was to borrow Le Fanu's setting for *Carmilla* – namely Styria, now part of eastern Austria. At some early stage he revised this location in favour of Transylvania further east, in what is now northern Romania. His notes indicate his familiarity with the writings of Emily Gerard, in particular her article 'Transylvanian Superstitions',[31] which sketched out the local beliefs on vampires and devilry. Much of Gerard's material would find its way into the opening chapters of *Dracula*. As Stoker says through his mouthpiece, Jonathan Harker: 'I read that every known superstition in the world is gathered into the horseshoe of the Carpathians' (D1:10), and it was there that Stoker eventually opted to base his vampire Count. Further research was undertaken at the British Museum, to supplement the many works listed in his notes as having been consulted.[32]

It is apparent from the novel that Stoker used a calendar. The journals and newspaper extracts all come from a particular year, but as he refers to dates, not days, there has been much speculation as to which year it was. Stoker's notes confirm the year to be 1893, for they contain the novel's time-span reproduced in a diary.[33] This discovery lends credence to the idea that Cruden Bay occupies a special place in the inspiration behind *Dracula*; for it was first visited by Stoker in 1893.

So much for the time and place of *Dracula*. There remains the origin of the name, for in his early notes Stoker refers instead to a Count 'Wampyr'. Popular wisdom apportions credit for the change to a Hungarian professor. Stoker's *Reminiscences* record that on 30 April 1890 he was introduced to Professor Arminius

Vambéry, a distinguished Orientalist from the University of Budapest. Vambéry had just returned from an expedition to central Asia tracing the steps of Marco Polo.[34] A further meeting took place two years later in Dublin.

The suspicion that Vambéry played some part in Stoker's crystallizing novel stems from the author's habit of taking real-life acquaintances and transplanting them, with little if any change of name, into his novels. In *Dracula*, when Van Helsing seeks a detailed picture of the demonic Count, he requests assistance from 'my friend Arminius, of Buda-Pesth University (D18:287-88; 23:359). This has led to the unwarranted presumption that fact mirrored fiction, that the *real* Arminius Vambéry supplied information on the *real* Dracula. Such presumption is dangerous because Stoker's use of names was often inconsequential. Another of the cast of *Dracula*, for example, took his name from a Lyceum painter and decorator.[35] What seems no less curious about Vambéry, *vis à vis* Stoker's researches, is that in most of the encyclopaedias Stoker would have consulted, the entries 'Vambéry' and 'vampire' are juxtaposed.[36] Unfortunately, nothing is known of the content of Stoker and Vambéry's conversations or correspondence, and if Vambéry ever wrote on the subject of vampires, or a so-called Dracula, no record has survived. What is, finally, the most persuasive argument against the primacy of the Vambéry connection is that all the important information in the novel concerning Dracula, or vampires in general, and which is attributed in *Dracula* to Arminius, can be found in the books and articles listed in Stoker's notes.[37] These notes do not mention Arminius Vambéry. *Dracula*, in other words, could have taken final shape without him.

Stoker's working notes tell us about his first known introduction to the historical Dracula. During his vacation at the Yorkshire port of Whitby in August 1890, Stoker did not content himself with local researches. In Whitby library he came across *An Account of the Principalities of Wallachia and Moldavia*, written in 1820 by William Wilkinson, one-time British Consul at Bucharest. On pages 18 and 19 Stoker would have read of the gruesome activities of a fifteenth-century Wallachian Voivode (Prince) – Dracula.

With this discovery, and the researches that followed, the necessary ingredients of the novel were established. In a note dated 29 February 1992, not only does the name 'Dracula' appear as an original entry, but basic locations found in the finished novel are mapped out: Whitby in England, and Bistritz and the Borgo Pass in Transylvania.

Modern Romania comprises three provinces: Transylvania and, to the east and south, Moldavia and Wallachia respectively. The links between these three regions date back to Roman times, from which Romania derives its name. In medieval Europe these states existed as semi-independent principalities, being squeezed between the Holy Roman Empire to the west, and the encroaching tentacles of the Ottoman Turks to the south. The Orthodox heritage of the Romanian peoples was therefore simultaneously threatened by Catholicism and Islam. In such circumstances it was difficult for any ruler to survive, let alone carve a name for himself in history; but 'Dracula' was such a man.

He was born around 1430 in the Transylvanian town of Sighisoara, but it was in the neighbouring territory of Wallachia that he, succeeding his father, made his reputation. Around the time of Dracula's birth his father was bestowed by Sigismund, the Holy Roman Emperor, with a title pledging him to wage war against the Czech Hussites and the Turks.[38] He was granted the throne of Wallachia and invested with the 'Order of the Dragon'; a semi-military, semi-monastic designation which may have been hereditary. The Romanian word for 'Dragon' happens to be 'Dracul' (pronounced Dra-cool), and the Order's escutcheon showed a dragon beneath a cross. The first holder of the office became popularly known as Vlad Dracul (Vlad the Dragon).[39]

Vlad Dracul presumably enjoyed something of a reputation: one source credits him with descending from the direct male line of Ghengis Khan.[40] In 1436 he seized the Wallachian throne, but his simultaneous appeasement of his patrons and the Turks could not endure. In 1447, together with his eldest son, Mircea, Vlad Dracul was put to death at Christian hands, whereupon the Wallachian throne passed to rival claimants.

The second son, Vlad junior, was in no position to contest the outcome. For some years he and another brother had been 'guests' of the Ottoman hierarchy.[41] It was while imprisoned in Anatolia that the teenage Vlad came to appreciate the weight of Turkish method, discipline, and barbarity. The Turks, when confident he had been cleansed of his father's duplicity, and was fully indoctrinated with Ottoman virtues, saw in young Vlad a suitably pliant ruler of Wallachia. With their connivance he snatched power for a few weeks in 1448. He was soon overthrown, however, and was forced to seek refuge until such time as he could win new sponsors.

In 1453 Constantinople fell to the Turks, the remnants of the Eastern Christian Empire crumbled, and surviving Christian nations shuddered at the prospect of an infidel empire sweeping all before it. Wallachia, hitherto subservient to Ottoman hegemony only to the extent of paying tribute, was now in the front line. Whereas it was the Turks who first propelled Vlad to take control over Wallachia, it was now the turn of his Hungarian neighbours to patronize him. He was, after all, duty bound to take up his father's mantle. From 1456 he ruled his principality with an iron hand, and in so doing acquired the sobriquet 'Dracula' – literally son of the Dragon[42] – the name by which he became known to Western contemporaries.

Such was the verve with which he set about centralizing his power that news of his exploits careered across Europe. In the process, he earned himself a more colourful nickname: Vlad Tepes (pronounced Tsepesh) – the Impaler. Torture and execution by impalement were hardly novel: such methods could be traced back to antiquity and were practiced by the Turks themselves. It was the sheer scale of Tepes' operations that caused a sensation. In its most 'artistic' form the stake would be rounded, greased, and introduced into the fundament with the weight of the body bearing down upon it. Death could take hours, or, preferably from Tepes' point of view, days. For variety, stakes could penetrate other parts of the body.[43] The methods varied according to the age, rank, sex, or nationality of the victim. For his entertainment, stakes would be arranged vertically in circles or other pleasing patterns, with the noblest perched highest of all. Woodcuts of the time depict Tepes seated at a table in the open, feasting alone amid rows of impaled and mutilated bodies.

In the absence of any centralized authority, the Romanian principalities were racked by factional feuding. Tepes' power remained tenuous until such time as he could emasculate two entrenched and privileged enemies – boyars and merchants. The boyars (landed noblemen) effectively lived as they pleased, immune to the demands of their princes and happy to foster the claims of any aspiring ruler sympathetic to their privileges. Tepes' rivals found sanctuary among the boyars, so he dealt with their 'treason' by impaling them in their thousands.

The economic infrastructure of the region was largely controlled by traders and merchants of Saxon descent. Their monopolistic privileges dated back to when the region was colonized from Germanic lands in the twelfth and thirteenth centuries.[44] Tepes sequestrated foreign merchants' trading rights and instituted protectionist measures designed to safeguard native Wallachian commerce. He promptly redistributed their properties among his acolytes as a means of forging new economic alignments beneficial to his consolidation of power.

Tepes was no less compromising when he turned his mind to the Turks. By 1459 he felt sufficiently secure to suspend payments of tribute, thus endearing himself to the Christian powers. Two years later, spurred by the demands of Pope Pius II for a fresh military campaign, he earned himself a place in the annals of Christian crusading by marching an army south across the Danube. He liberated those territories recently conquered, and impaled those Turks unfortunate enough not to escape or be killed outright.

By embarking on this crusade, Tepes was not declaring his devotion to Christ. He was a gifted military strategist, aware of the need to secure his southern gateway, across the exposed plains of the Danube.[45] Yet his situation remained precarious without material assistance from other Christian rulers. None was forthcoming. Maybe they feared a Turkish backlash, for Tepes was seized by Matthias Corvinus, King of Hungary. The king knew all about Tepes' military effectiveness: he had earlier received sacks of Turkish arms and legs, ears and noses, courtesy of his new prisoner. Corvinus may have feared Tepes' increasing autonomy: he was becoming too much his own man, showing too little deference to his Hungarian patrons. The boyars pressured Corvinus to act against their hated overseer; lowland peasants had been alienated by Tepes' scorched earth policy as he disengaged from the Turks; and he was rumoured to have adopted Islam, scandalously, in an attempt to save his own skin.

Imprisonment in Hungary spelled the end of Vlad Tepes' spectacular reign of terror. Between 1456-62 he had carved himself a niche in Europe's hall of fame. After twelve years' incarceration he was released by Corvinus, who was now anxious to display his magnanimity, renew the struggle with the Turks, and make use of the talented warrior in his custody. According to some, Tepes renounced his Orthodox faith and embraced Catholicism as his passport to freedom.[46] By the end of 1476 he was once again supreme ruler of Wallachia, but lost his life in combat with the Turks a few weeks later. What happened to his body is a matter of speculation. Some say his head was detached and presented to the Sultan in Constantinople.[47] Legend has it that his corpse, with or without his head, is buried in an island monastery at Snagov, outside Bucharest. Whatever the case, his legacy was to have personally authorized during his lifetime the deaths of perhaps one hundred thousand people[48] – equivalent to one fifth of the population of Wallachia at that time.

All rulers invite controversy. Few arouse such conflicting assessments as Vlad Tepes. He became a Renaissance legend in his lifetime. Largely inspired by boyar intrigues to discredit him, accounts of his misdeeds – real and exaggerated – were disseminated throughout Europe. Saxons, Hungarians, Turks, and Russians all had cause to despise him. Word of mouth, embellished in the telling, soon portrayed him as one of the great demented psychopaths of history. Wandering minstrels put his atrocities to song, and technological advances in German-speaking Europe spread the message further, as news-sheets tumbled off newly invented printing presses. The new medium had found a celebrity, and by the end of the century he was providing some of the favourite reading matter of the continent, vying for space with Columbus' discovery of America. One source maintains that, for a while, incunabula devoted to Dracula were outselling the Bible.[49] By 1558, news of Dracula's excesses even reached Britain, when Sebastian Munster's *Cosmographica* was translated into English.

There was however, another slant, that of a heroic Christian crusader. Unfortunately for his self-image, Tepes could not so easily be defended by his own people. Wallachian printing facilities lagged behind those of the West. Not until a century after his death were apologies for his acts available from his homeland.[50] In the interim, it was left to chroniclers in lands untouched by his ravages to present him in a less brutal light, and to rationalize his deeds as anticipating the ideas of Machiavelli, for whom almost any act was justifiable in the name of *raison d'état*. Even Machiavelli admitted it was better to be feared than loved.

As the centre of gravity in European affairs moved westwards, Vlad Tepes became a forgotten man. He would be resuscitated by two disparate developments. The first was Bram Stoker's novel, which sent researchers scurrying after its source. The second was the formation of the Romanian Socialist Republic in the 1940s, faced with the task of unearthing national heroes who could help ...... modern Romania to its past. Vlad Tepes had all the creden-
...... is not known inside Romania as 'Dracula', but as
...... his memory has been rehabilitated. He is the equivalent
...... d's Robin Hood, someone who took from the rich in
...... give to the poor; a freedom fighter who curbed foreign privileges; a man who virtually single-handed eliminated theft and other crime; and whose excesses are overlooked, considering the cruelty of the age in which he lived.[51] He is seen as a founding father of the Romanian nation-state; a hero of the Orthodox Church – a kind of Caesar and Pope all in one.

All this is fine for students of Vlad the Impaler. It is by no means clear that any or all of the foregoing was known to Bram Stoker. Whatever he did know would have been based on the earlier, harsher, Germanic accounts. But did he have access even to these? Wilkinson's book, for example, speaks of several Draculas. Neither Wilkinson nor any other of Stoker's named sources spare a word for Vlad the Impaler's atrocities. At the point where Wilkinson mentions 'Dracula's son', he refers the reader to Richard Knolles' *Generall Historie of the Turkes*

(1603). This reference is misleading, for the episode in question relates to Dracula's father and brother. But should Stoker have skipped to page 362 he would have unearthed a harrowing description of Wladus Dracula's tortures and executions – two square miles of gallows, wheels and stakes, upon which were broken some twenty thousand bodies.

Early in *Dracula* the Count gives a muddled and convoluted history of himself and of Transylvania from the time of Attila the Hun (D3:40-42). He says nothing of impalement. That would either be because Dracula prefers to skip over his own notoriety, or because Stoker knew little of it. This latter view is reinforced when Van Helsing surveys Dracula's life.

> He [Count Dracula] must, indeed, have been that Voivode Dracula who won his name against the Turks ... If it be so, then was he no common man; for in that time, and for centuries after, he was spoken of as the cleverest and the most cunning, as well as the bravest of the sons of the 'land beyond the forest' (D8:287-88).

The Professor seems quite blind to Dracula's darker side. He makes no mention of the name 'Vlad', nor his sobriquet 'the Impaler', nor his unspeakable cruelties. Indeed, he prefers to describe the Count as 'in life a most wonderful man'. At this, we begin to ask ourselves: did Van Helsing, or Stoker, really know who Dracula was?

Only circuitously, by using his named sources, could Stoker have come across authentic details of Vlad the Impaler. He would have needed to follow up one reference, then look elsewhere in the book referred to. He might then have discovered this account of the Impaler, tagged on behind an appreciation of another anti-Turk campaigner, John Hunniades – nicknamed 'the Devil'.

> As we have said, the Turks were so much afraid of Hunniades that they are said to have given him the name of 'the Devil', but the same designation, as well as that of the Impaler, has also been bestowed upon Vlad, a voivode of Wallachia, who was probably the ally of Hunniades, and who, if one-tenth of what has been related of him be true, has a much better claim to the title. He is represented to have been one of the most atrocious and cruel tyrants who ever disgraced

even those dark ages. One day he massacred 500 boyars who were dissatisfied with his rule. The torture of men, women, and children, seems to have been his delight. Certain Turkish envoys, when admitted into his presence, refused to remove their turbans, whereupon he had them nailed to their heads. He burned 400 missionaries and impaled 500 gypsies to secure their property. In order to strike terror into Mohammed II, he crossed over into Bulgaria, defeated the Turks, and brought back with him 25,000 prisoners, men, women, and children, whom he is said to have impaled upon a large plain called Praelatu.[52]

This reference states that Vlad was nicknamed 'the devil'. Stoker would have known of this from Wilkinson, who, in a footnote to one of the Draculas, states: 'Dracul in the Wallachian language mean Devil.'[53] In 'Transylvanian Superstitions', Emily Gerard makes the same point – for example 'Gania Drakuluj' (Devil's Mountain). Vampires are traditionally depicted in German-Romanian frontier regions as dragon-monster-serpents.[54] But the interlocking imagery of devil and dragon, and the overlapping etymologies of 'vampire' and 'devil' in other languages, may have provided Stoker with an ingenious concept: Vlad the Vampire.

In summary, from the books Stoker was known to have consulted, we cannot be over confident that Count Dracula is the resurrected Vlad the Impaler.[55] If he was, then Stoker's sources suggest he seized on the name 'Dracula' for no other reason than that it means 'Devil'.

Critics of the novel have seized on Stoker's historical and ethnological inaccuracies as confirming his slovenly use of source material. They point out that his potted Romanian history is distorted at best, exemplified by his fundamental 'error' in basing Dracula in Transylvania when his actual power-base was in neighbouring Wallachia. As a result of this discrepancy, a whole Dracula-industry has flourished, bedevilled by cross-purposes. True, Stoker *does* begin and end the novel in Transylvania; the climactic chase at the conclusion *does* take the characters through named places in Transylvania; and Castle Dracula – mythical though it may be – *is* sited in that province, near the Borgo Pass. The problem arises because the Romanian authorities, anxious both to capitalize on the tourist potential of *Count* Dracula and to dissociate him from their own hero, *Vlad* Dracula, have gone to great lengths to direct Western tourists to the castles of Vlad Tepes. These lie in Wallachia, far from the less accessible Borgo Pass in Transylvania, where perchance there are fewer suitably impressive castles to show off.[56]

Yet in a sense, discussion of Stoker's historical licence is immaterial. He was, after all, a novelist, not a historian. It was not his concern to portray an accurate picture of medieval eastern Europe. Besides, the sources available to him were fewer and less reliable than those of today. Rather, Stoker was concerned to gather enough insights into time and place to impart something of their flavour to the Victorian reader He even provides local recipes.

One further difficulty remains in linking Vlad Tepes with Count Dracula. Whatever the Impaler's crimes and inhumanities, nowhere was he accused of being a vampire. Spilling blood was more his style, not drinking it. Yet there existed other, tacit associations between Tepes and vampirism. His chosen method of execution – impalement – happened to be the same as that recommended for vampires; Tepes was eventually decapitated in the manner of accused vampires; and his alleged resting place in Snagov was itself opened up and pillaged[57] – suggestive that he had risen up. Stoker may even have learned of the legend that Tepes never really died, but was waiting to rise up and protect his homeland if threatened. He was, in other words, lying in wait – 'undead'. Again, according to Catholic sources, he had renounced the Orthodox faith in which he was baptized – an offence in Orthodox eyes that would indict others of vampirism. Evil persons were also reputed to turn into vampires, and Tepes' obsession with shedding human blood was in itself suggestive enough.

On the other hand, there are features of the fictional Count far removed from the known facts of the Impaler. Principally, they stem from Stoker's decision to label his vampire a 'Count', when Vlad Tepes had been a 'Voivode'. This is not simply a matter of semantics. The title 'Count' is alien to the Romanian social hierarchy but is native to Hungary. Tepes's principality,

Wallachia, is properly Romanian, whereas Transylvania was at that time a province of Hungary. Moreover, although later occupied by the Turks, by the time Stoker wrote *Dracula* Transylvania was once again administered by Hungary, within the Austro-Hungarian Empire. (Transylvania became a part of modern Romania after World War One.) Count Dracula, in other words, was Hungarian, not Romanian, and refers to himself as a 'Szekely' (D3:41) – a Hungarian race descended from Attila who guarded the frontier with Turkey.[58]

This Hungarian emphasis is appropriate not only in view of Stoker's reliance on Western (Saxon and Hungarian) sources on the Impaler, but also because Hungarian folklore is richer than Romania's in the expression of vampire superstition. Montague Summers asserts: 'Hungary [has] the reputation of being that particular region of the world which is most terribly infested by the Vampire and where he is seen at his ugliest and worst.'[59] In consequence, it is evident that Stoker's relocation of Dracula northwards from Wallachia to Transylvania was intentional, and not the product of careless attention to detail.

One further historical figure should be mentioned in this connection. Stoker's general focus on Hungary was enhanced by his reading in Sabine Baring-Gould's *The Book of Were-Wolves* of the exploits of Elizabeth Bathory. She was born 130 years after the Impaler and supplied the pieces absent in Tepes. She was Hungarian; she was a *Count*ess; her crest featured a dragon; and, unlike the Impaler, she actually drank blood – she was a living vampire. The *Guinness Book of Records* accredits the 'Blood Countess' with being the most prolific murderess in history, recording at least 610 confirmed victims. They were invariably virgins, tortured and killed in order to supply the Countess with fresh blood, which she believed possessed rejuvenating properties. Application of fresh blood made her look and feel younger; a coincidence borrowed by Stoker in the case of Dracula. When finally convicted of her abominations, Bathory was 'imprisoned' in her castle at Csejthe. She died in 1614, the most notorious and best authenticated practitioner of vampirism on record.[60]

So powerful were the twin influences of Le Fanu's fictional *Carmilla* and the real-life Elizabeth Bathory, that they were probably jointly responsible for Stoker's initial intention to base his novel in what is now Austria. One of the expunged chapters of *Dracula* (popularly known as 'Dracula's Guest') goes so far as to feature a vampire Countess from Gratz. Fortunately for the sake of *Dracula*'s originality, Stoker eventually distanced himself from the more obvious Carmilla/Bathory connections, though they remain potent sources of influence and inspiration.

Curiously, for all Stoker's debt to Vlad Dracula, it was not his intention to title his novel in the Impaler's honour. The manuscript which Stoker submitted to his publishers bore the working title 'The Un-Dead'.[61] Much of the novel's later success can be put down to Stoker's, or his publisher's, inspired last minute switch to bring the name 'Dracula' to the fore.

---

1   See, for example, Sir William Wilde, *Irish Popular Superstitions* (1853) and Lady Wilde, *Ancient Legends of Ireland* (1888).

2   Reproduced in Ludlam, pp.27-34.

3   In Street, pp.36-54.

4   ibid., pp.97-117.

5   Peter Haining, *The Leprechaun's Kingdom*, pp.91, 99.

6   Sean O'Sullivan, *Legends from Ireland*, p.72.

7   ibid., pp.21, 23.

8   Haining, pp.21, 25, 39. Consider Harker's experience with Dracula's coach (D:1:19-20).

9   ibid., p.107.

10   O'Sullivan, pp.114-15.

11   Phyllis A Roth, *Bram Stoker*, p.96; Raymond T McNally and Radu Florescu, *The Essential Dracula*, p.21.

12   See James B Twitchell, *The Living Dead: A Study of the Vampire in Romantic Literature*, pp.166-67; David Punter, *The Literature of Terror*, p.248.

13   Edouard Roditi, *Oscar Wilde*, p.115.

14   Nuel Pharr Davis, *The Life of Wilkie Collins*, p.211.

15   For example, the names Harkwright, Marian, and Laura in *The Woman in White* are easily turned into Harker, Mina and Lucy in *Dracula*. Similarly, both books feature a grotesque/lunatic.

16   See Mark M Hennelly Jr, 'Twice Told Tales of Two Counts' pp.26-27, also pp.15-18.

17 Reprinted in Raymond T McNally and Radu Florescu, *In Search of Dracula*, pp.177-78.
18 R A Gilbert, *The Golden Dawn: Twilight of the Magicians*, p.81.
19 Personal correspondence from R A Gilbert.
20 *Reminiscences*, Vol 1, pp.350-56.
21 Oswald Doughty, *A Victorian Romantic: Dante Gabriel Rossetti*, pp.416-17.
22 Ludlam, p.112 (see also p.107). Ludlam's date, 1895, for the commencement of Stoker's writing of *Dracula* has passed into many other secondary sources.
23 ibid., p.123.
24 *Reminiscences*, Vol 1, pp.107-8.
25 I am grateful to James Drummond for his insights into the many similarities between *Macbeth* and *Dracula*, which extend even to the cast. There is a Siward in *Macbeth* and a Seward in *Dracula*.
26 James Drummond, 'The Scottish Play', p.46.
27 Personal correspondence from James Drummond.
28 The Rosenbach Museum and Library.
29 Whitby Glossary, 1876, F K Robinson. Curiously, this dialect has many similarities to that of Cruden Bay (James Drummond, 'Bram Stoker's Cruden Bay', p.28).
30 F C and J Rivington, *Theory of Dreams*, 2 Vols.
31 *Nineteenth Century*, Vol 28, July 1885. This journal was edited by a friend of Stoker's, Sir James Knowles. Gerard's expanded researches were published in *The Land Beyond the Forest*, the literal translation of 'Transylvania'.
32 See Bibliography.
33 There is further internal evidence in support of 1893. In a diary extract of 26 September, Van Helsing speaks of the pioneer of modern hypnotism, Charcot, and adds 'alas that he is no more' (D14:230). Charcot died on 16 August 1893. Clearly, then, the book cannot be set earlier, and Van Helsing's expression of sadness suggests Charcot died very recently. Furthermore, a little cross checking confirms that 21 September must have fallen on a Thursday (D13:206; 14:221). This could only happen in 1893. Stoker's careless references to the moon previously threw researchers off the scent. He pays scant regard to the lunar cycle in *Dracula*, having the moon shine on the nights of 5 May, 15 May, 24 June, 11-13 August (when the moon is full), 17 September, 29 September, 1 October, and 3 October. Not only is this combination not possible, but on the nights of 11-13 August

1893, instead of there being a full moon, there was in fact, no moon at all.

34   *Reminiscences*, Vol 1, pp.371-72.

35   The decorator was Joseph Harker. Stoker kept his initials for his character Jonathan Harker.

36   Paul Dukes, 'Dracula: Fact, Legend and Fiction', p.45.

37   Joseph S Bierman reaches the same conclusion in 'The Genesis and Dating of "Dracula" from Bram Stoker's Working Notes', p.41.

38   Radu Florescu and Raymond T McNally, *Dracul: a Biography*, p.7.

39   See Grigore Nandris, 'The Historical Dracula: The Theme of his Legend in the Western and in the Eastern Literatures of Europe' p.370.

40   Gabriel Ronay, *The Dracula Myth*, p.57.

41   One view is that the brothers had been handed over to the Turks by their father as a sign of his goodwill (Florescu and McNally, op. cit., p.36).

42   Grigore Nandris, 'A Philological Analysis of Dracula and Rumanian Place-names and Masculine Personal Names in -a/-ea', pp.371-72.

43   For a catalogue of Tepes' tortures and cruelties see Nicolai Stoicescu, *Vlad Tepes: Prince of Walachia*, p.157.

44   Even today many Romanian towns are known by a German/Saxon equivalent. Sibiu was, and is, also known as Hermannstadt; Brasov is Kronstadt, and Sighisoara is Schassburg.

45   Stoicescu, p.77.

46   Florescu and McNally, op. cit., p.114. This claim is vigorously denied by Stoicescu, p.43.

47   Florescu and McNally, op. cit., p.121.

48   McNally and Florescu, *In Search of Dracula*, p.115.

49   Ronay, p.74.

50   Andrew MacKenzie, *Romanian Journey*, p.110.

51   The Renaissance era produced many cruel statesmen: Richard III, Cesare Borgia, Ivan the Terrible, to name some. See Nandris, 'The Historical Dracula', pp.370-71.

52   James Samuelson, *Roumania: Past and Present* (1882) p.170. Another episode in Samuelson was referred to in one of Stoker's sources: Major Johnson, *On the Track of the Crescent*.

53   William Wilkinson, *An Account of the Principalities of*

Wallachia and Moldavia, p.19.

54   Nandris, 'The Historical Dracula', p.377.

55   The foregoing discussion on Dracula's background is covered in
     Clive Leatherdale, *The Origins of Dracula*, chapter 5. See Ronay,
     pp.58-59; Nandris, 'The Historical Dracula', pp.371ff. It is
     possible to suggest several contemporaries of the Impaler as
     possible sources for Count Dracula.

56   Local legend insists that 36 ruined battlements can be found in
     Szeklerland. See Clive Leatherdale, *The Origins of Dracula*,
     p.128.

57   McNally and Florescu, *In Search of Dracula*, p.180.

58   see Clive Leatherdale, *The Origins of Dracula*, chapter 6.

59   Montague Summers, *The Vampire in Europe*, p.132.

60   See Raymond T McNally, *Dracula Was a Woman*.

61   See Richard Dalby, *Bram Stoker: A Bibliography of First
     Editions*, p.26.

6

FROM VLAD DRACULA
TO COUNT DRACULA

[Dracula's] face was a strong – a very strong – aquiline, with high bridge of the thin nose and peculiarly arched nostrils; with lofty domed forehead, and hair growing scantily round the temples, but profusely elsewhere. His eyebrows were very massive, almost meeting over the nose, and with bushy hair that seemed to curl in its own profusion. The mouth, so far as I could see it under the heavy moustache, was fixed and rather cruel looking, with peculiarly sharp white teeth; these protruded over the lips, whose remarkable ruddiness showed astonishing vitality in a man of his years. For the rest, his ears were pale and at the tops extremely pointed; the chin was broad and strong, and the cheeks firm though thin. The general effect was one of extraordinary pallor.

Jonathan Harker's Journal,
Dracula 2:28.

Before attention turns to some of the deeper themes of Stoker's most famous novel, it will be helpful to look more closely at the characters he created and the purposes they fulfil – beginning with Count Dracula himself. Stoker spared no effort to present his demonic vampire as dramatically as possible. Other, mortal, figures, he leaves under-sketched, relying on the reader's imagination to fill in the flesh on the bones he provides, but Dracula is painted with enormous attention to detail. After the first four chapters he is 'off-stage' for most of the rest of the novel,[1] yet not for a moment is the reader allowed to forget the Count's awesome presence.

Visually, aside from his facial features (described above), Dracula is clean shaven save for a long white moustache, and dressed without a single speck of colour about him anywhere. He is a tall, old man. He could not have been uncommonly tall, however, for Dracula makes off wearing Harker's clothes – which presumably fit satisfactorily – and Harker, himself, when later described by others invites no comment as to his size. Moreover, the accepted notion of Dracula's ever-present black cloak would seem to be an invention of the cinema. Only once is such a garment mentioned (D3:47) and the more usual description 'clad in black from head to foot' (D2:25) would hardly be appropriate to a single item of clothing.

Compare Harker's description of the Count with the only surviving description of Vlad the Impaler:

> He was not very tall but very stocky and strong with a cold and terrible appearance, a strong and aquiline nose, swollen nostrils, a thin and reddish face, in which the very long eye lashes framed large wide-open green eyes; the bushy black eye brows made them appear threatening. His face and chin were shaven, but for a moustache. The swollen temples increased the bulk of his head. A bull's neck connected his head [to the body] from which black curly locks hung on his wide shouldered person.[2]

Consider, too, a description of Henry Irving: 'a tall, spare man ... a peculiarly striking face, long grey hair thrown carelessly back behind the ears, clean shaven features remarkable for their delicate refinement, united with the suggestion of virile force [and] rather aquiline nose'.[3]

As a fictional character, Count Dracula is an alloy: he combines in his persona certain qualities taken from his real-life namesake; from Elizabeth Bathory; the tradition of the literary vampire descended from Lord Ruthven and Sir Francis Varney; the great myths of Romantic literature from which Stoker liberally borrowed; the wealth of Continental folklore to plant the novel firmly back in its roots; as well as an original flourish by Stoker to turn his Count into a master magician – as we shall see.

Being a literary vampire, Dracula conforms to the requirement of belonging to the ranks of nobility. He boasts of having a distinguished lineage, possessing in his veins the blood of Attila the Hun. In some respects, Dracula's behaviour is what one might expect of the conventional literary aristocrat. He exudes charm of manner; he is contemptuous of the common man; and he speaks several languages – German excellently, and more impressive English than the Dutch professor, Van Helsing. At intervals, Stoker puts in little touches which increase Dracula's sense of refinement. The Count is seen wearing white kid gloves and a straw hat, and he carries a brush for his clothes and a brush and comb for his hair. But on other levels he does not act like a nobleman at all. He lacks the typical aristocrat's high standard of living and conspicuous over-indulgence. He does not eat or drink to excess, nor does he pursue women (as normally understood). His lifestyle does not revolve around fashionable clothes, the theatre, or hunting; he does not hold receptions or build stately homes. He actually chooses to live in a Gothic ruin. Not even his violent pastimes are undertaken purely for pleasure.[4] Most unusual of all, for a thriving aristocrat, is the absence of servants. Dracula is not averse to performing all the necessary menial tasks – driving the calèche, preparing meals, and even making beds – to prevent Harker, his guest, from deducing that he employs no domestic staff.

By way of character, Dracula conveys more than a vague presence of malice. Stoker endows him with a personality, of sorts. He has a mannerism of tugging his moustache during animated discourses on his family history – the only subject touched on in the book capable of making him pleasantly excitable (D3:40). He exhibits a full range of powerful emotions: hate, passion, anger, disdain, baffled malignity, vanity. His mental gifts are largely taken from those of his namesake. The Count, like the Voivode before him, has a mighty brain, is fearless, remorseless, a shrewd leader and cunning soldier – not averse to executing a strategic retreat in the face of disadvantageous odds, as the handbooks on guerrilla warfare dictate. Stoker plays down the tyrannical aspects of Dracula's pre-vampire life, for when speaking of his own past the Count naturally does not see himself as a merciless psychopath, but as a stern, principled statesman. And Van Helsing concedes: 'he was in life a most wonderful man. Soldier, statesman, and alchemist ...' (D23:359). In this, of course, Dracula resembles Mephistopheles in Goethe's *Faust*, whose portrayal of Irving left such a deep impression on Stoker.

Overall, legal-minded Harker is so impressed by his host's great foresight and intellectual prowess that he utters the book's most memorable understatement: Dracula, if he had chosen, 'would have made a formidable solicitor' (D3:44).

This intelligence and urbanity, while allowing Dracula to be firmly located within the tradition of the literary vampire, only partly accounts for his all-pervading menace. He also partakes of the characteristics of the vampire of folklore. Stoker is keen to highlight the animalistic quality of his master-vampire, taking full advantage of the folkloric connection between vampires and werewolves. Besides having pointed ears and protruding canine teeth, Dracula possesses coarse, broad hands with squat fingers – as werewolves are described. His palms, too, are hairy and the nails cut to a sharp point. His eyes glow red. The stench which clings to his places of rest, and which produces a feeling of nausea to those in proximity, is the stench of excrement, of all the ills of mortality, of death, of arrested decay – augmented, when his thirst has been slaked, by the sickly-sweet, acrid smell of blood. Even his persona is animalistic: anti-rational, childlike, instinctive. His vitality is shown as feral, and his cunning is that of an animal that resorts to swift physical action to counter any errors of judgment.

Dracula enjoys the gymnastic abilities of reptiles, animals, and birds. He can climb face-foremost down a castle wall, gripping the vertical surface with toes and fingers – though he does not fear death should he fall, for he is immune to the natural laws of mortality. These wall-descending activities are described as 'lizard-like' (D3:47). Later, Dracula's agility is expressed as 'panther-like'; he has a 'snarl' on his face; and he shows 'lion-like disdain' (D23:364). His empathy with the animal world is demonstrated by his control over lower forms of life: rats, bats and wolves.

In many ways Dracula is obedient to the vampire specifications of European folklore. Being undead, his flesh is icy to the touch; he casts no reflection in the mirror, and when standing in front of flames does not obstruct a view of them. He is unable to impose his presence on a victim at the time of first contact, unless his prey shows complicity in some form. This is evident in Harker's stepping over the threshold at Castle Dracula (D2:26), and in the Count's later visits to Lucy and Renfield (D21:332). Dracula possesses enormous physical strength and speed of movement; his eyes can induce hypnotic effects; and with selective victims he is capable of psychic transfer.

Dracula can direct the elements around him, such as creating a puff of wind. He can see in the dark and vaporize himself at will. He is able to change into a dog, wolf, or bat; he can dematerialize to be transported as mist; and he can take shape from phosphorescent specks riding on moonbeams – whose whirring motions weaken powers of resistance. He is restricted by the presence of running water, being unable to cross it except at the slack or flood of the tide, unless with manual assistance. He sleeps and wakes with the precision of clockwork – dawn and dusk being calculated to the second. While sleeping, Dracula appears to be dead, eyes open and no pulse or respiratory motion. All the while he is 'conscious' of activity around him, although searching hands cannot 'wake' him (D4:67).

Crucially, although Dracula can be repelled by garlic and other pagan safeguards, he is essentially a vampire of the Christian mould. In other words he is a representative/client/manifestation of the devil (in London he aptly assumes the alias 'Count *de Vil*le' (D20:326). He must therefore be shown to be vulnerable to Christian icons and imagery. The crucifix – arch-symbol of the Christian faith – makes him recoil and cower, and the application of holy wafer sterilizes his places of rest.[5]

But Stoker did not wish to restrict his vampire-king within the parameters prescribed by folklore. Dracula would have to be special, both in his attributes and in his manner of becoming a vampire. Several of Dracula's qualities differentiate him from more common varieties of his ilk, for example Stoker's insistence that Dracula can sleep only in consecrated earth: 'in soil barren of holy memories [he] cannot rest' (D18:288). This requirement would seem to possess neither folkloric nor historic antecedent.[6] According to Orthodox superstition, the undead, if excommunicated, were unable to rest in hallowed soil. So what were Stoker's motives? Maybe he intended Dracula's 'sacrilege' to heighten the reader's sense of outrage. Stoker's innovation makes the Count's lairs harder to locate, for he is 'sleeping' deceitfully among God's true dead. And, of course, Vlad Tepes himself was buried in consecrated earth.

Another example of Dracula's uniqueness is his immunity to the rays of the sun. The vampire of superstition is the quintessential apparition of night; it being believed that sunlight could pass through, or harm, sensitive tissue. Dracula, however, cannot be destroyed by direct sunlight as film versions would have us believe. That would make him too vulnerable. Once he is strong and vigorous from the consumption of fresh blood, he is permitted in the novel to wander the streets of London quite naturally. Dracula's only handicap is that his vampire powers become neutralized during daylight, when he reverts, to all intents, to being a mere mortal. He must therefore take care that at the moment of sunrise he is in the place and form that he wishes to be for the coming day. Otherwise he must await the precise moment of noon or sunset to effect the desired transference (D22:347-8).

Most important, Stoker could not allow his arch-fiend to have become a vampire by any of the standard procedures of folklore, for all imply falling victim in some manner. Count Dracula can be a victim of nobody and nothing. If he is a vampire, it must have been through his choice and his power. He was neither bitten whilst alive by another undead, nor was he sentenced to a vampiric punishment for any of the appropriate transgressions. In his human life, Count Dracula was an alchemist and magician. He had studied the secrets of the black arts and other aspects of devilry when enrolled as a student at the Scholomance (D18:288; 23:360) – a mythical academy situated high in the Carpathian Mountains, overlooking the town of Sibiu (known in Saxon as Hermannstadt).[7] The patron of the academy is the devil himself, who instructs on the dark secrets of nature: thunder and lightning, the language of animals, magical spells. Those who studied natural phenomena were assumed to be capable of mastering them. Legend has it that the Scholomance would admit students ten at a time. Upon acquisition of the devilish insight, nine would return to their everyday lives, leaving the tenth to be taken up by the devil as group payment. He would be mounted on an *ismejeu* (dragon – a merging of Dracula's devil/dragon associations) and recruited as the devil's aide-de-camp.[8] Needless to say, Dracula was the tenth student, whose arcane wisdom is demonstrated by Stoker early in the novel. The Count inspects mysterious blue flames flickering in the forest, which, according to folklore, conceal treasure and gold.

Stoker does not permit Dracula's transition from man to vampire to be left to the reader's imagination. Such were the resources of Dracula's brain that, together with the magical powers gleaned from the Scholomance, his mental faculties survived physical death (D23:360). But they did not survive intact. He paid the price of having much of his memory destroyed, and has to engage in the re-learning process almost in the manner of an infant. Van Helsing, the guru of Dracula's adversaries, is an exponent of the scientific method of 'experimentation'. He appreciates the Count's emerging mental powers because he, Van Helsing, also employs scientific method, reaching out to acquire knowledge slowly but surely, one step at a time. Van Helsing's fears are twofold: that Dracula has acquired immortality through forging a special, yet undisclosed relationship with the devil; and that he has centuries ahead of him to sharpen his cunning and his intellect. Dracula undergoes a dramatic shift in power during the course of the novel. At the outset he appears as a cautious old man, not yet sure of the powers at his command. Despite his longevity, he is in the position of a fledgling bird about to leave the nest and fly for the first time. He has not yet employed the full range of vampire powers which are about to be unleashed.

Count Dracula is physically dead. But if he is, as it were, living in death, then it might be asked whether he is more dead than alive, or more alive than dead. If he is really dead, then why does he never speak of life beyond the grave, or communicate its wonders or its terrors? The only time Dracula reflects on his past is when recalling his martial exploits during his pre-vampire existence. He has nothing to say about the four hundred years since he signed up with the devil. It would appear that his only aspect that is dead is his body, for his mind has never travelled beyond the experiences of this earth.

To reinforce Dracula's grasp of black magic, Stoker invests the Count's native Transylvania with suitably mysterious rocks and waters. It might easily be a lost world inhabited by dinosaurs, for it is a land

> full of strangeness of the geologic and chemical world. There are deep caverns and fissures that reach none know whither. There have been volcanoes, some of whose openings still send out waters of strange properties, and gases that kill or make to [sic] vivify. Doubtless there is something magnetic or electric in some of these combinations of occult forces which work for physical life in strange way [sic] (D24:380).[9]

These gases are discovered at first hand by Van Helsing when he sniffs sulphurous fumes inside the chapel of Castle Dracula (D27:438). Stoker's Transylvania, in other words is not only a land beyond the forest, it is also a land beyond scientific under-standing – a netherworld – where the known laws of nature are suspended. It is a fitting haunt for an agent of diabolism.

Awareness of Dracula's vampire origins leads to the next, vital, question – his motives. He is no zombie-like automaton driven solely by a blind lust for blood. The relationship between Dracula and blood is much more subtle. For one thing, its consumption actually alters his appearance. Absorption of blood changes him from an old, into a younger, stronger man with dark, not white, hair. In just three days between 'meals' his hair reverts to showing white streaks (D11:167).

Dracula is not out to bite the neck of every victim who comes his way. He does not patrol nightly in search of liquid nourish-ment. Rather, his is the addiction of the junkie or the alcoholic. Dracula will not die if no blood is available, any more than will the alcoholic if deprived of spirits. In each case just one substance supplies vigour, energy. It is not that Dracula *likes* drinking blood. He *needs* blood – not for life (with which he is blessed/cursed) but for power. It functions as a stimulant.

The only exception is when his taking of blood is tactical. Dracula's blood-banks are always female.[10] His szgany (gypsy) henchmen, who do his earthly bidding, do not go in fear of his teeth. Renfield, similarly, becomes a servant of Dracula, not his blood supply. Still more illuminating is Dracula's trivial interest in Jonathan Harker, who serves as his estate agent and English language tutor, not his provider of nourishment. When Harker cuts himself shaving, Dracula only momentarily loses control of himself. This suggests that the sight of blood induces in him a love-hate ambivalence, not dissimilar to the reactions stimulated in the alcoholic by the prospect of liquor.

Dracula's strategic, as opposed to his biological, interest in blood is to ensnare female victims. These, in turn, will ensnare their menfolk, so that his vampire empire enlarges evermore through incestuous expansion. Here, Stoker, acknowledges the folkloric requirement that vampires always seek their nearest and dearest: 'The holiest love was the recruiting sergeant for their ghastly ranks' (D22:354). Dracula is aware of how he can turn this to advantage: 'Your girls that you all love are mine already: and through them you and others shall yet be mine – my creatures, to do my bidding, and to be my jackals when I want to feed' (D23:365).

In no instance does he destroy the lives of his victims for pleasure, but always in order to make use of them. As bloodlessness is not life-threatening to Dracula, his search must stem from a deeper, psychological drive. Dracula tells an unsuspecting Harker of his ambitions: 'I long to go through the crowded streets of your mighty London, to be in the midst of the whirl and rush of humanity, to share its life, its change, its death, and all that makes it what it is' (D2:31).

This confession is revealing. In the Europe of the 1890s Dracula has become outdated.[11] Transylvania is depicted as a peasant land in decline, unfitting as the continued habitat for a proud descendant of Attila. Admittedly, it is Dracula's bloodsucking over the centuries which is partly responsible for the enfeeblement of his native land, for its depleted population flout his authority by immunizing themselves with garlic and crosses. He feels cheated and deprived. No longer can he wage war against invading Turks: instead he is reduced to hunting defenceless children. In the meantime, Britain has become the hub of Western industrialism. By switching his arena and his methods of operation, Dracula sees new opportunities to be exploited.

His objective is therefore to establish a contemporary vampire empire in Britain. In this he will be aided by British laws and customs. The rational West will not suspect him. Its contempt for Eastern superstitions will leave him free; its democratic customs will enable him to flourish undetected; and its legal principle of presumption of innocence will work to his devious advantage. Jails cannot hold vampires. British society will unconsciously provide both his sheath and his armour, and 'the doubting of wise men would be his greatest strength' (D24:382).

Notwithstanding, Dracula's motives contain a more personal element. When narrowly escaping ambush in London he reveals his burning grievance: 'My revenge has just begun! I spread it over centuries, and time is on my side' (D23:365). Revenge? Revenge for what? Stoker seems to be harking back to Vlad Tepes, who was undoubtedly driven by revenge when he became ruler of Wallachia. He needed to avenge the deaths of his father and brother, and his own adolescent incarceration at the hands of the Turks. If Count Dracula could not take revenge against the Turks, the superpower of his time, he could at least direct it against the modern superpower. Britain must pay the penalty for the crimes of the Ottomans. Further, Britain has come to symbolize the ingratitude and treachery of Christian Europe, which betrayed Dracula while he was fighting the Turks in their interests (D21:343).

This desire for revenge, however, is not totally persuasive. Like the Wandering Jew, Dracula is doomed to wander the earth for eternity unless his heart be pierced. The Count is bored. It is sport he craves. He toys with his adversaries, taunting them, almost defying them to pit their puny wits against him. Despite this range of motives, it is not Stoker's aim to elicit sympathy for Dracula, or reveal him a victim as much as a victimizer. Stoker portrays him as incarnate evil, without any redeeming features, someone deserving not the least vestige of sympathy.

Presumably, Stoker's intention was that the reader breathes a sigh of relief when Dracula meets his doom. But can we be so sure? Clearly his pursuers think they have destroyed Dracula, and continue to think so several years afterwards. But have they? This is how Mina describes that climactic moment:

As I looked, the eyes [of Dracula] saw the sinking sun, and the look of hate in them turned to triumph. But, on the instant, came the sweep and the flash of Jonathan's great knife. I shrieked as I saw it sheer through the throat; whilst at the same moment Mr Morris's bowie knife plunged in the heart ... the whole body crumbled into dust and passed from our sight ... in that moment of dissolution there was in the face a look of peace such as I never could have imagined might have rested there (D27:447).

This might seem conclusive enough, until it is recalled that Van Helsing had earlier given precise instructions on how to be rid of the vampire. Folklore, too, insists on ritualistic observation of prescribed rites. These are not followed in the case of Dracula, who is despatched as if he were human, with cold steel. No wooden stake is used; his head is not detached from the body; and no corpse remains to be properly treated or devoured by flames. Initially it seems that Dracula's look of 'triumph' is premature, but could it be the attackers' sense of satisfaction that is misplaced? Stoker had already informed his readers that vampires have the power of dematerialization and can transform themselves into specks of dust. Conceivably, then, the Count dematerialized just in time. Realizing his narrow escape he prefers to lay low, until such time as Stoker resurrects him in a sequel.

---

1   The Count, in fact, has only two speaking parts once he arrives in England. Stoker's final decision to have Dracula 'on view' as little as possible appears, from his notes, to have been reached in a late draft. Earlier drafts show Dracula on-stage more frequently.

2   Nicholas Modrussa, in Radu Florescu and Raymond T McNally, *Dracula: A Biography*, p.50.

3   Newspaper report from *New York Tribune*, November 1883, reprinted in Austin Brereton, *The Life of Henry Irving*, Vol 2, p.14.

4   Franco Moretti, *Signs Taken for Wonders: Essays in the Sociology of Literary Forms*, pp.90-91.

5   Stoker's working notes show that Dracula was meant to register fear only when presented with relics older than himself.

6   Leonard Wolf, *A Dream of Dracula*, p.264.

---

7 Most of Stoker's information on the Scholomance came from Emily Gerard's 'Transylvanian Superstitions'.

8 Gerard, op. cit.

9 Here again, Stoker may have consulted the works of Emily Gerard, *The Land Beyond the Forest* and *The Waters of Hercules.*

10 The only possible exception is Dracula's 'attacks' on the crew of the *Demeter*. Whether he merely kills them, or kills them for their blood, or they throw themselves overboard in terror, is not made clear.

11 See Thomas P Walsh, '*Dracula*: Logos and Myth'. p.230.

7

'THANK GOD FOR
GOOD BRAVE MEN'

[Stoker] has in the first place the deficiency commonly found among writers who concern themselves almost exclusively with occult themes, of having either no interest in human personality, or no ability to analyse it. Despite the fact that he uses with unsurpassed skill the technique most suited to revelation of character [namely diary entries and the like], the people in the story are totally unconvincing, with the partial exception of the demon himself, whose personality is of course inhuman.

Glen St John Barclay,
Anatomy of Horror: Masters of Occult Fiction, p.44.

It is a commonplace criticism of Gothic romances that they lack vividness of characterization, that their heroes and heroines are stereotypical, and that this failing stems from the principal preoccupation of the genre – the threat of the supernatural. Other-worldly beings inevitably take precedence over this-worldly ones. *Dracula* has not escaped from this line of attack; indeed, it has received particular vituperation from some critics. Even those otherwise well-disposed to the novel have flayed Stoker's inability to give greater substance and credibility to the mortals lined up against the Count.

It cannot be denied that the novel would have been strengthened had Stoker paid as much attention to his living beings as to his vampire. Yet Stoker did not lack the ability to inject life into his characters. One of the reasons for Dracula's deserved reputation as a horror classic is the masterly way the author paints his central creation. So omnipotent is Count Dracula, so all-encompassing is his evil, that it is necessary for the cast of mortals to pale beside him. When Dracula sneers at his adversaries, 'You think to baffle me, you – with your pale faces all in a row, like sheep in a butcher's' (D23:365), he is speaking for Stoker. Compared to the Count they are like sheep – pitiful, lacking depth and substance. They must be that way. Had Stoker laboured to present them with greater vigour, the essential imbalance between good and evil would have shifted, and Dracula's omnipotence diluted. None of them is a match for him; they are mere putty in his hands. Only collectively do they possess any strength, and that fact is central to the novel. The typical antagonist of the literary monster is 'a distillation of complacent nineteenth-century mediocrity: nationalistic, stupid, superstitious, philistine, impotent, self-satisfied'.[1] All this can be applied to the adversaries of Dracula.

Because Stoker's characters are so flimsy, readers must make of them what they can. The resulting portraits are by no means mutually consistent. We should bear in mind Stoker's objective in choosing particular names for his characters. Sometimes it appears he gave no thought to the matter, conjuring up names at whim; but on other occasions it is clear that his names were carefully selected.[2] Only when Stoker's characters have been discussed and their functions ascertained will it be possible to dissect the novel in terms of its multi-faceted symbolism.

Jonathan Harker

It is fitting that a discussion of the cast of Dracula begins with Jonathan Harker. It is he who is responsible for bringing the Count to London, who suffers irredeemable guilt for so doing, and who fittingly severs the villain's throat at the conclusion. Harker probably acquired his name from one Joseph Harker, who had occasional assignments as scenic designer and painter for the Lyceum.[3] This has not prevented speculation. 'Hark', it has been suggested, refers to a danger signal,[4] or an injunction to heed and listen.[5]

Like Bram Stoker, Jonathan Harker is a man of the law. To be exact, he is a recently qualified solicitor in his early twenties, practising in Exeter. Whether he is Exeter born and bred is not clear. Most likely he is not. Stoker is fastidious about accent and dialect, but Harker's does not draw comment. When the Count requests lessons in English, so that when in London he will not stand out, he is not concerned that he might be absorbing a west-country lilt that would defeat his purpose.

Like Stoker, too, Harker is a Protestant. He possesses a clever, strong, youthful face, and a quiet, frank, business-like manner. He has the virtues of discretion associated with his profession. His hair at the outset is dark brown, but Stoker has the aim of pivoting Harker and Dracula around their common 'wife' – Mina. As Dracula's vitality increases, Harker, once his wife has been 'visited', is drained in reverse. He becomes haggard, his spirits are sapped, and his once dark hair turns white as his energy is transferred, via his wife, to the Count.

This visible deterioration has contributed to conflicting views as to what kind of person Harker is. To some, Harker is simply not much of a man, often appearing in a passive or supine state.[6] He is something of a half-witted creep, a goody-goody; someone who puts duty before all else. He is a provincial philistine, is no connoisseur of food and drink, and is a creature of monotonous habit – insisting that he winds his watch before going to bed and folds his clothes in a certain way. He harbours a naïve and simplistic belief in the value of the English legal system, with a criminal's right of protection under the law. Even his wife describes him as 'sweet and simple', though in a way that is meant to be flattering. He has evidently never had to face any real responsibility in his life, prior to his Transylvanian ordeal. His very existence in the novel is almost apologetic: a 'sufficient substitute' to act for his employer who was too ill to undertake the trip himself (D2:27). Throughout, Harker knows his humble place, particularly in the company of the other, socially superior Dracula-hunters. Morally, he is something of a prude: he objects to the tight-fitting clothes of Transylvanian women. He is intellectually curious only in the bigoted way of an insular Englishman who wants his preconceptions confirmed and is completely nonplussed otherwise.

But there is another, more positive, side to Harker. Even though this is his first trip abroad, he is no Little Englander. He appears fascinated by foreign places and customs. The fact of his travelling to a virtually unknown land gripped by superstitious mania testifies to his adventurous spirit. He can converse in German and his diary reveals him as both observant and alert. When imprisoned in the castle he ascertains his plight through his own mental and physical resources: he cannot take advantage of Van Helsing's guiding light. Harker demonstrates initiative and immense personal courage in trying to outwit the Count. Evidently he works better under strain. Moreover, he has a healthy contempt for snobbery and is adept at playing 'prigs' at their own game if the occasion demands (D20:317).

What is most remarkable is the way in which this unassuming, placid solicitor, who gives the impression of never having lifted a finger in anger, resorts to extreme physical violence when aroused. Not only is he prepared to take a shovel to the sleeping Count's face, but at the climax the outraged husband wields a great Kukri knife to sweep past Dracula's armed gypsy bodyguards. Awestruck, they step aside to permit Harker to slice the throat of their master. When motivated, Jonathan Harker is no mouse. Overall, his most enduring achievement, and the one by which he is best assessed, is that he is one of the few fictional characters to have been imprisoned by vampires, and through his own guile and courage survived to tell the tale.

In several respects, Harker is a projection of Bram Stoker. Like Stoker at a comparable age, Harker is a provincial Protestant man of law. Harker reveals to the reader how both he and Stoker came by their knowledge of Transylvanian history and customs – through the British Museum. Furthermore, Harker's sexual fantasies, we shall see, are undoubtedly an extension of Stoker's.

Harker also highlights a major riddle in *Dracula*. One of Stoker's posthumously published short stories was called 'Dracula's Guest'. The tale speaks of an unnamed young man who, en route to visiting Count Dracula, is exposed to perilous adventures in Munich. These occur on Walpurgis Nacht, 1 May. As the novel *Dracula* opens with Harker's departure from Munich, it is evident that the two tales are related. It is widely believed that 'Dracula's Guest' (published in 1914) is the excised opening chapter of Dracula.

In fact, the relationship between 'Dracula's Guest' and *Dracula* cannot be so straightforward. Stoker's papers dated 29 February 1892 reveal that the Munich events, scheduled to span two chapters, were themselves to be preceded by another chapter pertaining to property transactions. It would appear that the entire introductory section of the novel, comprising three chapters, was at some stage (or stages) discarded. Confirmation of these excisions can be found in the page-numbers of Stoker's now-discovered typescript of *Dracula*: page '3' overrides a crossed out type-written page '103'.

Stoker's original framework for *Dracula* shows he intended three separate incidents to befall Jonathan Harker in Munich. Taken in sequence these are, firstly, an adventure in a snowstorm with a wolf; secondly, a visit to the theatre to see a production of *The Flying Dutchman* (presumably an aperitif for the real-life immortal he was about to meet); and thirdly, a spooky encounter in a 'Dead House', in which Harker confronts an apparition of the Count.

A deleted reference to the 'Dead House' appears near the beginning of Stoker's *Dracula* typescript. But as neither the Dead House nor the Flying Dutchman episodes feature in 'Dracula's Guest', that short story cannot function as the prelude to *Dracula*.

'Dracula's Guest' concerns itself solely with the first of Harker's three Munich experiences, when he shelters from a snowstorm in an eerie, forbidding tomb, catches sight of a beautiful woman within, and is 'rescued' by a wolf. Stoker constantly switched his ideas around: originally it was to have been the Dead House incident which took place on Walpurgis Nacht. That of the snowstorm, the tomb, and the wolf was scheduled earlier, for 27 April. Stoker's typescript, however, contains an deleted reference to the woman 'in the tomb on 'Walpurgis Nacht'. Unfortunately, the intended boundaries between the three episodes become increasingly blurred, and it is difficult to sift one from the others.

The uncertainty surrounding the timing and original contents of 'Dracula's Guest' is heightened by oddities in its published format. For one thing, the narrative style employed in the short story is different from that found in *Dracula*. 'Dracula's Guest' is not a diary entry, but a first-person account with much dialogue. The central motifs are also quite distinct. In *Dracula*, the 'wolf' is shown as savage and destructive: the animal familiar of the Count. In 'Dracula's Guest', however, a wolf warms the body of the insensible guest to protect him from the cold.

More critically, the unnamed 'guest', although identified in Stoker's notes as Jonathan Harker, is unrecognizable from the Harker of the finished novel. In the course of the various drafts Harker's personality undergoes a radical change. In 'Dracula's Guest' he is aggressive, insensitive, and brash, sufficiently impulsive to go sauntering off on his own on Walpurgis Nacht – an act quite out of keeping with the introverted Harker of the novel.

Crucially, Dracula's guest does not speak German: the Harker of *Dracula* does. This discrepancy is enlightening because Stoker originally intended to base his novel in German-speaking Styria. Stoker noted in March 1890 that the Count will insist that his English go-between should not be able to speak German. Otherwise, of course, the locals will be able to warn him of his peril and convince him of the need to return home. By 1892, by which time Stoker had relocated his Count to Transylvania, there was no longer the same pressing demand for Harker's ignorance of the language. Though many Transylvanians speak German, their superstitious nature undermines the force of their warnings. In any case, Harker cannot escape Dracula's all-seeing powers once he enters Transylvania (in 'Dracula's Guest' he was unable to escape them even in Munich). Besides, in his mature drafts, Stoker clearly wanted Harker to be aware of the risks he was running – by allowing him to communicate in German – and embrace his fate by disregarding them.

In summary, it can be maintained that if at some late stage an opening chapter of Stoker's typescript was excised, that chapter could not be anything like that published seventeen years later under the title 'Dracula's Guest'. More probably, that particular tale is a self-contained episode reworked from the earliest, 1890-92, phase of Stoker's ideas. It is not clear how, or when, 'Dracula's Guest' came by its published name.

Van Helsing

A second outlet for Stoker's own character is Professor Abraham Van Helsing, who is allowed to borrow Stoker's Christian name. He is the only character in the book, Dracula aside, to warrant a careful physical description. Van Helsing is

> a man of medium height, strongly built, with his shoulders set back over a broad, deep chest and a neck well balanced on the trunk as the head is on the neck. The poise of the head strikes one at once as indicative of thought and power; the head is noble, well-sized, broad and large behind the ears. The face, clean-shaven, shows a hard square chin, a large resolute, mobile mouth, a good-sized nose, rather straight, but with quick, sensitive nostrils, that seem to broaden as the big, bushy eyebrows come down and the mouth tightens. The forehead is broad and fine, rising at first almost straight and then sloping back above two bumps or ridges wide apart; such a forehead that the reddish hair cannot possibly tumble over it, but falls naturally back and to the sides. Big, dark blue eyes are set widely apart, and are quick and tender or stern with the man's moods (D14:218-19).

His countenance is repeatedly described as 'of iron'. Van Helsing is old (we are not told how old), grey, and lonely – his wife is insane and his son is dead (D13:210, 12). He remains faithful to his wife's memory and finds a substitute for companionship in work, though he comes to 'love' each and every one of the little band afflicted by Dracula, and views them as his sons and daughters. He treasures old-fashioned virtues, and (evidently like Bram Stoker) is unsettled by the sceptical, selfish, late-Victorian age in which he lives (D14:226).[7] Van Helsing is the remote, aged specialist. Like Father Lankester Merrin in *The Exorcist*, he is the Catholic scientist, the superbrain waiting to be called for one final battle against the forces of evil. These wise men appear on the scene only when ordinary 'medicine' has failed, when it is necessary to seek recourse in the 'witch doctor' who has access to less orthodox remedies.

Many readers see Van Helsing as the hero of *Dracula*. The Dutch professor is the repository of worldly wisdom; the guru and shaman without whose intervention Dracula's evil schemes would doubtless have succeeded. As a doctor of Medicine, of Philosophy, and of Letters – and a lawyer into the bargain – he is portrayed as the all-round intellectual and free thinker. His philosophical breadth of mind may reveal how Stoker thought of himself. Van Helsing knows something of many languages and has 'revolutionized therapeutics by the discovery of the continuous evolution of brain matter' (D18:292). When he is introduced, the reader is left in no doubt that here is the man to do battle with the Count. Van Helsing

> knows as much about obscure diseases as anyone in the world ... He is a seemingly arbitrary man, but this is because he knows what he is talking about better than anyone else. He is a philosopher and metaphysician, and one of the most advanced scientists of his day; and he has ... an absolutely open mind. This, with an iron nerve, a temper of the ice-brook, an indomitable resolution, self-command and toleration exalted from virtues to blessings, and the kindliest and truest heart that beats – these form his equipment for the noble work that he is doing for mankind – work both in theory and in practice, for his views are as wide as his all-embracing sympathy (D9:137).

He is, in other words, almost too good to be true: a paragon of professional and personal virtues.[8] He is the Sherlock Holmes who will tackle Moriarty. Both the professor and the sleuth are detached, purposeful, and gifted with superior intellects. Likewise, both the Count and Moriarty are cold and cunningly evil, have total control over their underlings, and possess brilliant, if twisted, minds.[9] For all its supernatural content, *Dracula* is as much a tale of detection as of horror. It is therefore not surprising that Stoker's super-hero began life in the early drafts of the novel as three different people: a German philosopher and historian, a psychical research agent, and a detective. Such is the range of talents necessary to offset the Count's mastery that all three were eventually encapsulated in one composite embodiment of power, knowledge and virtue – Abraham Van Helsing.

Unfortunately, Van Helsing is not always the inspiring presence Stoker intends him to be. Despite having been a student in London, his spoken English is on occasions heavily accented. This often makes him difficult to understand, and because it is Van

Helsing's critical function to elucidate the behaviour of vampires, the reader is put to some inconvenience every time he speaks.

Although capable of discretion and sensitivity towards the sufferings of Dracula's victims, Van Helsing is not above thoughtless remarks, and his sense of humour can be distasteful, even macabre. At times, he seems to taunt those he loves with the perilousness of their position. On one occasion he tactlessly reminds Mina that the Count has 'banqueted heavily' from her body (D22:352). Presumably even Van Helsing must be permitted some lapses, given the strain he is under. He is, after all, fighting for the salvation not just of his comrades, but, in all likelihood, mankind. On the other hand, his moral severity is central to the Christian ethic that underpins the book: his duty is to stand firm against moral weakness, especially sexual desire. His name 'Abraham' is not only Stoker's, but also that of the first biblical patriarch. Combining his scientific eminence with his Vatican contacts, Van Helsing has connections with two of the dominant forces of Western culture.[10]

Van Helsing, of course, is principally a medical man: he is not a trained vampire hunter. He has to learn quickly the nature of the crisis confronting him. He relishes the challenge presented by Dracula's brain, and feels not a little intellectual affinity with him: 'I too am wily and I think his mind in a little while' (D23:373). Even when he fully comprehends, his secretive nature prevents him from imparting his understanding to others until they are able to discern the light for themselves. Through his own arcane researches he has a pretty shrewd idea of what he is up against, but like the true initiate he refuses to tell.[11] Although the professor cannot yet be sure, he evidently suspects the presence of a vampire from the outset (D9:139; 10:150). However, he is slow to make use of his suspicions, and his tardiness contributes to Lucy's death, which could have been averted given the extent of Van Helsing's knowledge at the time. Afterwards he defends himself by maintaining he had not guessed the horrific cause of her malady (D18:283).[12] He then compounds the errors made over Lucy, operating a conspiracy theory when he learns of the attack on Mina which, it turns out, could easily have led to a second tragedy.

Van Helsing, the more the microscope is turned on him, entertains somewhat illiberal attitudes and beliefs. What liberal-minded doctor, for example, would refer to mental illness as a 'defect' (D18:294)? Moreover, he is a devout Roman Catholic who upholds the strictest moral values. He constantly urges 'trust' and 'belief' in his ideas on the nature and causes of vampirism. His supposedly 'open mind' is in fact a sham. Everything is seen through the narrowest spectacles of Christian dogma, and goodness and evil interpreted in the light of Vatican strictures. He is basically a kind, avuncular old man, but one for whom the path of righteousness is narrow and the consequences of deviating unthinkable.

Nor is he in the least constrained by the conventions of science and medicine, being quite prepared to turn to non-scientific thinking for inspiration. When modern science and Christian faith prove inadequate for the task in hand, he readily resorts to folklore and superstition. Van Helsing, of all people, should know that superstitions are not systematic, and that vampire traits vary from region to region. He turns vampire lore into vampire law, yet solves that particular difficulty by declaring such superstitions to have their roots in 'faith' (D24:390). As a consequence, Van Helsing leads the forces of God with a bizarre combination of modern science and superstition, and he warns his fellows against their materialist, bourgeois prejudices (D18:285). By his use of garlic with Host and crucifix, Van Helsing takes science across the frontiers of witchcraft. Whereas Mary Shelley's Frankenstein, eighty years earlier, had been a 'magician-turned-scientist', Van Helsing becomes a 'scientist-turned-magician'.[13]

Renfield

The most unexpected human character in the novel is R M Renfield, an inpatient in a lunatic asylum. He stands outside the little band opposed to Dracula, being psychically in tune with the Count and, initially, anxious to serve him. In that sense he, too, can be viewed as a manifestation of Stoker – Renfield being the minion of a vampire, Stoker of an actor.

Renfield is fifty-nine, of ruddy complexion, and with pleading eyes. He possesses great physical strength; is selfish, secretive, and purposeful; and he is morbidly excitable, being prone to violent spasms (D5:78; 6:87; 9:131-32). He is also, it transpires, surprisingly well-educated and articulate.

One of Renfield's functions in the novel is to form a triangular relationship. He connects with Dracula, on the one hand, and his pursuers on the other – which helps to clarify the reader's understanding of both.[14] A second function arises when Stoker uses Renfield to expound a pseudo-scientific theory of vampirism. The patient gives the lie to those who would believe vampirism to be the product of simple-minded peasants in distant lands. Renfield is himself a living vampire, serving his vampire apprenticeship while confined within the walls of an asylum. He consumes blood by consuming life. Consider the children's song:

There was an old lady who swallowed a fly
I don't know why she swallowed a fly – perhaps she'll die.
There was an old lady who swallowed a spider
[bird, cat, dog, goat, cow, horse].

Renfield is like that old lady, and throughout Stoker's notes he is referred to as the 'Flyman' or the 'Fly Patient'. Incarcerated in his cell he takes to catching flies and eating them, seeking justification and explanation in the scriptural phrase 'the blood is the life' (D11:171; 18:280). Not content with flies he turns his attention to spiders, which have previously caught and digested flies. Next he contrives to gorge sparrows, jubilant in the various accumulated lives he is ingesting. He asks for a cat – but does not get one – and even tries to kill a human solely for the purpose of lapping his blood. He believes that flesh and blood from living creatures will grant him immortality, and for his pains he is medically classified as a 'zoophagous (life-eating) maniac' (D6:90).

Another role for Renfield is that of barometer of the Count's presence. As will be explored, Renfield takes on a John the Baptist identity, prefiguring the arrival of his 'Christ'.[15] Renfield's eccentric behaviour starts attracting attention while the Count is still hundreds of miles from England, although it is not clear whether it is he who senses Dracula, or *vice versa*. His tantrums thereafter coincide with dawn, noon, and dusk, the times when Dracula's powers are changing or at their weakest.

Finally, Renfield is included to highlight the issue of madness. Is it really he who is mad for acknowledging the existence of Dracula, when other, 'saner' persons must sooner or later come to the same conclusion? Like Harker, Renfield yearns to distinguish between nightmare and grim reality. As with Harker, too, truth eventually wins through, confirming what Van Helsing once observed: 'I may gain more knowledge out of the folly of this madman than I shall from the teaching of the most wise' (D19:305).

Strange to say, although Renfield is the most unconventional character in the novel, apart from Dracula, he is also the most convincing.[16] The same could not be said of the three young, worldly heroes – Seward, Holmwood, and Morris.

Dr Seward

Dr John (Jack) Seward shares with Jonathan Harker the fact of being a compulsive diarist. Many of the events in the book are seen through his eyes – or, rather, mouth, for Seward records his thoughts on to the newly invented phonograph. Seward functions as a link man, being the catalyst which brings four of the other male characters together. His relationship with Van Helsing (his master) and Renfield (his patient), for example, is central to the unfolding of the plot.

Seward is a twenty-nine-year-old psychiatrist, running a large, private lunatic asylum – a profitable industry in late-Victorian England. He is of good birth, handsome, with a 'strong jaw and good forehead', and eminently marriageable. He has had his share of youthful adventures, hunting and travelling the world, though he nonetheless appears inexperienced and nervous in the company of women. Seward has studied under Van Helsing in Amsterdam (he was his favourite pupil), and the admiration evidently goes both ways. But the personal bond goes deeper than shared professional competence. Seward once saved his master's life, in circumstances which cast a shadow over an already deepening plot. Van Helsing suffered a gangrenous wound inflicted by a knife, which Seward had to suck clean (D9:138). Seward, in other words, has sucked Van Helsing's blood, a second instance (added to Renfield's) of human blood-sucking in the novel.

Seward serves as the representative of all that Van Helsing rejects: materialist, rationalist science – panacea of the late-Victorian age. Seward finds it difficult to have faith or trust in anything or anyone. He does not trust people he does not know well (D17:265), and in the case of Van Helsing not even someone he does. His role is also that of social commentator. Through him, for example, the reader learns that tearful breakdowns are considered unmanly, and if unavoidable are best performed in the company of women (D17:275).

Notwithstanding Seward's prejudices, Van Helsing presumably admires his ex-student's intellect, just as Sherlock Holmes respects Dr Watson's. Seward occupies the same position *vis à vis* Van Helsing as Watson does for Holmes. Seward and Watson have the same Christian name and same profession. Both are given to 'half-baked philosophizing'.[17] Seward is the foil in *Dracula*, the vehicle by which Stoker explains everything to the reader through someone who cannot comprehend unless everything is reduced to first principles. Seward is the last of the characters to understand and accept the presence of the supernatural in their midst. *Punch*, in reviewing Dracula, summarized Seward as: 'the Inquiring, Sceptical, Credulous, Noodle ... the devoted admiring slave of the philosophic astute hero, ever ready to question, ever ready to dispute, ever ready to make a mistake at the critical moment, or to go to sleep just when success depends on his remaining awake'.[18]

In fact, Seward is more than just a 'noodle'; for one thing, his medical ethics are questionable. He admits to a certain cruelty in his handling of Renfield, his pet lunatic (D5:78). Although familiar with Renfield's violent mania, Seward encourages him to escape so that his behaviour can be studied while at large. Nor is Seward averse to offering Renfield the live cat he had earlier demanded, though his patient this time declines it. Seward even demonstrates a happy disregard for the law when expedient to do so; for example, sidestepping the need for an inquest into Lucy's death – although he has at that time no inkling of what caused it.

Just as Van Helsing is partly responsible for Lucy's death, so Seward ultimately fails as Renfield's physician – both in the diagnostic sense, and by contributory negligence which results in his patient's death. When Renfield, with the unexpected lucidity of sanity, tries to show others what he alone can see, he is disregarded. He is mortally wounded by Dracula, but is abandoned by Seward, who does not even summon an assistant to care for him. So concerned is the doctor for the plight of the sane that Renfield is left to die alone and untended.

If Seward is a somewhat unprincipled doctor, he is even more pitiful in his private life. Early in the book he is driven to distraction by his love for Lucy. His proposal of marriage is turned down, and within weeks he confesses to a 'savage delight' at the prospect of beheading her (D16:253). Worse, as the hunt for Dracula nears its climax, this respectable man of healing comes to feel 'wild with excitement' as battle approaches. He imagines he knows 'what men feel in battle when the call to action is heard' (D25:399). Unbeknown to Seward, that feeling is usually abject terror.

To compound matters, Seward not only fails to perceive his limitations, medical and otherwise, but instead harbours a disconcerting personal ambition. The fact of running his own lunatic asylum while so young testifies to his conventional medical abilities and entrepreneurial aptitude. Yet he yearns to promote his own claims to medical research, and sees Renfield as the key to his success. He even envies his patient's sense of purpose. Seward's ego is sufficiently swollen for him to contemplate whether he might enjoy a congenitally exceptional brain (D6:90). But eventually, depressed and unsettled by unrequited love, obsessed by Renfield's behaviour, and mentally tortured by the supernatural intrusion into his tidy, scientific mind, he is forced to tackle the nature of sanity – his own and Van Helsing's – head on. His innate nineteenth-century belief in progress clashes with his increasing doubts about himself and his motives. Not surprisingly, given his inner torment, he is usually ineffectual when it matters most.

Arthur Holmwood (Lord Godalming)

The most shadowy and under-developed of the major characters is the Hon Arthur Holmwood – Lord Godalming as he becomes. It is obligatory for Stoker's young heroes to be physically attractive, and Holmwood conforms, being 'tall, handsome and curly-haired' and possessing 'stalwart proportions'. 'Buoyant' by nature, he is devastated by the double death of his fiancée. Although he can handle dogs and steam launches, he seems otherwise to have no worthwhile qualities at all – save those of inherited wealth, for which he takes no credit. True to his privileged upbringing he is preoccupied with his honour as a gentleman and his faith as a Christian (D15:246) – though neither prevents him using his title or his money to win whatever favours he wants. His Lordship's practical suggestions are usually cause for hilarity: to assist in the under-cover operation to unearth Dracula's whereabouts in the rundown East End of London, he offers to provide his heraldic adorned coaches (D22:350); and when the action shifts to the primitive vastness of the Black Sea hinterland he fancies he can hire a 'special' train (D25:402).

Holmwood, in fact, has only two justifications for being in the book. The first is his wallet. A six-person expedition chasing Dracula across Europe costs a great deal – but Holmwood happily and without question provides the cash. The second is his title. Holmwood's elevation to the peerage on the eve of Lucy's death promotes him to a platform opposite Count Dracula: two aristocrats fighting for possession of the same woman.

Both Holmwood's name and his title give insights into Stoker's thinking. The name 'Arthur' highlights the chivalrous nature of his role as England's archetypal hero and saviour.[19] It is possible, furthermore, that 'Holmwood' was taken from 'Ringwood' – a character in *Varney the Vampire*. In *Dracula*, the Holmwood family home is at Ring. An alternative source for the name 'Holmwood' can be found in an 1892 edition of *Lloyd's Weekly Advertiser*, wherein the story is told of a certain Mr Holm, who, in the company of a Mr Wood, broke into a vault in St Mary's churchyard, Hendon, to sever the head from his mother's body.

This incident appeared on the same page as a review of Irving's *King Lear*, so was likely to have come to Stoker's attention.[20] Whatever the source, Holmwood's title transforms him into 'LORD GODalming'. God has come to fight Count DE VILle.[21]

Quincey P Morris

Quincey P Morris, the American from Texas, has deliberately been left to last, because with him lie most of the uncertainties relating to the male cast. As a personality he is painted by Stoker with almost invisible strokes. Almost nothing is known about him. He does nothing of note throughout the book: nothing, that is, until its concluding lines. Then he dies, giving his life in the successful assault on Dracula.

The reason for Morris's death is a major mystery. He is the most superfluous character in the drama, being neither a victim of the vampire's kiss, nor a grieving partner out to settle accounts. It is difficult to imagine the novel being impaired were he to be struck from it altogether (several film versions fuse Morris and Holmwood into a single personality). Morris's role seems simply to complete the trio of Seward and Holmwood, all suitors of the same girl, to mirror Dracula's three vampire mistresses. Yet this nonentity not only plunges his knife into Dracula's heart: he is the only pursuer to lose his life. It is also he who gives his name to the Harkers' son – Quincey Harker. Morris thereby gains vicarious immortality, and as a result takes pride of place in Stoker's puzzling climax.

The problem lies in seeking to unearth Stoker's intention. As Morris is the most peripheral of the initiates, his sacrifice is neither as telling, nor indeed as logical, as that of any of his companions. Dracula has no particular quarrel with Morris. Before the possibilities are explored, it will be useful to recap what is known about Quincey Morris. He is pure cardboard, a complete stereotype; the fresh breezy, all-American boy; the bubbling well of good spirits; the brash, vulgar Texas millionaire. He appears in the mould of Teddy Roosevelt, conforming to Victorian Britain's condescending view of the raw-edged but genuine American – dependable yet banal. At the practical level, Morris, as the gun-totin', knife-waving campaigner, provides the brawn to complement the European's monopoly of brain. (He is the only member of the pursuing party who can speak no foreign language [D26:412]). He is the calm, phlegmatic, tobacco-chewing man of action in a gang otherwise composed of medics, aristocrats and city slickers; he is a born leader in hunting expeditions (D16:251; 23:363). So stereotypical is he, that Morris appears, cloned almost, in one of Stoker's earlier short stories.[22]

In sum, Morris is much travelled and a man of countless adventures. This makes him, in a sense, the most attractive, the most romantic, the most uncomplicated, the most identifiable of the little group. He is the only one who can die a hero's death, for he has no personal axe to wield against Dracula. Perhaps, then, it is just these qualities of friendship, loyalty, and reckless courage that Stoker is trying to celebrate.

Of course, Stoker was fond of America and recognized the courage of her menfolk, though why Morris should hail from Texas is less apparent. There are, in fact, extended similarities between Morris and that real-life Texan freedom fighter, Jim Bowie. These go beyond the arming of Dracula's attacker with a Bowie knife. Stoker might have constructed Morris upon that earlier hero of the Lone Star State, who met his end, along with William Barratt Travis and Davy Crockett, in the Mexican assault on the Alamo in 1836. To begin with, there is the similarity of personality and lifestyle. Both Bowie and Morris were adventurers, hunters who relished entertaining massive odds. Both were urbane, polished and rich. They were quietly spoken and gentle, qualities which contrasted with the more belligerent aspects of their personalities. Each was pragmatic, generous, extravagant, loyal to an espoused cause, and a born leader.

In their financial affairs both men lived unscrupulously. Jim Bowie won his immense personal fortune by wheeler-dealing, slave trading with pirates, and indulging in fictitious or fraudulent land titles.[23] Similarly, for all his dashing heroism, Quincey Morris is aware of not having always lived by the Book: 'I'm only a rough fellow, who hasn't perhaps lived as a man should', he admits (D25:393). He is also a teller of tall stories which, less charitably, could be another way of saying he does not know truth from fiction.

In the company of women both were shy and ill at ease. Both fell in love with a member of the local social élite (Bowie with a nineteen-year-old Mexican girl; Morris with the similarly aged, similarly privileged Lucy), and both lost them in dire circumstances (cholera in the case of Bowie's wife and children; the bite of Dracula in the case of Lucy).

Thereafter both men dedicated themselves to combating their malefactors. Jim Bowie took up with fellow Texan settlers to stand firm against Santa Anna, while Quincey Morris risked all in the hunt for Dracula. Not only did Morris wield a Bowie knife against his tormentor but, like Bowie, he paid the ultimate sacrifice. Each fell to the cold steel employed by their antagonist's troops/bodyguard.

At the very least, Morris bears passing resemblance to Jim Bowie. As for the name 'Morris', Stoker may have learned that Bowie's youthful notoriety first came to prominence with the knifing of a Major Morris Wright,[24] or that immediately following the Alamo's fall, Senator Thomas Morris of Ohio presented a petition to Congress demanding the recognition of Texan independence.[25]

The difficulty with Stoker's borrowing from Jim Bowie is that by reincarnating the Alamo's first commander half a century later, the circumstances which gave rise to Bowie are less germane. Given that the year in which Dracula visits England is 1893, and that Morris is no more than twenty-five (Seward is twenty-nine and he refers to Morris and the others as younger men [D25:403]), one can pinpoint Morris's birth as the late 1860s – hard on the heels of the American Civil War.

With his choice of Texas, Stoker alighted on an area so vast and the product of so many disparate influences that efforts to place Morris in his native environment are easily frustrated.[26] He comes, Stoker says, 'from' Texas; he does not specifically say he is a Texan. He may have been a second- or third-generation Texan, or, along with thousands of others, been an immigrant from another State. Either way, the pre-Civil War methods of profiteering in Texas were succeeded by decades of comparative austerity. This was one consequence of the emancipation of the slaves and the resultant disruption of the cotton industry. The value of land collapsed, and most Texans were more concerned with staying alive than with striking it rich. Among other problems, they had to guard against the Indian menace and roaming, lawless unpaid veterans of the war. The Ku Klux Klan made their first appearance in Texan history at this time. The commonest Texan pastimes in these troubled years were said to be drinking, card-playing, and shooting.[27] By and large, Texas had to wait until the twentieth century before recapturing the money-making opportunities of its pre-Civil War heyday. Not long before Morris's death in 1893 Texas was still viewed by many Americans as a marginal region almost at the edge of civilization.

It is therefore probable that Morris's fortune was the product of his parents' or grandparents' endeavours, and that he was something of a globe-trotting playboy. This would not leave much time for money-making, other than by speculation of one kind or another, and it rules out any kind of professional career.

If, however, Morris was more than simply a playboy son of affluent stock, how did he come by his fortune in post-reconstruction Texas? Oil had little significance until the twentieth century, and manufacturing was only just becoming profitable by the 1880s. He might have been a cattle baron or a railroad entrepreneur. One film adaptation of *Dracula* casts Morris as a diplomat, exploiting the tradition of Texan frontiersmen dabbling in politics – though 'politicians' were one species of American known not to have impressed Stoker.[28] In his working notes, Stoker mentions an American 'inventor' from Texas, though this is crossed out.

The reason for this emphasis on one of Stoker's minor personages is to prepare the ground for a radical conjecture. Several critics have been puzzled by the incongruity of a nobody like Quincey Morris taking precedence in the final pages of *Dracula*. This incongruity is made congruous if Morris was in league with the Count. This hypothesis has already been presented by Moretti, who notes the inexplicability of Morris's death, and that it seems out of keeping with the logic of the narrative. Moretti takes a close look at the American's activities in the novel, for Morris is shrouded in mystery:

'He looks so young and so fresh that it seems almost impossible that he has been to so many places and has had such adventures' [D5:74]. What places? What adventures? Where does all his money come from? What does Mr Morris do? Where does he live? Nobody knows any of this. But nobody suspects. Nobody suspects even when Lucy dies – and then turns into a vampire – immediately after receiving a blood transfusion from Morris. Nobody suspects when Morris, shortly afterwards, tells the story of his mare, sucked dry of blood in the Pampas by 'one of those big bats they call vampires' [D12:183]. It is the first time that the name 'vampire' is mentioned in the novel: but there is no reaction. And there is no reaction a few lines further on when Morris 'coming close to me ... spoke in a fierce half-whisper: "What took it [the blood] out?"' But Dr Seward shakes his head; he hasn't the faintest idea. And Morris, reassured, promises to help. Nobody, finally, suspects when, in the course of the meeting to plan the vampire hunt, Morris leaves the room to take a shot – missing, naturally – at the big bat on the window-ledge listening to the preparations; or when, after Dracula bursts into the household, Morris hides among the trees, the only effect of which is that he loses sight of Dracula and invites the others to call off the hunt for the night. This is pretty well all Morris does in *Dracula*. He would be a totally superfluous character if, unlike the others, he were not characterised by this mysterious connivance with the world of the vampires. So long as things go well for Dracula, Morris acts like an accomplice. As soon as there is a reversal of fortunes, he turns into his staunchest enemy.

... And at the moment when Morris dies, and the threat disappears, old England grants its blessing to this excessively pushy and unscrupulous financier, and raises him to the dignity of a Bengal Lancer: 'And to our bitter grief, with a smile and silence, he died, a gallant gentlemen' ... These, it should be noted, are the last words of the novel, whose true ending does not lie – as is clear by now – in the death of the Romanian count, but in the killing of the American financier.[29]

Following Moretti's lead, one can unearth other incidents to support his contention. When Lucy dies upon receiving Morris's blood, he abets her 'death' which the Count is trying to bring about. Once the decision is taken to exclude Harker's wife from the hunt for Dracula, it is Morris who ensures that she is left alone, thereby enabling the Count to visit her without hindrance (D18:290). It is Morris who discovers (beckons?) Dracula's rats in the chapel (D19:300-1). Dracula's advances to Harker's wife behind a locked door are actively encouraged by the Texan, who tries to avert Van Helsing's intrusion by *twice* protesting against violating a woman's bedroom (D21:335) – the only occasion in the book in which he is concerned with propriety. In the ensuing chase Morris is in a good position to give false directions to assist the Count's escape. After Renfield is mortally wounded by Dracula and been abandoned by the doctors, the next person to see him is Morris, who 'reports' his death (D21:340). Finally, when Dracula is almost cornered in a house in Piccadilly, it is Morris's self-imposed function to prohibit escape through the window. How does Dracula escape? – through the window (D23:365).

Though the present writer is not contending that Morris ended up as Dracula's accomplice, one cannot be so confident regarding Stoker's earlier intentions. His notes left clues. In the novel's early drafts, the Texan (whose name went through several changes[30]) was forever coming and going. Once, Seward was supposed to receive two visitors together: the Count and the Texan. Chapters three and four of Book Three were supposed to have the Texan journey to Transylvania alone and at his own request. Although this was later scrapped from the finished novel, the question remains: what did Stoker intend should happen to him there?

---

[1]   Franco Moretti, *Signs Taken for Wonders: Essays in the Sociology of Literary Forms*, p.84.

[2]   For example, Dracula recruits the services of a wolf named 'Bersicker'. Stoker had noted from *The Book of Were-Wolves* that Berserkers were particularly fierce Norse warriors who fought with seemingly supernatural strength and ferocity.

[3]   Harry Ludlam, *A Biography of Bram Stoker: Creator of Dracula*, p.110.

[4]   Mark M Hennelly Jr, 'Dracula: the Gnostic Quest and the

Victorian Wasteland', p.20.

5 Thomas P Walsh, '*Dracula*: Logos and Myth', p.233.

6 See Leonard Wolf, *The Annotated Dracula*, p.24.

7 Van Helsing fulfils similar functions in Dracula to Baron Vordenburg in *Carmilla*, and his name is similar to Dr Hesselius in another of Le Fanu's tales, 'Green Tea'. In view of his battle with Dracula, Van Helsing has also been identified with 'Hell Singer', Hennelly, op. cit., p.22

8 The expression is from Leonard Wolf, *A Dream of Dracula*, p.215.

9 See E Randolph Johnson, 'The Victorian Vampire', p.210.

10 Stephanie Demetrakopoulos, 'Feminism, Sex Role Changes, and Other Subliminal Fantasies in Bram Stoker's *Dracula*', p.104.

11 Ronald Schleifer, 'The Trap of the Imagination: the Gothic Tradition, Fiction, and the "Turn of the Screw",' p.299.

12 He may even have caused her death more directly. See Chapter 9.

13 Robert Dowse and David Palmer, '"Dracula": the Book of Blood', p.428.

14 See Royce MacGillivray, '"Dracula": Bram Stoker's Spoiled Masterpiece', p.525.

15 In this connection, one Dracula etymologist has suggested that 'Ren' means to 'clear a way for' a pastoral area (a 'field'), Walsh, p.234.

16 This view is not universally held. MacGillivray, for example, thinks that the portrayal of Renfield is unsuccessful, p.525.

17 Johnson, op. cit., p.209.

18 *Punch*, 26 June 1897.

19 See Walsh, p.233.

20 Philip Temple, 'The Origins of Dracula'.

21 Indeed, the full title is nearly Lord God Almighty, and the 'alming' implies *noblesse-oblige* pedigree, or alms to God, Walsh, p.233. The present writer is not generally impressed by much of the linguistic speculation employed on characters' names. The striking nature of 'Lord Godalming', however, prevents a powerful exception.

22 In 'The Squaw', Elias P Hutcheson hails from Nebraska. He is a 'cheery stranger, full of racy remarks and a wonderful stock of adventures'. He has fought grizzlies and Injuns and carries a pistol illegally. The middle initial 'P' is transferred to Morris, and the only perceptible difference from Morris is the state of origin.

23 Walter Lord, *A Time to Stand*, p.26.

24 ibid.

25 L W Newton and H P Gambrell, *A Social and Political History of Texas*, p.224. As for the word 'Quincey', this is similar to the name for a throat disease, quinsy – a Victorian description for bronchitis (Walsh p.234). Dracula could also be said to bring about a disease of the throat.

26 The flood of immigrants from the 1830s into Texas came from as far as Britain, Germany, and France. There was an indigenous Mexican population, but they were soon submerged by waves of Americans moving west. Among them were farmers, artisans, and professional men, cultivated and educated southern gentlemen. The harshness of life on the frontier, however, soon encouraged a tough, independent, empire-building spirit that is still encapsulated in the name 'Texan' today. Interestingly, Texas was one of the few States with which Stoker was hardly acquainted, and it is not even known if he went there. Not until early 1896, on the Lyceum's fifth tour of North America, were performances given in the Deep South, and even then New Orleans was the nearest venue to Texas (Austin Brereton, *The Life of Henry Irving*, Vol 2, p.226). Farson, in contrast, asserts that the Lyceum performed for the first time in New Orleans in 1884 (Daniel Farson, *The Man Who Wrote Dracula: A Biography of Bram Stoker*, p.74).

27 Newton and Gambrell, p.224.

28 Bram Stoker, *A Glimpse of America*, p.28.

29 Moretti, pp.94-96.

30 For example, Brutus M Moris and Quincey P Adams (which comes rather too close to John Quincy Adams, the sixth President of the United States).

8

'SWEET, SWEET, GOOD, GOOD WOMEN'

There is no head above the head of a serpent: and there is no wrath above the wrath of a woman. I had rather dwell with a lion and a dragon than to keep house with a wicked woman ... All wickedness is but little to the wickedness of woman ... What else is a woman but a foe to friendship, an unescapable punishment, a necessary evil, a natural temptation, a desirable calamity, a domestic danger, a delectable detriment, an evil of nature, painted with fair colours! ... women are naturally more impressionable and more ready to receive the influence of a disembodied spirit ... they have slippery tongues ... since they are feebler both in mind and body it is not surprising that they should come more and more under the spell of witchcraft ... Women are intellectually like children ... she is more carnal than a man as is clear from her many carnal abominations ... for the sake of fulfilling their lust they consort evil with devils ... she is a liar by nature.

Malleus Maleficarum, Part 1, Question 6.

Male fear and suspicion of women is as old as time. Was not the act of childbirth the greatest and most inexplicable act of magic? And why, provided they survived childbirth, had women always outlived men, and been more immune to plagues and pestilence?[1] What other unknown powers of sorcery did they possess? While their menfolk fought and died in countless battles, women stayed at home to pass on their mysteries to their daughters. Classical Europe was contemptuous of women: Seneca (*Tragedies*) wrote of their lust, hatred, pride and evil; Cicero (*The Rhetorics*) complained of their avarice; and even Socrates referred to them as a confounded nuisance, necessary only for producing heirs.

The Christian religion lent a new dimension to misogynous persecution. From St Paul onwards women were accused of being the temptresses of men. Woman, after all, was not created in God's image, but was a mere bent rib from Adam's breast. Eve was shown to be fickle and weak-minded, and these qualities were taken to be true of women in general. The Bible discriminates against the weaker sex, and the extraordinary language of the *Malleus Maleficarum* (above) testifies to the official Church view of womankind in fifteenth- and sixteenth century Europe. Women not only attracted the devil; they bore his mark on their bodies. The dissected woman's belly revealed two sweeping Fallopian tubes – surely the horns of the devil.[2] Woman, in short, was the source of all man's evil – soiling his 'reason' with her 'desire'.

The problem for the Church was how to reconcile the perceived abomination of most women with the divine perfection of the Virgin Mary.[3] The dilemma was solved by cutting out the middle ground. Women were either fallen creatures, with treacherous minds and lecherous bodies – a recruiting ground for the devil, or they were saintly, obedient to the commands of men, and exalted for their spiritual and bodily purity. Women, in other words, knew no moderation: they were either sacred beyond belief, or whores from the pits of hell.

English literature has always reflected this dichotomy. Chaucer's Criseyde is fickle; Shakespeare's Hamlet sees Gertrude as weak and disgusting; Milton's temptresses are iniquitous; and Restoration Comedy depicts flirtatious behaviour by older women with contempt. By the eighteenth century, novelists such as Richardson and Fielding became custodians of public morality. Female purity was celebrated by their heroines resisting seduction. In Fielding's *Tom Jones*, the hero has his fling with loose women, but finally marries a 'pure' one. Pope and Swift look upon female sexuality almost with disdain, and Richardson conveys paranoia at its very existence. His Clarissa, bereft of her virginity through rape, and as yet unmarried, has no recourse but to take her own life.

With the coming of the nineteenth century, sexual liaisons produced such embarrassment that it became almost impossible to express them openly in fiction. The division between the idealized purity of 'good' women and the defiled untouchables was never so marked. Throughout Victorian literature flirtatious women rarely earn sympathy, while overt sexuality barely breaks the surface. *Jane Eyre* is one of the few Victorian novels to portray a rampantly sexual woman (and even here the suggestion is made obliquely). Charlotte Brontë clearly loathes the romps of Bertha Rochester, whose sexual appetite all but deprives her of her humanity. Naturally, Bertha's promiscuity can have just one explanation: she is deranged. Only the mad and the sick can behave as she does. Brontë's description of this lewd woman is enlightening:

> I never saw a face like it! It was a discoloured face – it was a savage face. I wish I could forget the roll of the red eyes and the fearful blackened inflation of the lineaments! ... The lips were swelled and dark; the brow furrowed; the black eyebrows widely raised over bloodshot eyes. Shall I tell you of what it reminded me? ... of that foul German spectre – the Vampyre.[4]

This passage makes clear that Brontë and her readers understood the association between female lust and demonic blood-sucking. The implication could hardly be more explicit: sexually active women were associated in the Victorian mind with mental derangement and devilry.

Typical Victorian heroines are the opposite of Bertha Rochester. They are angelic souls existing only to be loved, and rescued from malicious adversaries, by good, brave men. This holds true for *Dracula*. As we shall see, Stoker believed women to be inferior to men. Seward, for example, says this about Van Helsing:

> He laughed till he cried and I had to draw down the blinds lest any-one should see us and misjudge; and then he cried till he laughed again; and laughed and cried together, just as a woman does. I tried to be stern with him, as one is to a woman under the circumstances; but it had no effect. Men and women are so different in manifestations of nervous strength or weakness! (D13:209-10).

Upon first meeting Harker's wife, Van Helsing says: 'Ah, then you have a good memory for facts, for details? It is not always so with young ladies' (D14:219). He is obviously used to scatterbrained females, but he is relieved to find 'that there are good women still left to make life happy' (D14:222). One of the book's minor characters is given the words: 'you can't trust wolves no more nor women' (D11:167).

Lucy Westenra

Dracula, in fact, illustrates both contempt for women, and adulation of them. In the novel we meet two young ladies, both targets of the Count, and both acting as windows on the tensions aroused by male-female relations in the 1890s. Lucy Westenra is nineteen and, despite being cast as a joyous *ingénue* – a worthy prize for any worthy man – she comes over to the modern reader as devoid of admirable qualities. She is a pampered, upper-middle-class child with the silver spoon still showing. One critic describes her as 'silly, transparent, gushy, giggly, beautiful and good';[5] another as 'a fragile, porcelain, simple-minded creature'.[6] All Lucy seems concerned about is her own pleasure. She is a kept woman whose idle life involves no more than trivial recreations: picture galleries, walking and riding in parks; rowing, tennis and fishing (D5:71; 9:131). She is overburdened even by writing regularly to her best friend. The only aspect of her life to arouse curiosity is infuriatingly left unexplained. Stoker tantalizingly lets slip that, like her late father before her, Lucy was in childhood an habitual sleep-walker (D6:91; 9:137), a subject to which we shall return. Dracula sensibly takes advantage to make her acquaintance during their nocturnal jaunts.[7] So inclined, she makes an ideal 'Eve' for the visiting serpent, for as her friend says of her: She is of too super-sensitive a nature to go through the world without trouble' (D7:110).

If her sleep-walking is the key to her relationship with Dracula, it is her good looks that spark the emotional entanglements which bind the story together. Three long-standing friends – Seward, Holmwood and Morris – fall hopelessly in love with her. This, in itself, says much about courtship patterns a century ago, when marriage involved economics, class, and arrangement. Many a modern man will see Lucy – despite her beauty and financial resources – as less than a desirable companion for the rest of his days, and will feel little sympathy for Seward and Morris, whose proposals are turned down. Holmwood is the (un)lucky one. He himself is so unremarkable that they make a good match.

Throughout the book, Lucy shows such a dearth of character that the *Malleus Maleficarum* might have targeted her for special opprobrium. She is, as it declared of her sex in general, totally gullible. She is duped by Quincey Morris's tall stories into believing that he 'is really well educated'. She confides: 'We women are such cowards that we think a man will save us from fears, and we marry him' (D5:74). Lucy is not the most selfless of girls. She is forever reminding Mina of how exciting her love-life is, oblivious to the anxiety of her friend, without news from Jonathan in Transylvania. Nor has Lucy the slightest intention of remaining faithful to her beloved. She might say she loves Arthur: but she hardly hinders the amorous Count. She *can* have her cake and eat it.

Here, not for the first time, the author's intentions and the modern reader's perceptions diverge. Stoker intends his stricken characters to be the embodiment of Victorian virtue, unaware that their plastic, antiseptic goodness repels more than it attracts. Lucy somehow has men fawning all over her and she revels in it. She almost admits to being a 'horrid flirt', and acknowledges feelings of 'exultation' at collecting proposals (D5:75). Perhaps she is exercising a form of power, an insatiable appetite for counting suitors. Victorian women were not above collecting marriage proposals and flaunting them as a sign of their desirability, as Lucy acknowledges (D5:73). Some male readers may identity her, euphemistically, as a 'phallic' teaser.

To be fair, Lucy does have a rebellious streak. After all, she chooses her husband for herself, without discussing the matter beforehand with her mother. She also sighs with frustration that she cannot marry all three suitors. Deep in her unconscious she maybe resents her dull conformity, and yearns to rebel and allow her as-yet-poorly-developed sensuality free rein.[8] A girl with no destiny, she finds one only through Dracula's kiss. She would have passed through life leaving no shadow, until a chance encounter turns that metaphor into reality.

Attention is often turned to that most unusual of surnames – 'Westenra'. Possibly it is an amalgam of 'the West' (being under attack from the East) and 'Ra' (the pagan sun-god). Lucy, in other words, symbolizes the Light of the West. Other critics have fastened on her Christian name, perhaps a derivative of Lucifer: she does indeed become a servant of the devil.[9]

Curiously, Stoker resists detailed physical description where his heroines are concerned, confining his descriptive efforts to the central antagonists, Dracula and Van Helsing. All we are told is that Lucy is pale and thin long before Dracula gets near her, and Quincey Morris speaks of her 'little shoes', so she may have been of slight build. She has rippling black hair to offset her fragile countenance.[10]

Mina Harker

Lucy's friend Mina is made of sterner stuff. Christened Wilhelmina Murray, she marries Jonathan Harker, whom she has known since childhood, during the course of the novel. Mina is referred to as a 'sweet-faced, dainty looking girl' (D17:26).[11] She is merely attractive, in contrast to Lucy's stunning looks. Mina wears her hair long and loose, so that she can pull it round to hide her face if upset (D22:353). On one occasion she lends Lucy her shoes, so presumably the two girls were similarly petite. Mina is no weakling, however, chasing around Whitby in the middle of the night, up and down its cliffs, in a way that would tax a trained athlete. She is deeply religious, offering a prayer of thankfulness after surviving the slightest adventure.

The two girls have been intimate friends since childhood, though considering their differences this is somewhat surprising. Mina is probably an orphan, since she knew neither her father nor her mother. Unlike Lucy, Mina is a working girl, a productive member of society and of lower social class than her friend. Their respective pairings underline their class status: Lucy becomes betrothed to the aristocracy (twice – to a future Lord, then a Count), while Mina takes on a humble solicitor's clerk. When the reader meets her, Mina is an assistant school-mistress teaching 'etiquette and decorum' in Exeter. She must be a year or so older than Lucy, and may even have taught her, for she was once Lucy's 'friend and guide when [she] came from the schoolroom to prepare for the world of life' (D9:130).

The girls' personalities are strikingly different. Mina is as resourceful as Lucy is resourceless. What Mina sees in Lucy to warrant her patient affection is almost as mysterious as the infatuation of the male trio with her vacuous friend. Mina shows much forbearance, probably acting out of a sense of duty towards her ill-fated companion. Given Mina's caring, maternal nature, it would be in keeping for her to overlook Lucy's faults and see only her good qualities. Mina is the nearest thing to a saint that Stoker can conceive of. She has shown no hint of malice in her life. She cuddles and comforts all the men in their distress over Lucy, and always puts the welfare of others before herself. Even in her darkest agonies she says this of her tormentor, Dracula:

> Jonathan dear, and you all my true, true friends, I want you to bear something in mind through all this dreadful time. I know that you must fight - that you must destroy ... but it is not a work of hate. That poor soul who has wrought all this misery is the saddest case of all. Just think what will be his joy when he, too, is destroyed in his worser part that his better part may have spiritual immortality. You must be pitiful to him, too, though it may not hold your hands from his destruction (D23:367).

Here she comes close to the Virgin Mary, interceding with God on behalf of sinners. She insists that even Dracula can be redeemed.[12] All the men think of Mina as an angel on earth though it is Van Helsing who speaks for them all: 'She is one of God's women, fashioned by his own hand to show us men and other women that there is a heaven where we can enter, and that its light can be here on earth ... so true, so sweet, so noble, so little an egoist' (D14:226). Stoker was not untypical in handling his heroines in this fashion. When Charles Dickens describes Rose Maylie in *Oliver Twist* he could easily have had the future Mina as his model: '... cast in so light and exquisite a mould: so mild and gentle; so pure and beautiful; that earth seemed not her element, not its rough creatures her fit companions'.[13]

Stoker demands that Mina be exposed to evil, in order that she may consciously choose 'good'.[14] Her faith is to be tested to the utmost. For such a 'sweet, sweet, good, good woman' (D23:367), chivalrous men will move heaven and earth to lighten her suffering. Female readers may be irritated by Van Helsing's (Stoker's) repeated insistence that women cannot endure pain and hardship: 'We are men and able to bear, but you [Mina] must be our star and our hope, and we shall act the more free that you are not in danger such as we are' (D18:289). When, in the postscript to the novel, he looks back on the nightmare and surveys Mina's son, he declares: 'Already he [the child] knows her sweetness and loving care; later on he will understand how some men so loved her that they did dare much for her sake'. Not many books – even in the Victorian age – could exalt women solely for being passive inspirations to men.[15]

But Mina is much more than the embodiment of purity and virtue: unlike Lucy, she has a mind. Mina is, in fact, the real star of the show: the moral honours go to her, not to Van Helsing. For all the Dutchman's brain-power, the pursuers are outfoxed by the Count until Mina's intuition and practical thinking turn the tables against him. Van Helsing reveals more about his (and Stoker's) prejudices than about Mina's talents when he concedes: 'Ah that wonderful Madam Mina! She has a man's brain – and a woman's heart' (D18:281; 25:404). She must in any case be almost unique: after all, she survives the bite of a vampire.

It is this unexpected attribute of Mina being able to think for herself that highlights Stoker's ambivalence towards women. Much recent interest in *Dracula* has been sparked by feminist concern for the ways in which women have historically been portrayed in the English novel. In *Dracula*, Stoker's treatment of women encourages one feminist critic to identify him as a fellow feminist.[16] Others, however, perceive deep hostility towards female sexuality,[17] together with a desire to control women.[18] Dracula is the only male vampire in the novel, whereas the assortment of she-vampires are collectively portrayed as devilish, inhuman, wildly erotic, and motivated solely by a craving for blood/sex. (The term 'vamp' is used today of a highly sexed woman.) The first half of the novel, climaxing with the vampire death of Lucy, has been held up to demonstrate Stoker's pathological aversion to women.[19]

It is Stoker's complex treatment of Mina that invites a reassessment. She is the mouthpiece for an exploration of a social phenomenon of the 1890s – the emergence of the so-called 'New Woman'. The 1890s was a decade much reviled by guardians of good taste and public morality. The late nineteenth century was felt to be 'wandering between two worlds, one dead, the other powerless to be born'.[20]

The New Women were the Victorian equivalent of today's feminists. They took issue with a range of social restrictions imposed by male dominance and prejudice. They objected to being encased in whalebone. Some dared to pedal around on bicycles, which required disposing of petticoats and chaperons.[21] Certain women were striving for financial independence and careers of their own. This meant deferring or abandoning the traditional Victorian roles of marriage and child-rearing. Motherhood had been held to constitute a woman's natural function and destiny. Now, these New Women were turning their backs on their 'rightful' place – in the home – and opting for novel vocations, such as medicine or business.[22]

All this was radical enough, but what really riled conservative opinion was the New Woman's challenge to accepted sexual values. She was accused of destabilizing society and accelerating moral decay. The New Women were hardly homogeneous – they embraced varying shades of opinion – but what united them in the public image was their willingness to speak more frankly than before on sexual matters from a female perspective.[23] Some openly contemplated sexual liaisons prior to marriage. Nor were they coy about discussing contraception, or that greatest of Victorian taboos, venereal disease. Novelists of the time, both male and female, fuelled the movement. They highlighted the perceived drudgery of the average woman: sexually repressed and subservient in marriage.[24]

Mina's background and circumstances make her a potential New Woman. She discusses New Women in the novel, but is far from convinced about their values. She feels them to be more intolerant than men. Moreover:

> If Mr Holmwood fell in love with [Lucy] seeing her only in the
> drawing room, I wonder what he would say if he saw her now.
> Some of the 'New Woman' writers will some day start an idea
> that men and women should be allowed to see each other asleep
> before proposing or accepting. But I suppose the New Woman
> won't condescend in future to accept; she will do the proposing
> herself. And a nice job she will make of it too! There's some
> consolation in that (D8:111).

Mina's sarcastic tone clearly distances her from the New Woman.
And yet she is educated and has embarked on her own teaching
career. Such opportunities would not have been widely available
to women much older than Mina, so she might be expected to
show some sympathy with the New Woman ethos.

Nonetheless, she is no subservient, stay-at-home housewife.
True, she sacrifices her career upon marriage (this is not stated,
but assumed unquestioningly), but she then makes good use of her
talents to assist her husband in his legal work. In today's terms,
she would make an outstanding secretary. She learns railway
timetables off by heart (as Stoker would have done for Irving);
and becomes skilled in the stenographic arts – typing and
shorthand. These aptitudes were novel for women in the 1890s,
and her desire to assist her husband other than through domestic
chores was almost revolutionary.[25]

Only intellectually is Stoker prepared to grant Mina equality
with men, 'etiquette and decorum' scarcely being the most radical
subject on the curriculum. One critic contends that Stoker reveals
Mina at her most liberated only when imitating masculine pseudo-
rationality and gentlemanly stoicism.[26]

Mina, then, is constructed as a dual-faceted creature. She
adopts certain modern trappings associated with the New Woman,
while remaining at heart a devoutly traditional female. Mina
knows woman's proper place: she refers to the taste of the
original apple that remains in all women's mouths (D14:220). On
matters of sexual expression, Stoker keeps the wraps firmly
around her. Her repression is typically Victorian: she even feels it
improper for Jonathan to take her arm in public (D13:207).
Whereas Lucy offers no obstacle to Dracula's advances, Mina
resists with all the mental powers she can muster. The girls' after-

reactions to the Count's 'visits' could not be more contrasting. Lucy recalls only the bitter-sweet sensation of his presence, yet looks and feels refreshed for the experience (D8:115). But Mina, with her greater intelligence, strength of character – and repression – refuses to countenance what she has done. She is filled with revulsion, and never becomes wantonly sexual in the manner of Lucy. Mina's anguish, it is important to note, is not the anguish of rape, for she (like Jonathan and Lucy before her) knows the all-powerful temptation of the vampire. Mina confesses: 'I did not want to hinder him' (D21:342). As her spirit gradually succumbs during the following weeks, she adopts a more passive role, falling back on remarks straight from Stoker's heart: 'Oh, thank God for good brave men!' (D23:370).

If the time should come, she instructs that the others destroy her according to the prescribed ritual, rather than allow her to join the undead. Even here, her courage has been observed to possess a sexist element. She assumes it is the duty of men to kill those they love to prevent their falling into the hands of an enemy. Other women – Cleopatra, for instance – were quite capable of taking their own lives when faced with a fate worse than death.[27]

Lucy, the privileged but sexually liberated (fallen) woman, is portrayed as constantly inferior to Mina. In the context of the New Woman, Lucy's wish to sleep with/marry three men (four, if we include the Count) indicts her of the most venal of the New Woman's sins – promiscuity. To Stoker, and to common decency as he saw it, she must pay the ultimate price for her depravity. Van Helsing turns her body into a moral battlefield. She has stepped out of line. For her overt sexuality, for stepping beyond the bounds of chastity and showing desire, she must be persecuted, even destroyed.

This is not to say that Stoker conceives of Lucy as a villainess. Rather, she is a woman/angel violated by the devil. Although the memory of the 'real' Lucy never fades, her vampiric eroticism offends Victorian males' sensibilities. Men effectively dominated women, but in the vampire world the unthinkable happens: women turn the tables and try to enslave the men who once enslaved them.[28] Perhaps that is why Seward yearns to decapitate Lucy.

But Stoker's moral indignation goes deeper than this. Concerns over motherhood lie at the heart of his strictures against the so-called freedoms of the New Woman. Domesticity was assumed to constitute the Victorian woman's sole desire. Influential medical opinion of the period could state: 'Love of home, children and domestic duties, are the only passions [women] feel'.[29] Stoker suggests that the traditional family structure can survive the threat of New Women/vampirism. He shows this by contrasting Lucy's and Mina's acquiescence to the prospect of motherhood.

The plot of *Dracula* hinges on the fate of these two women. Some critics have proposed that essentially it is the same story told twice:[30] first through Lucy, then Mina. By way of preamble, Stoker introduces the Count's three vampire consorts in Castle Dracula. Through them Stoker proposes that women who are flauntingly sensuous are on a par with child molesters. Deprived of Harker's blood, these she-vampires are appeased by the gift of a small child. Blessed children, in other words, are not to be cherished: they are to be eaten! Lucy, likewise, commences her career as a London vampire by snatching children, preparatory to graduating to adult males. This callousness towards infants, this reversal of female function, is meant to appal the reader. Not only are sex roles reversed in New Women/vampires, but mothering roles too. Conceivably, some deep-seated trauma is being hinted at: a mute protest at the intolerable strains large families put on the Victorian mother.[31]

When Lucy is finally destroyed, the novel could logically have ended.[32] (Upon her 'first' death Seward declares 'Finis' [D13:212]). But now Dracula turns his foul attentions to a different calibre of woman. Unlike Lucy, Mina does not reject men: on the contrary she accepts and comforts them all. Soothing Arthur in his grief she says: 'We women have something of the mother in us that makes us rise above small matters when the mother-spirit is invoked; I felt this big, sorrowing man's head resting on me, as though it were that of a baby that some day may lie on my bosom, and I stroked his hair as though he were my own child' (D17:275).

There is nothing sexually threatening about Mina. Even the child which eventually does grace her life is named after those who fought Dracula on her behalf, as if a multi-platonic love affair has conceived it. This offers another link with the Virgin Mary, for Mina's son can be seen as the product of immaculate conception: she has not defiled her body through succumbing to the sexual act. Whatever the circumstances, she crowns the novel by bearing a son on its concluding page. The little band return to England to live happily ever after, closing their minds to the brief threatening interlude when women tried to rise above their station. The maternal has beaten off the challenge of the carnal.

Mina's purity stems from her knowing her place *vis à vis* men, and her absence of threatening 'appetites'. She blends the best in what is traditional and what is modern. Mina probably symbolizes perfection to Stoker's conscious mind; Lucy to his unconscious. Stoker wrestles with the conflict between what is right and proper, and what is illicit and irresistible. It will be recalled that Stoker himself was surrounded by strong, challenging women.[33] Beginning with *Dracula,* his fiction turns increasingly to portraying heroines who are anything but meek and submissive – though they happily relinquish their independence for the pleasures of marriage. His villainesses, by contrast, radiate eroticism. In general, greater sexual expression was permissible in the literature of the 1890s onwards, but not for Bram Stoker. Nowhere in his fiction do his chaste heroines experience sexual pleasure.

Let us conclude this chapter by examining Lucy and Mina in relation to hypnosis. Several of Stoker's named sources contain disquisitions on hypnosis and mesmerism,[34] and so entrenched are these phenomena in *Dracula* they almost provide a plot within a plot. Two other works of Stoker reveal his interest in the subject. In *Famous Impostors*, he writes an unflattering chapter on the wiles of Anton Mesmer; while in his fictional *Lair of the White Worm*, Stoker constructs a scene around the discovery of Mesmer's magic chest. In *Dracula*, however, Stoker speaks always of 'hypnosis', never 'mesmerism', as to distance himself from the latter's connotations of black magic and quackery.

It is part of Dracula's armoury that he can induce submission in his victims by applying his hypnotic, animalistic stare. Harker,

Lucy, Mina, and Renfield are all victims of those power-sapping, blazing eyes. Renfield, for example, states: 'his eyes burned into me, and my strength became like water'. Even when vampires dematerialize into phosphorescent specks, they 'hypnotize' Harker, and put a 'spell' on Lucy.

But Stoker's use of hypnosis in *Dracula* goes much deeper than this. Lucy, we have remarked, as a young girl was prone to sleep-walking, a kind of trance. Although Van Helsing demands she meets the fate of all vampires, Stoker wishes to exonerate her from full complicity. Her somnambulism provides him with the means to do so. Somnabulism provided grounds for acquittal in Victorian courts: it can therefore aquit Lucy of immorality. She meets Dracula in trance. She also dies in trance. Let Van Helsing explain, as he examines her vampire body:

> Here, there is one thing which is different from all recorded; here is some dual life that is not as the common. She was bitten by the vampire when she was in trance, sleep-walking ... and in trance could he best come to take more blood. In trance she dies, and in trance she is Un-Dead, too. So it is that she differ from all other. Usually when the Un-Dead sleep at home ... their face show what they are, but this so sweet that was when she not Un-Dead [sic] she go back to the nothings of the common dead. There is no malign there ... (D15:241).

The reason Lucy is only partly innocent is that somnambulism was widely assumed to enable activities secretly desired at other times, and was a means of fulfilling the fantasies of dreams. It was, in any case, rare for the disorder to persist after twenty years of age, from which birthday Lucy is just weeks away.

Likewise, trance states produce analgesic effects. Dental and surgical operations may even be undertaken painlessly in certain cases. Lucy, we must remember, has had the sensitive skin of her throat chewed by four canine teeth, yet she insists 'she did not even feel it' (D8:115). Unless one imagines that Dracula's teeth are like mosquitoes, anaesthetising as they insert, we must assume it is her state of trance that shields her from undue discomfort.

Dracula feasts upon Lucy times without number between 10 August and 17 September. He does not make fresh holes with each visit but reopens the old ones. Lucy has her own orifices which are available to him and to none other. Even before she breathes her last, her neck wounds disappear, sealing her fate as a vampire. From now on she will be Dracula's platonic companion, no longer his concubine/nourishment.

Stoker's ambivalence towards Lucy is further demonstrated when we consider late Victorian attitudes to those who sleepwalked. Their behaviour harboured powerful associations with epilepsy, nightmares, and the incubus: 'Somnambulism generally forbodes, when it does not betray, insanity ... Dreams assuming the shape of incubus or nightmare, are very frequent in the earliest stages of insanity, and they constantly agitate the sleep of epileptics.'[35] Clearly, Stoker was conscious of both the sexual and the insane potential of Lucy's malaise.

When it comes to Mina, she is 'hypnotized' first by the Count, then by Van Helsing as a means of locating him. The Count's methods are not spelled out: his presence and eye contact are enough in themselves to weaken her will. For the professor, however, Stoker describes more conventional hypnotic procedures. Van Helsing demonstrates his knowledge of the subject by mourning the death of the celebrated neurologist and hypnotist Charcot. He categorizes hypnosis alongside other supposedly verifiable phenomena, such as corporeal transference, astral bodies, and thought reading (D14:230).

Given his knowledge of such matters, it is puzzling that the initiative to hypnotize poor Mina comes not from him but from her. Even more puzzling is the way he sets about the induction process. He makes 'passes in front of her, from over the top of her head downward, with each hand in turn' (D23:371). Hey presto, Mina is hypnotized.

This induction procedure comes as a shock. It relates more to the largely discredited methods of Mesmer and the animal magnetists than to hypnosis as usually practised in the 1890s. Hypnosis attunes to the power of suggestion, and practitioners in Van Helsing's day were less likely to imitate mesmeric passes than to invite their subjects to fix their gaze while listening to droning commands for progressive relaxation. The prerequisites for hypnosis, in the 1840s as today, are stillness and privacy. Van

Helsing commands none of this. He arrives in his dressing gown at Mina's bedroom with the sun not yet risen, with Godalming, Seward and Morris peering in at the door, and her husband making mental notes for his diary.

Stoker could hardly have been ignorant of the hypnotic procedure. Why should he go to such lengths to research the medical background of *Dracula*, only to ride roughshod over hypnotic induction? Possibly he is insisting that medicine must take account of the unorthodox. Tellingly, Harker notes as the induction proceeds: 'my own heart beat like a trip-hammer, for I felt that a crisis was at hand.' 'Crisis' is the outmoded language of mesmerism. Its cathartic convulsions provided the hoped-for cure.

Mina opens her eyes without being instructed to. She displays no convulsions, but 'has a faraway look in her eyes'. She 'does not seem the same woman'. But, of course, she is not the same woman. She is a vampire woman in telepathic communictaion with Dracula.

Notwithstanding Van Helsing's cavalier attitude towards hypnotic induction, the foregoing passages raise important questions about the attitudes of *Dracula*'s author towards his heroines. Charcot was indeed an eminent authority on hypnosis, except that he believed that only morbid personalities, of hysterical temperament, were susceptible to it. Lucy's capacity for somnambulism, and Mina's succumbing to Van Helsing's hand-passes, appears to label them both in Stoker's eyes as hysterics. It was common wisdom in Victorian Britain that women of hysterical disposition were susceptible to imagining themselves in the presence of the supernatural. From this perspective, it was not only Lucy who aroused Stoker's misogyny, but Mina too. It is Mina's valiant insight while under hypnosis that restores her worth, enabling her to betray her tormentor and instigate his destruction.

Now that the cast of *Dracula* and their functions have been introduced, we are ready to tackle the underlying themes of the novel. In view of the foregoing discussion of Lucy and Mina, it is appropriate to begin by examining *Dracula*'s sexual symbolism.

1   Jeffrey B Russell, *A History of Witchcraft: Sorcerers, Heretics, and Pagans*, pp.113-15.

2   Penelope Shuttle and Peter Redgrove, *The Wise Wound: Menstruation and Everywoman*, p.225.

3   Though venerated by the early Church, from the twelfth century onwards the cult of the Blessed Virgin proliferated all over Europe.

4   Charlotte Brontë, *Jane Eyre*, Chapter 25.

5   Leonard Wolf, *A Dream of Dracula*, pp.208-9.

6   Stephanie Demetrakopoulos, 'Feminism, Sex Role Changes, and Other Subliminal Fantasies in Bram Stoker's *Dracula*', p.104.

7   In Stoker's notes Dracula reactivates Lucy's sleep-walking by means of a magic brooch which he has deposited, and she discovers, on Whitby beach.

8   Carol A Senf, '"Dracula": Stoker's response to the New Woman', p.42.

9   Stoker was fond of using the same initials in his fictional works. Lucy Westenra re-emerges as Lilla Watford, and Mina as Mimi, in *The Lair of the White Worm*. Stoker seemed particularly fond of the initial 'M'; other heroines of his being Margaret and Marjorie.

10   At least she has dark hair as a vampire (D16:252). Beforehand, things may have been different. The first edition of novel and some modern reprints refer to her 'sunny' ripples. The second, and subsequent, editions were published under copyright: they speak instead of 'shiny' ripples (D12:194). See Roger Johnson, 'The Bloofer Ladies' in The Dracula Journals, Vol 1, No 4, 133.

11   Dracula etymologists have suggested that the name 'Wilhelmina' implies a wish for protection, and 'Murray' derives from the name for a plague, dead flesh, or the infliction of death (Thomas P Walsh, '*Dracula*: Logos and Myth', p.234). Matthew Lewis, author of *The Monk*, had also known of a vampire tale called 'Mina' (Christopher Frayling (introduction), *The Vampire: Lord Ruthven to Count Dracula*, p.70).

12   Judith Weissman, 'Women and Vampires: *Dracula* as a Victorian Novel', p.399.

13   See Carrol L Fry, 'Fictional Conventions and Sexuality in Dracula', p.21.

14   Senf, op. cit., p.48.

15   Weissman, p.398.

16   Demetrakopoulos, p.104.

17 Phyllis A Roth, 'Suddenly Sexual Women in Bram Stoker's *Dracula*', p.113.

18 Weissman, p.405.

19 See Senf, op. cit., p.34.

20 In Brian Murphy, 'The Nightmare of the Dark: the Gothic Legacy of Count Dracula', pp.10-11.

21 Gail Cunningham, *The New Women and the Victorian Novel* p.2.

22 Senf, op. cit., p.46.

23 A R Cunningham, *The New Women in Fiction of the 1890s*, p.178.

24 See, for example, the attitudes of Herminia Barton in Grant Allen's *The Women Who Did*.

25 Demetrakopoulos, p.110.

26 ibid., p.104.

27 Weissman, p.399. This point is stronger in principle than in practice. Mina would not know when the time had come: she would have to leave that decision to others.

28 See Senf, op. cit., p.39.

29 Peter T Cominos, in Demetrakopoulos, p.107.

30 See Phyllis A Roth, *Bram Stoker*, p.102. Stoker's notes lend support to this connection, for Lucy and Mina were originally scheduled to perform acts eventually undertaken by the other.

31 By rejecting prescribed feminine roles, New Women/vampires become social outlaws – even 'sexual sociopaths', Demetrakopoulos, p.107.

32 Roth suggests that such an ending would disconcert the reader because the destruction of Lucy hints at matricide, and this anxiety must be assuaged (Roth, 'Suddenly Sexual Women', p.117).

33 Although Stoker dedicated *Dracula* to a man (Hall Caine), almost all his other novels are dedicated to women.

34 See Clive Leatherdale, *The Origins of Dracula*, chapters 13 and 14.

35 Journal of Mental Science, January 1879, p.574.

9

'KISS ME WITH THOSE RED LIPS'

I was afraid to raise my eyelids, but looked out and saw perfectly
under the lashes. The fair girl went on her knees and bent over me,
fairly gloating. There was a deliberate voluptuousness which was
both thrilling and repulsive, and as she arched her neck she actually
licked her lips like an animal, till I could see in the moonlight the
moisture shining on the scarlet lips and on the red tongue as it lapped
the white sharp teeth. Lower and lower went her head as the lips
went below the range of my mouth and chin and seemed about the
fasten on my throat. Then she paused, and I could hear the churning
sound of her tongue as it licked her teeth and lips, and could feel the
hot breath on my neck. Then the skin of my throat began to tingle as
one's flesh does when the hand that is to tickle it approaches nearer –
nearer. I could feel the soft, shivering touch of the lips on the
supersensitive skin of my throat, and the hard dents of two sharp
teeth, just touching and pausing there. I closed my eyes in a
languorous ecstasy and waited – waited with beating heart.

Jonathan Harker's Journal,
Dracula 3:52.

That *Dracula* exudes a sexual quality will by now be evident,
though the suggestion sounds, at first, preposterous. On the face
of it, what could be less erotic than a mouldy corpse; less enticing
as a nest of love than a cobweb-infested coffin or a crumbling
castle? Further, given Victorian paranoia at the idea of 'sex', how
could an erotic book have been published, let alone sold by the
thousands? For erotic Dracula certainly is. 'Quasi-pornography'
one critic labels it.[1] Another describes it as a 'kind of incestuous,
necrophilious, oral-anal-sadistic all-in-wrestling match'.[2] He is
being reticent. A sexual search of the novel unearths the
following: seduction, rape, necrophilia, paedophilia, incest,

adultery, oral sex, group sex, menstruation, venereal disease, voyeurism – enough to titillate any sexual appetite. It is necessary only to substitute intercourse for kisses, and semen for blood to be left with a novel as sexually explicit as any of the time.

Count Dracula was hardly the first vampire to exude sexuality. The ancient lamias of folklore did so; as did several literary vampires of the nineteenth century. But the question remains: despite the pretence at vampire subterfuge, how could explicit sexual acts come to be portrayed at this period? No obscenity laws existed, though there was strict control over the contents of circulating libraries. The invisible jury of public opinion regulated what was publishable and what was not.[3]

Yet what could not be conveyed directly could be explored allegorically, and at this level *Dracula* is alive with sensuality. Because the dead cannot logically indulge in sex, Stoker could not be accused of prurience, and *Dracula* was not acknowledged for its eroticism among readers of the day. No contemporary reviewer questioned the novel's sexual content, though there had been a near-hysterical reaction a few years earlier when Ibsen's *Ghosts* alluded to sexual relationships and even venereal disease. Evidently, it was all a matter of camouflage, and evidently Stoker camouflaged his eroticism effectively. Nevertheless, *Dracula* can be seen as the great submerged force of Victorian libido breaking out to punish the repressive society which imprisoned it.[4]

The novel epitomizes Twitchell's summary of sexual vampirism: 'The myth is loaded with sexual excitement; yet there is no mention of sexuality. It is sex without genitalia, sex without confusion, sex without responsibility, sex without guilt, sex without love – better yet, sex without mention'.[5] The erotic preoccupation is obsessively oral, for vampires are sexually inoperative from the neck down.[6] Their 'kiss' is a euphemism for deeper intimacy, and throughout Stoker's notes he refers to vampire 'kisses', not 'bites'. Three lengthy episodes alert the reader to the erotic undercurrents of *Dracula*. The first arrives when the imprisoned Jonathan Harker strays upon the Count's three 'mistresses'. As befits vampires, their outward objective is to suck Harker's blood, but the entire sequence is overlaid with sexual imagery. The extract quoted at the opening of this chapter comes from this episode, but let us look at how Stoker introduces Harker's erotic encounter:

> I suppose I must have fallen asleep ... In the moonlight opposite me were three young women, ladies by their dress and manner ... Two were dark, and had high aquiline noses, like the Count's, and great dark piercing eyes, that seemed to be almost red when contrasted with the pale yellow moon. The other was fair, as fair as can be, with great, wavy masses of golden hair and eyes like pale sapphires. I seemed somehow to know her face, and to know it in connection with some dreamy fear, but I could not recollect at the moment how or where. All three had brilliant white teeth, that shone like pearls against the ruby of their voluptuous lips. There was something about them that made me uneasy, some longing and at the same time some deadly fear. I felt in my heart a wicked, burning desire that they would kiss me with those red lips. It is not good to note this down, lest some day it should meet Mina's eyes and cause her pain; but it is the truth. They whispered together, and then they all three laughed – such a silvery, musical laugh, but as hard as though the sound never could have come through the softness of human lips. It was like the intolerable, tingling sweetness of water-glasses when played on by a cunning hand. The fair girl shook her head coquettishly, and the other two urged her on. One said:-
> 'Go on! You are first, and we shall follow; yours is the right to begin. The other added:
> 'He is young and strong; there are kisses for us all.' I lay quiet, looking out under my eyelashes in an agony of delightful anticipation. The fair girl advanced and bent over me till I could feel the movement of her breath upon me. Sweet it was in one sense, honey-sweet, and sent the same tingling through the nerves as her voice, but with a bitter underlying the sweet, a bitter offensiveness, as one smells in blood (D3:50-52)

There is not much of the squalid, grunting vampire of Montague Summers here. In any other language, Harker is being seduced. If the she-vampires wanted only his blood they would simply have taken it, but they are obviously desirous of something else. Indeed, the passage reveals more than a thinly-veiled focus on seduction. This is a woman making advances to a man – unheard of according to the Victorian code, yet probably the ultimate male fantasy. It is the stuff of dreams, and sure enough

Harker does think he is dreaming. Note, too, the ambivalence of his response, the 'longing' coupled with a 'deadly fear'. This conflict is crucial to vampire sexuality: attraction versus repulsion. Coleridge wrote of it a century previously in an exquisite phrase: 'desire and loathing strangely mixed'.[7] Harker's head tells him to resist. He describes his desire as 'wicked', and thinks of how hurtful his moment of pleasure would be to Mina, should she discover. But as inevitably happens when faced with vampire temptation, his physical yearning is bound to triumph.

The exchange of sex roles extends even to Harker's manner: peering out from under the eyelashes is what one popularly expects from a coy female who does not wish to 'encourage' her lover. Moreover, there are *three* women vampires, all queueing up to get at him – a kind of demoniacally inversed 'gang-bang': 'There are kisses for us all'. Harker must be virile indeed. To the Victorian mind, Harker's anguish mirrors the suffocating repression that consumed his society. He is being offered, on a plate, instant sexual gratification, no strings attached – the utopia of the permissive society. His culture, however, has conditioned him to wait until marriage, and the matronly Mina is hardly the type of woman to relieve these frustrations.[8] Throughout the book it is the female vampires who are sexually alive and endowed with greater potency, reversing the idea that men possessed insatiable sexual appetites, while the female function was to passively appease it.[9]

It is here appropriate to introduce another of Stoker's long-standing riddles. Setting eyes on the blonde vampire, Harker later writes: 'I seemed to know her face, and to know it in connection with some dreamy fear, but I could not recollect at the moment how or where.' Harker never does recollect, so who was she? Some critics have suggested the arch-temptress Lucy, though Lucy was dark-haired, and in any case it is unclear from the novel whether Harker had ever met her. Alternatively he sees a fantasy view of Mina: not as she is, but how he subconsciously wishes her to become. Van Helsing, however, later destroys the blonde vampire and he recognizes in her no resemblance to Lucy or Mina (D27:440). Other critics have proposed that Harker is confronted by a mythological temptress, Medusa, or the original wife of Adam, Lilith – the first and archetypal lamia.[10]

Only with the unearthing of Stoker's typescript has the riddle been solved. The fair beauty is she whom Harker encountered in the tomb of Countess Dolingen of Gratz, in the episode 'Dracula's Guest': 'I saw, as my eyes were turned into the darkness of the tomb, a beautiful woman, with rounded cheeks and red lips, seemingly sleeping on a bier'.

Whatever the source of Harker's vision, all that has so far been described is a simple role-reversal of heterosexual sex. But when the Count intervenes to protect Harker from the ravages of his three companions, a host of new relationships emerges. Two of the women are said to resemble Dracula: this suggests they are biologically related in some way – probably his daughters. The third, whom Harker recognizes, has the right to head the queue and is presumably their mother. Expressed in human terms, the Count's fury is that of jealous husband and irate father; in vampire terms it is an expression of incest. His women taunt him: 'You yourself never loved; you never love! To this he rejoins: 'Yes I too can love; you yourselves can tell it from the past. Is it not so?' (D3:53).

With this exchange Stoker seems to make two points: first, that the vampire's sexual inhibitions extend even to that most rigid of taboos, incest; and second, by not having 'loved' his creatures, except in the distant past, the Count is not interested in 'kisses'. His 'love' is restricted to the warm-blooded living. With fellow vampires, he is impotent.

Only once does Harker hint at something beyond seduction, when he describes the vampire's breath as possessing 'a bitter offensiveness as one smells in blood'. Here, too, his language possesses hidden meaning. In some societies blood is an aphrodisiac. Nor is it unheard of for some people to derive sexual satisfaction from shedding blood.[11] This is most obvious in the love-bite, which in extreme cases can draw blood. More generally, the colour 'red' invites sexual connotations, illustrated by applying lipstick to the mouth and rouge to the face, not to mention the haunts of prostitutes – 'red light' districts.[12]

Dracula's women prepare the reader for Lucy's promiscuity. This is perceived as so devilish it must be resisted by all the powers available to Van Helsing *et al.* That is why the battle to

save Lucy from Dracula's clutches is so protracted and critical to
the novel's structure. In these sequences blood becomes a direct
analogy for semen. Their association in vampire mythology is not
arbitrary. The vampire craves blood for its life-giving properties,
yet semen, too, is a fluid without which procreation cannot occur.
The lamias and succubi of folklore depend on this ambiguity –
sucking the 'vital spirits' out of man. The convertibility of the two
fluids has even been calculated: forty ounces of blood are needed
to recompense the loss of one ounce of semen.[13] Cold-blooded
demons, moreover, possessed cold semen. In the annals of folklore
it was possible to detect seduction by the devil (incubus), for his
sperm was as cold as ice. The wider psychological relationship
between blood and semen has been summarized by Ernest Jones:

> The explanation of these fantasies is surely not hard. A nightly visit
> from a beautiful or frightful being, who first exhausts the sleeper with
> passionate embraces, and then withdraws from him a vital fluid; all
> this can point only to a natural and common process, namely to
> nocturnal emissions accompanied with dreams of a more or less
> erotic nature. In the unconscious mind blood is commonly an
> equivalent for semen.[14]

Harker's fantasy alludes to the surreal nature of a 'wet dream';
when a male awakes to find sperm emitted in his sleep, it is easy
to imagine that 'someone' took it out.

With this in mind, we may now turn our attention to the battle
for Lucy's life. Her admirers are compelled to put in what
Dracula has taken out – blood. She receives no fewer than four
blood transfusions: from her fiancé, the two rejected suitors, and
Van Helsing – who despite his age retains a keen eye for female
beauty, and can rise to the demands made upon him. Giving blood
can instil pride and wonder on the part of donors, who may feel
they have escaped the confines of their body and become part of
another's.[15]

Pursuing the theme of Lucy's sexual liberation, her sequence of
blood transfusions symbolizes successive acts of sexual
intercourse, as she attains the freedom she dreamt of in life ('Why
can't a girl marry three men?'). On her death-bed her wish comes
true, for she takes a series of 'lovers'. Holmwood, her fiancé,

heads the queue to donate his blood/semen. In his later grief he interprets his blood mingling with hers as a symbol of marriage in God's eyes. Their relationship, in other words, has been consummated. Holmwood knows nothing of her later transfusions, and his friends agree to silence regarding their contributions to save him pain and jealousy (D10:156; 13:209).

But Van Helsing (and Stoker) knows perfectly well what has really happened. Using Holmwood's analogy of marriage, Lucy has become a polyandrist and he, Van Helsing – still married in the eyes of the Catholic Church, though his wife is deranged – an adulterer and bigamist. Worse, he has described Lucy as like a daughter to him. There may be no vampire component to this episode, but blood exchanges are still portrayed as though charged with sexual potency. Nor would Stoker claim anything novel in this metaphor. John Donne's seventeenth century poem 'The Flea' was dependent on the understanding that the mingling of two people's blood *was* sexual intercourse.[16]

Lucy, we know, was beautiful when alive. Though Stoker hides the fact, she must also have had exuded eroticism, judging from her effect on the men she came across. In her living death, however, Lucy's beauty changes from that of a virgin to that of a whore. Her 'sweetness was turned to adamantine, heartless cruelty, and the purity to voluptuous wantonness': indeed the apparition is 'like a devilish mockery of Lucy's sweet purity' (D16:252-53). Lucy's attacks on small children smack of paedophilia. Even her apparel reflects her new-found liberation: gone is the restricting corset presumably worn in life; instead she revels in a free flowing, unhampering shroud.[17]

Lucy's nocturnal existence climaxes in another of Stoker's passages saturated with sexual meaning. On that day, had she lived, she would have married Holmwood (now elevated to Lord Godalming). Now she taunts him: 'Come, my husband, come!' and the following night Godalming is given the task of freeing his wife's soul by driving a (phallic) stake through her:

> He struck with all his might.
> The thing in the coffin writhed; and a hideous, blood-curdling screech came from the opened red lips. The body shook and quivered

and twisted in wild contortions; the sharp white teeth champed together till the lips were cut and the mouth was smeared with a crimson foam. But Arthur never faltered. He looked like a figure of Thor as his untrembling arm rose and fell, driving deeper and deeper the mercy-bearing stake, whilst the blood from the pierced heart welled and spurted up around it. His face was set, and high duty seemed to shine through it ...

And then the writhing and quivering of the body became less, and the teeth ceased to champ, and the face to quiver. Finally it lay still. The terrible ordeal was over.

The hammer fell from Arthur's hand. He reeled and would have fallen had we not caught him. Great drops of sweat sprang out on his forehead, and his breath came in broken gasps (D16:258-59).

Little imagination is required to interpret this as thinly disguised passionate intercourse. This is indicated by Holmwood's post-coital exhaustion (the folkloric prescription of the vampire being destroyed by a solitary thrust is conveniently overlooked). But Stoker's language dares to portray another Victorian unmentionable – the female orgasm. In probably no other literary form of the time could such a taboo be depicted. Though Dracula has enjoyed previous sexual access to Lucy, thereby enslaving and freeing her simultaneously, her reactions to being 'staked' suggest the painful deflowering of a virgin, followed by her first and last orgasm. The passionate display is also performed on-stage, so to speak. Lucy and Arthur's only moment of intimacy is not performed in private. All his friends are gathered around, admiring and cheering him on. The mutilation of an unresisting female body offers the book's clearest example of sexual sadism. It contrasts with Lucy's masochistic self-destruction as she repeatedly gave herself to Dracula.

The notion of a 'pecking order' surfaces once more. Just as one of Dracula's vampirellas had first claim on Harker, so Godalming has the 'right' to stake Lucy. Notwithstanding the sadism, the assembled gentlemen conduct themselves with uneasy restraint and civility. All except Godalming must take their pleasure vicariously, voyeuristically. Later, Mina will force a pledge from her husband that he will be the one to set her free should the need arise (D25:394). Once again, 'love' is equated with being staked.

Attention now switches from Lucy to Mina. Though her bond with Jonathan is fundamental to the novel, no aspect of their physical relationship is touched upon. She appears totally sexless, until the Count awakens her submerged instincts. Whereas Lucy had merely to await his amorous touch, Dracula has a fixed purpose in mind for her friend. He wishes to immobilize his enemies by striking at Mina, symbol of all their values. By so doing he takes revenge on Harker, who escaped his clutches in Transylvania and joined forces with Van Helsing. Rather than go for the troublesome solicitor, Dracula inflicts greater suffering by making for his wife:

> Kneeling on the near edge of the bed facing outwards was the white clad figure of [Mina]. By her side stood a tall, thin man, clad in black … With his left hand he held both Mrs Harker's hands, keeping them away with her arms at full tension; his right hand gripped her by the back of the neck, forcing her face down on his bosom. Her white nightdress was smeared with blood, and a thin stream trickled down the man's bare breast, which was shown by his torn-open dress. The attitude of the two had a terrible resemblance to a child forcing a kitten's nose into a saucer of milk to compel it to drink (D21:336).

This incident is so packed with erotic meaning that Stoker wants his readers to hear it twice, for Mina then tells of her ordeal in her own words. (Her own words, but not her diary. It is Dr Seward who reports her viewpoint.)

> [Dracula] pulled open his shirt, and with his long sharp nails opened a vein in his breast. When the blood began to spurt out, he took my hands in one of his, holding them tight, and with the other seized my neck and pressed my mouth to the wound, so that I must either suffocate of swallow some of the – Oh, my God, my God! what have I done? (D21:343)

Mina's reaction is to rub her lips as though to cleanse them from pollution. The victim has sucked from the vampire, a reversal apparently without precedent in folklore.[18] Except for underground pornography, the Victorian public was starved of erotic literature. One can only speculate what readers must have made of these passages. Not content with voluptuous ladies breathing down Harker's neck and Godalming hammering Lucy until she climaxes, Stoker is here bold enough to describe fellatio. Lapping a saucer of milk lends visual strength to the analogy.

The posture of Mina's husband adds to the intrigue. He is lying on the bed, flushed and breathing heavily. Is Dracula responsible for his stupor, or is it Mina, acting under instruction, who 'exhausts' her husband during love-making? If the latter, then Mina has become a succubus, draining Jonathan in order to nourish her own incubus, Dracula. She thereby assists in the process of energy exchange between her two 'husbands', for it is now that Harker's hair begins to turn white. But there is more symbolism to come:

> She shuddered and was silent, holding down her head on her husband's breast. When she raised it, his white night robe was stained with blood where her lips had touched, and where the thin open wound in her neck had sent forth drops. The instant she saw it she drew back, with a low wail, and whispered amidst choking sobs:-
>
> 'Unclean, unclean! I must touch him or kiss him no more. Oh that it should be that it is I who am now his worst enemy, and whom he may have most cause to fear.' (D21:338-39)

Here, her words, 'Unclean, unclean!' take us beyond the language of the vampire. They are strangely suggestive of the menstrual taboo. Even Stoker's description of the wound conveys a distinct change. Hitherto in the novel, Dracula's canine teeth have left twin puncture marks, but in this instance Mina bears a 'thin open wound'. Such a 'wound', penetrated by an elongated canine tooth, is as near as Stoker can come to describing intercourse. Dracula enjoys the ultimate sexual power: he doesn't need a vagina – he makes his own holes. Stoker is also describing a narrow slit as presented by a menstruating vagina. Blood is no longer employed as a substitute for semen, but refers more directly to the menstrual flow itself.[19]

On the face of it, this might seem a gratuitous diversion by Stoker. On closer inspection it is not. The ancients perceived a connection between menstrual blood and semen. The miracle of childbirth could be explained by simple observation. A child emerged from its mother nine months after the injection of one fluid (semen) and the ceased emission of another (menstrual blood). Logic dictated that a baby was a concoction of the two: menstruation was to women what ejaculation was to men. We might at this point refer to Freud:

> The primitive cannot help connecting the mysterious phenomena of the monthly flow of blood with sadistic ideas. Thus he interprets menstruation, especially at its onset, as the bite of a spirit-animal [vampire?] or possibly as the token of sexual intercourse with this spirit. Occasionally the reports reveal this spirit as one of an ancestor, and then from other knowledge we have gained we understand that it is in virtue of her being the property of this spirit-ancestor that the menstruating girl is taboo.[20]

Count Dracula might not be Mina's ancestor, but he does claim her as his property. It is also his bite which causes the unclean flow of blood – token sexual intercourse, according to Freud. Another consequence of combining semen with menstrual blood is the freedom to indulge in coitus during a woman's period. Mina benefits from a kind of calendar liberation, so important to Victorian women, when they could enjoy their liaisons without fear of pregnancy. Again, the onset of menstruation is frequently accompanied by personality changes – and Mina is certainly acting rather differently to what is normally expected of her.

But why should Stoker have sought to incorporate menstrual imagery in *Dracula*? One theory, aired to explore his deeper impulses in writing the book, concerns his wife. One biographer would have us believe that Florence was frigid from the time of her son's birth.[21] As with other sexually dissatisfied women, she might have experienced troublesome periods. The hypothesis continues: 'was it some image of these that gave Stoker's subliminal mind the hint that formulated a myth of formidable power, out of the ferocity of a frustrated bleeding woman crackling with energy and unacknowledged sexuality?'[22]

The further one probes *Dracula*, the more sexual allegories are unearthed. Stoker even provides alternative methods of destruction for male and female vampires. Lucy, and Dracula's consorts, are extirpated by the application of the stake/phallus. Their destruction, and release, is accompanied by expressions of quasi-orgasm. For Dracula, the only male vampire, transfixion does not appear to be mandatory. The decapitation of the women is performed almost as an afterthought, once the full poignancy of their violent penetration is exhausted. The decapitation of the Count, by contrast, is shown as crucial. Harker's knife goes for the throat, not for the heart.

The knife-blade enjoys psychological connotations as a phallic symbol. It sadistically imitates the bodily penetration of the penis. It is notable that Harker strokes the blade of his knife as he contemplates the final assault on Dracula. The solicitor's own sexual responses have come full circle. His masochistic instincts, as he yielded himself to the Dracula harem, are replaced by sadistic impulses as he sets about mutilating his tormentor.[23]

Psychologists are aware that in nightmares pertaining to castration fears, the head can represent a penis-substitute.[24] Dracula is thereby neutralized, symbolically castrated, suffering the ultimate sexual revenge. This is affirmed by Van Helsing's use of the term 'sterilize' – in the sense of ridding the world of Dracula's menace – to hint at a sexual operation.[25] Nor should we overlook Harker's escape from Castle Dracula as illustrative of his own castration fears. In descending the castle's sheer walls, rather than be captured by the vampire women, his valedictory diary entry reads: 'At least God's mercy is better than that of these monsters, and the precipice is steep and high. At its foot a man may sleep – as a *man*' (D4:69; author's italics). As for Dracula's own anxieties, his great wooden boxes filled with native earth from Transylvania have been proposed as womb-substitutes. These are as necessary as blood for sustaining the vampire's life in death.[26] His tomb becomes the womb.

Notwithstanding its perversions and inversions, in one respect *Dracula* remains within the traditional bounds of literary eroticism. Its sexual framework is rigidly heterosexual.[27] Dracula acquires she-vampires, who in turn pursue males. Although Dracula is undead at the preternatural level, on a more earthly plane he is little more than a continuation of a literary stereotype. The Count is recognizable as the archetypal rake – the classic Gothic villain emanating from his mist-shrouded castle with its locked and secret rooms. He even looks the part, right down to the 'glittering eye' of the sexual tyrant. In this, he is aligned with other corrupt but courtly seducers of fiction, such as Lovelace in Richardson's *Clarissa*, from whom sexual conquests are to be expected. Dracula's visits to Lucy pre-empt the claims of her fiancé.[28] If blood is an aphrodisiac, so is power.

Dracula and his fellow literary rakes can ruin respectable women with impunity. In this Dracula is the envy of other men, who are jealous of this outsider's erotic power. He seduces their women with a potency they cannot equal, then moves on to further conquests. His is the classic expression of 'love them and leave them'. Curiously, both the rake of fiction and the vampire of folklore pass on their condition to their victims – moral depravity and acquired vampirism respectively. Both sets of victims become social outcasts, doomed in their differing ways to what amounts to a nocturnal existence. Dracula's consorts stalk the land under cover of night, while the fallen women of fiction frequently turn to prostitution, or serve as the chattel of their seducer.[29] 'Creatures of the night' fits them all. Dracula, we might say, is a moral degenerate, a disciple of carnal fun without responsibility.[30] He offers a glimpse into another world, the Eastern world – a leisured potentate selecting his harem.

This harem is socially discriminating. Dracula is not interested in low class women. As Harker observes, the Count's mistresses are not common whores but 'ladies by their dress and manner'. Lucy conforms to this pattern – as does a mysterious beautiful girl wearing a fashionable cart-wheel hat whom Dracula sets eyes upon in London (D13:207). Mina, however, does not conform, for the Count's interest in her is less erotic than strategic. In any case, her bourgeois repression prevents her welcoming his embrace. To the middle class, like Stoker, it appeared that both the upper and the lower tiers of society enjoyed greater sexual licence than themselves.[31]

Nor is it simply well-bred women who attract Dracula. He appears fussy about their marital status. This highlights his moral offensiveness, for he seduces Lucy and Mina when one is betrothed and the other newly married. The awakening of female sexuality on the threshold of marriage makes them more

167

vulnerable, and unlocks the key to his and their desires. He takes his 'brides' as his own, emasculating the jilted grooms. Harker may have been rendered impotent by his ordeal in Transylvania: in which case, does Mina's 'frustration' weaken her resistance? In the case of Holmwood, it is suggested that Lucy needed to be destroyed before she could enslave her 'husband' – for that would have been more than a Victorian readership could stomach.[32]

Aside from Mina's account of fellatio, the novel's sex scenes are portrayed from the male perspective. The slaughter of the women vampires highlights the evil of sex. Erotic women will annihilate honourable men if they are not destroyed.[33] Victorian culture assumed that men bore sexual responsibility; that of women was to submit in order to reproduce. Male dominance was 'confirmed' by Victorian science. Biologists claimed female births were the product of a passive, dormant energy cell, leaving responsibility for sexual potency with the male.[34]

Despite, or maybe because of, this institutionalized male superiority, there is evidence of a Victorian reaction against it – and not just on the part of the New Woman. Many men might wish, like Harker, to lie back passively and soak up the pleasure. Victorian prostitutes pandered to male masochism, while underground pornography catered for every taste.[35]

Dracula conforms to the timeless Christian crusade against indulgence in physical pleasure. Yet the vocation of Dracula's principle assailants lends a new dimension to the sexual theme. On the surface, vampirism is portrayed as supernaturally induced, to be countered by supernatural procedures: demonic possession requires spiritual as well as practical antidotes. But by introducing medical men into the arena, Stoker opens up a further interpretation. Vampirism, in Victorian terms, is revealed as a disease, a physical and mental disorder, which can be 'cured' by doctors rather than 'exorcised' by priests.[36] Stoker labours this point in several passages: Lucy and Mina are afflicted by a 'disease'; are 'infected'; and have 'poison' in their veins (D9:140; 24:380-1, 383). God-fearing physicians should uphold ethical standards and counter sexual affliction.

The sexuality with which *Dracula* seethes was able to titillate Victorian readers by being symbolic and hidden. It could therefore be enjoyed without admitting the nature of the pleasure. But to what extent Stoker was aware of all this? Was he writing pornography, confident that he had found the key to its possible expression? Or was he oblivious to *Dracula*'s eroticism, in the same way as were its reviewers? Some critics claim that nothing known about Stoker's life would have led him to consciously write prurient fiction. Others object to the patronizing implication that each new generation assumes it has discovered sex for the first time. This latter view claims that it stretches credibility to insist that Stoker had no appreciation of *Dracula*'s sexual underpinnings.[37] Thornburg, for example, insists that on every other criterion (folklore, occult, Christian,) Stoker shows himself to be totally in control of his material. So why the exception when it comes to sexual imagery?[38]

To some extent this is undoubtedly valid. Unconsciously, Stoker' mind was evidently replete with hallucinatory sex. On the conscious level, one need hardly imagine his outrage at the accusation. Indeed, so incensed was he at the smutty literature issuing forth in his later years that, in 1908, he launched a vehement attack on the moral standards of fiction. He came close to advocating formal censorship, at times his language straying closer to that of the pulpit than of the critic:

> A close analysis will show that the only emotions which in the long run harm are those arising from the sex impulses ...
>
> Within a couple of years past quite a number of novels have been published in England that would be a disgrace to any country even less civilized than our own. The class of works to which I allude are meant by both authors and publishers to bring to the winning of commercial success the forces of evil inherent in man ... As to the alleged men who follow this loathsome calling, what term of opprobrium is sufficient, what punishment could be too great? ... For look what those people have done. They found an art wholesome, they made it morbid; they found it pure, they left it sullied ... In the language of the pulpit, they have 'crucified Christ afresh' ... such works as are here spoken of deal not merely with natural misdoing based on human weakness, frailty, or passions of the senses, but with vices so flagitious, so opposed to even the decencies of nature in its crudest and lowest forms, that the poignancy of moral disgust is lost

in horror. This article ... is a deliberate indictment of a class of literature so vile that it is actually corrupting the nation.[39]

Improbable as it may seem, that outburst was penned by the same hand that wrote *Dracula*. The contrast, not to say hypocrisy, surely lends credence to the notion that *Dracula* stemmed from severe sexual repression. Let us now subject the novel and its author to some of the insights of psychoanalysis.

1   C F Bentley, 'The Monster in the Bedroom', p.27.

2   Maurice Richardson, 'The Psychoanalysis of Ghost Stories', p.427.

3   Bentley, p.27.

4   David Pirie, *The Vampire Cinema*, p.26.

5   James Twitchell, 'The Vampire Myth', p.88.

6   See Raymond T McNally, *Dracula was a Woman*, p.93.

7   James Twitchell, *The Living Dead: A Study of the Vampire in Literature*, p.136.

8   See Bentley, p.28.

9   Judith Weissman, 'Women and Vampires: *Dracula* as a Victorian Novel', p.404.

10   Dante Gabriel Rossetti, in 'Eden Bower', had written of Lilith's vengeance on Adam and Eve. Lilith also appears, fleetingly, on Walpurgis Nacht in Goethe's *Faust*.

11   Ornella Volta, p.33.

12   Many nineteenth-century poets and writers exploited the erotic symbolism entailed in the colour red. See, for example, Keats' 'The Eve of St Agnes'.

13   C S Blinderman, 'Vampurella: Darwin and Count Dracula', p.422.

14   Ernest Jones, in Christopher Frayling, *The Vampyre: Lord Ruthven to Count Dracula*, pp.323-24.

15   See, Volta, p.23. The practice of performing blood-transfusions was extremely dangerous in the 1890s. Not until 1901, with Landsteiner's discovery of different blood groups, could it be made safer. Van Helsing's transfusions were likely to (did?) kill Lucy.

16   See Brian Murphy, 'The Nightmare of the Dark: the Gothic Legacy of Count Dracula', p.10.

17   Penelope Shuttle and Peter Redgrove, *The Wise Wound:*

Menstruation and Everywoman, p.267.

[18] Twitchell, *The Living Dead*, p.138.

[19] See Bentley, p.30. Stoker may have known of the belief held in parts of Italy that a young girl could secure the attentions of her lover by his drinking some of her menstrual blood (Volta, pp.26, 92).

[20] Sigmund Freud, 'Contributions to the Psychology of Love: the Taboo of Virginity', in *Collected Papers* IV, pp.221-22.

[21] Daniel Farson, *The Man Who Wrote Dracula: A Biography of Bram Stoker*, p.214.

[22] Shuttle and Redgrove, p.266.

[23] See Burton Hatlen, 'The Return of the Repressed/Oppressed in Bram Stoker's *Dracula*', pp.86-87.

[24] Sigmund Freud, 'A Connection between a Symbol and a Symptom', in *Collected Papers* II, pp.162-63. In the Marquis de Sade's *Justine* a sexual embrace often involved the decapitation of the partner.

[25] Bentley, p.31.

[26] ibid., p..32.

[27] Leonard Wolf dissents from this view, interpreting Lucy's three suitors as linked by dimly homosexual bonds. (*A Dream of Dracula*, p.210).

[28] This has been described as an echo of the medieval *jus primae noctis*: the Count acts as a feudal lord exercising his *droit de seigneur*. See Bentley, p.32.

[29] Carrol L Fry, 'Fictional Conventions and Sexuality' p.21

[30] See Blinderman, p.422.

[31] See Hatlen, pp.93, 95.

[32] Thomas P Walsh, '*Dracula*: Logos and Myth', p.231.

[33] Phyllis A Roth, 'Suddenly Sexual Women in Bram Stoker's *Dracula*', p.119.

[34] Jill Conway, in Stephanie Demetrakopoulos, 'Feminism, Sex Role Changes and Other Subliminal Fantasies in Bram Stoker's *Dracula*', p.106.

[35] See Demetrakopoulos, pp.106, 108.

[36] See Bentley, p.32.

[37] See Murphy, p.10.

[38] Thomas Ray Thornburg, 'The Quester and the Castle: the Gothic Novel as Myth, with Special Reference to Bram Stoker's *Dracula*', p.146.

[39] Bram Stoker, 'The Censorship of Fiction', pp.483-85.

10

FREUD, ORALITY, AND INCEST

Complex and ... fundamental emotions are at work in the
construction and maintenance of the vampire superstition. It is one
more product of the deepest conflicts that determine human
development and fate – those concerned with the earliest
relationships to the parents. These come to their intensest expression
in anxiety dreams and ... a number of features ... point
unequivocally to the conclusion that the terrible experiences there
must have played an important part in moulding the beliefs in
question: ... the occurrence of the supposed events during sleep, the
evident relation of the events to nocturnal emissions resulting from
sexual – particularly perversely sexual – experiences, the vampire's
capacity for transformation, his flight by night, his appearance in
animal form and, finally, the connection between the belief and that
in the return of dead relatives ... The essential elements are ...
repressed desires and hatreds derived from early incest conflicts ...
[especially] hate and guilt.

Ernest Jones, 'On the Vampire', in Christopher Frayling (ed.),
The Vampyre: Lord Ruthven to Count Dracula, p.330.

The sexual aspects of *Dracula* demand closer examination. The
1890s witnessed the climax of Victorian decadence and the dawn
of psychoanalysis. The year 1897 marked *Dracula*'s publication
and the commencement of Freud's psychoanalytical researches.
For advocates of psychoanalysis *Dracula* yields a rich harvest.
One critic insists that *Dracula* must be seen from a Freudian
standpoint: 'from no other does the story really make any sense'.[1]
Another sees *Dracula*, in its relation to our darkest fears and
desires, as presaging the attempts of psychoanalysis 'to dissect
the human soul and penetrate into its arcana by a secret door
opened by a magic key'.[2]

According to Freud's complex model of human behaviour, the erotic drive is an important component of psychic energy. When that drive is repressed, guilt and neuroses may result unless other 'healthy' defence mechanisms come into play. Freud's hypotheses confronted Western society with the neurotic consequences of suppressing erotic impulses. He postulated a series of overlapping stages in psychosexual development, each stage marked by preoccupation with certain parts of the body. The infant first enters the 'oral' stage, using the mouth and teeth to derive pleasure and to explore the world. The child takes delight in suckling the breast and, following the arrival of teeth, attempting to eat it.

This oral phase is not pre-sexual: it is intensely sexual. *Dracula* derives much of its impact from its 'orality', and in this sense illustrates what may be termed regressive infantilism. The English language is rich in the association of sexual and digestive pleasures. Colloquial terms for a lover include 'honey', 'sweet', 'sugar'. The admission of sexual desire can take the words 'I could eat you up'. The practice of the love-bite probably stems from an unconscious urge to devour the partner. 'Sex' and 'food' may even be substituted for one another, as when a person falling in love loses his appetite.

Following the 'oral' stage comes the 'anal' stage, when the child enjoys physical gratification through withholding and expelling faeces. Later, according to Freud, at some point between the third and fifth year the male child will exhibit a fixation with his penis. During this 'phallic' stage the child matures from his narcissistic perspective on life and enters the realm of the Oedipus complex. His emotions towards his mother acquire sexual overtones, with corresponding sensations of rivalry and hostility towards his father. The child harbours deep-seated fears that he will be 'castrated', removing his threat to his father.[3] The application of psychoanalysis to *Dracula* will highlight the novel's obsession with infantile sexuality and its preoccupation with death. Freud maintained that morbid dread, such as fear of vampires, is likely to point to repressed sexual instincts.

Vampire visits in folklore are largely confined within the family. Incest, therefore, is written into the very expression of vampirism. Likewise, the triangular Oedipal configuration of mother, father, and son is redolent of incest and the threat of parricide. (Compare the function of the dhampire, who suffers no pangs of guilt from destroying his vampire father.) *Dracula*'s use of family metaphors, particularly its handling of competing father-figures, establishes the novel as woven around the Oedipus complex. There exists in the book an endogamous motif which, other than the Count, links nearly all the main characters as members of one large, figurative family.[4] Most couplings can be slotted into parent-child or brother-sister relationships. Even Dracula's harem approach Mina with the words 'Come, sister' (D27:436). Quasi-ceremonies bind Dracula's pursuers together, for example Lucy's blood transfusions, and the bundle of names given to Harker's son, so that the whole book takes on an incestuous air.

The Count himself is the obvious father-figure, endowed with unequalled potency. He is the patriarch of his domain, having one family resident in his castle, while seeking to extend his blood-ties by acquiring colonies of subservient vampires. He will sire them not through his sperm but through his bite.

Van Helsing is also recognizable in the father role. He views the young men and women around him as replacing his own lost son. One critic suggests that by having two father-figures in the novel, Stoker permits the Count's contempt for the family to contaminate the professor, who becomes tinged with a certain moral ambiguity.[5] Seen from another perspective, the existence of two competing fathers resolves the Oedipal complex: the 'sons' are simultaneously allowed to kill the one, while respecting and obeying the other.[6]

Equally, there exists an obvious sibling rivalry between the 'brothers' (the rivals for Lucy's hand), though Stoker plays this down. All hint of jealously is expunged, so their passions may be channelled against the evil father who steals their women. In so doing, these Victorian avengers are reminiscent of Freud's 'primal horde'.[7] They concert their energies against the 'father' who seeks the women for himself.

When Dracula is destroyed, he is not the first father-figure to perish, for parricide is endemic in the novel. Old Mr Swales, who had conveyed his wisdom to Lucy on Whitby cliffs, is killed; Holmwood's father also passes away; as does Harker's employer and 'second father' Mr Hawkins. In his bereavement, the 'fatherless' Harker begins to doubt himself (D12:190). He is then 'adopted' by Van Helsing, but his Oedipal trauma is resolved only with his slaying of Dracula.[8] To compound matters, Quincey Morris also dies, to become a retrospective 'father' in giving his name to Quincey junior. As one critic has noticed, these father-deaths are gratuitous: they are not central to the plot, tending in fact to detract from it.[9] It is as if Stoker is driving home his own Oedipus complex: anybody remotely 'fatherish', other than Van Helsing, must be destroyed.

Actually, it is truer to speak of parenticide rather than parricide. Mother-figures die too. First to do so is a peasant woman, pleading for her child outside Dracula's castle, but upon whom he summons the wolves. Next is Lucy's mother, followed by Lucy herself. The teenage beauty who rejected two of the novel's 'sons' and later molested 'toddlers' is herself a victim of quasi-matricide.

Of greater consequence is the intended fate of the central mother-figure, Mina. It has been maintained that Stoker's need to dispose of mother surrogates extends even to the goddess Mina. Coexistent with the need to protect her lies a submerged instinct to visit destruction upon her. How else, the argument goes, could her guardians so persistently expose her to the Count's preda-tions, almost inviting him to violate her, unless this is their uncon-scious wish?[10] If her husband has been sexually incapacitated by his Transylvanian ordeal, then she remains a virgin. To pursue this line of thought, one need only recall the custom in several cultures of sacrificing virgin wives to the aristocracy.[11]

The many instances of parenticide in *Dracula* are matched by infanticidal parallels. Two mothers are responsible for the death of their child. In Whitby, Dracula sleeps in the grave of a suicide, George Canon, the only son of his widowed mother. Twenty years earlier Canon had blown his head off with a musket to prevent his 'hell-cat' of a mother claiming the life-insurance she had taken out (D6:85). As her piety would send her to heaven, Canon shot himself so he'd avoid her in hell.

The second murderous mother is Mrs Westenra. Whenever she is encountered she acts in some way to Lucy's detriment. Her selfishness is commented upon by Seward: 'She was alarmed [at Lucy's deterioration], but not nearly so much as I expected ... the terrible change in her daughter [does] not seem to reach her' (D10:146-47). For reasons that are unconvincing, Mrs Westenra even disinherits her daughter in favour of Holmwood (D:13:201). Finally, it is Mrs Westenra who *twice* removes the protective garlic that Van Helsing has wreathed around Lucy's neck (D11:162, 174). On the first occasion, she opens the window to Dracula. On the second, no one but she could have drugged the servants with her medicine so Dracula might not be interrupted.

On a figurative level, the Count is the clearest example of murderous parent, for he must kill before he can recruit vampires into his 'family'. He even provides a living child to be consumed by his wife/daughters. But there are other, less obvious, instances. For example, Dr Seward's negligence promotes the death of the 'child' in his care, Renfield. One commentator suggests that perhaps Quincey Morris's demise is necessitated by his anti-social independence. In Freudian terms, Morris is punished for his non-conformity, figuratively castrated, and then reinstated into family-based relationships via Harker's son.[12] Dracula's downfall can even be taken as infanticide, this time supervised by the good father, Van Helsing. Not for nothing has the professor insisted on treating the Count as a 'child-brain' who looks upon his crates of Transylvanian soil as surrogate wombs – to which he is tied as effectively as by an umbilical cord.

Dracula's 'childishness' is abetted by his sexual proclivities. The Count is not only a child-brain: he is markedly childlike in his psychosexual development. His sexual activity is not yet phallic, for it has not yet progressed beyond the oral and anal stages. To his preoccupation with biting and sucking can be added Stoker's references to the stench which emanates from the Count's resting places: these suggest the malodour of excrement – 'the mephitis of cloaca and the charnel house'.[13] It would seem that Dracula's only non-infantile aspect is his age – he is over 400 years old.

In view of his infantility, perhaps it is misleading to attribute to Dracula the source of the novel's terror. More persuasively, that accolade should fall to the vampire women. Harker clearly knows (as does Stoker) where the source of his own terror lies: 'It is maddening to think that of all the foul things that lurk in this hateful place the Count is the least dreadful to me' (D3:49-50). The male reader, one suspects, agrees with him. What is most to be feared, unconsciously, is the devouring woman; the mother-figure who threatens by being desirable. This claim can be supported, firstly, by reference to Stoker's three other horror novels. In each, the supernatural presence is erotic and feminine. Secondly, it is necessary only to recall Mina's mouth being pressed down upon Dracula's breast. In that act it is *he* who becomes the threatening mother, forcing Mina to suckle from him. Roth has summarized this terror of women:

> The threatening Oedipal fantasy, the regression to a primary oral obsession, the attraction, and destruction of the vampires of *Dracula* are, then, interrelated and interdependent. What they spell out is a fusion of the memory of nursing at the mother's breast with a primal scene fantasy which results in the conviction that the sexually desirable woman will annihilate if she is not first destroyed.[14]

Moretti offers a perceptive explanation for the threats engendered by the male, as opposed to the female, vampire in literature. High-brow poets and writers have usually employed female vampires (for example, the vampires of Goethe, Keats, Poe, Le Fanu). The vampires of mass, popular culture, on the other hand, were more usually male (such as Sir Francis Varney and Count Dracula). The foregoing discussion has proposed that literary vampirism is rooted in the Oedipus complex. Consequently, to present the threat as female is appropriate, since the sex of the threatening mother and the threatening vampire coincide. By deploying a male vampire, however, the parental threat is displaced: 'the unconscious source of perturbation is hidden.'[15] In short: 'the vampire is transformed into a man by mass culture, which has to promote spontaneous certainties and cannot let itself plumb the unconscious too deeply.'[16]

This central hypothesis, that terror springs from the female vampire, is tied in with expressions of unconscious guilt –

particularly sexual guilt – on the part of the male child. Freud propounds that incest is in all likelihood the primordial sin from which all others derive: that adults' unconscious guilt stems from infantile incestuous desires. Males most affected by the Oedipus complex – those who failed to come to terms with their father's rivalry – are often the most jealous in their love affairs.[17] In extreme cases, their guilt is projected from the living to the dead, who, it is supposed, cannot rest in their graves but feel compelled to rise and return to their loved ones. Those resting in peace, ironically, are permitted an incestuous relationship of their own, measured by their decomposition and integration with 'Mother Earth'.[18]

Persons most afflicted by visions of the vampire are, therefore, those most afflicted by sexual guilt. Sexually rejected, their love of mother turns to hate, in turn leading to fear of retribution after her death. This illustrates the fundamental warring triangle – love, hate, guilt – through which Freudian psychoanalysis postulates each of us must contend with in infancy. In later life, whenever healthy sexual outlets are repressed, there is a tendency to regress to an earlier stage. Repression invites fear and dread, which then connect with aggressive instincts to be expressed, for example, in oral sadism.

Central to the vampire phenomenon lies a preoccupation with teeth. Oral sadism stems from an infant's discovery of his ability to use them to inflict pain. The mouth that first sucked the breast is able to bite and try to eat it – in other words, to practice cannibalism (and draw blood, not milk). The acquisition of teeth provides the baby's first opportunity to cause pain and to demonstrate aggressive instincts. The original sucking impulse is not abandoned, but is adapted in adult life in the form of kissing, thereby retaining its sexual significance. Suckling at the breast has obvious parallels with sexual intercourse. Both acts involve the swelling of an organ, the emission of a precious white liquid, followed by a physical and mental sense of well-being in both participants. This adds to the psychological association between milk and semen. The cutting of a child's teeth, however, assumes a critical place in his emotional development, for if teeth can inflict pain on the mother, her teeth can also inflict pain on the child. When in time he comes to expect retribution for his earlier cannibalistic tendencies, it is castration that is his unconscious fear.

At this point it is appropriate to introduce the concept of *vagina dentata*; a sexual myth found in many folk tales around the world, and bound up with Freud's castration complex. The male child's obsession both with his mother and with teeth gives rise to psychological displacement, creating in his mind an unconscious fusion between her mouth and genitals. The vagina is envisaged as mouth-shaped, complete with lips and 'teeth'. During menstruation the horrific image is intensified. (As blood is so precious, its loss without visible cause is traumatic enough.) The menstruating 'mouth' becomes blooded, presenting an horrific image of the penis being devoured by the mouth/vagina. (The concept has parallels at plant level, as when the brightly coloured Venus Flytrap tempts insects inside before snapping shut around them.) Almost every culture regards coitus during menstruation as taboo, a blooded penis being too fear-provoking for most men to entertain. Likewise, many societies regard women as being in some way castrated men. They are viewed as less worthy for that reason, and it is hardly surprising that the idea of 'penis-envy' on the part of women became fashionable.

Psychoanalytically, *vagina dentata* is conditioned by the menstruating mother, which invokes both sexual excitement and terror.[19] The threat of castration cannot be neutralized until the 'teeth' are extracted – symbolically (or actually) removed. In 'Berenice', Edgar Allan Poe demonstrates an obsession with her teeth and the necessity to extract them from her dead body:

> The teeth! The teeth! They were here, and there, and everywhere, visibly and palpably before me, long, narrow and excessively white, with the pale lips writhing about them … I shuddered as I assigned to them, in imagination, a sensitive and sentient power … I felt that their possession could alone ever restore me to peace in giving me back my reason.

Teeth, like any sharp elongated instrument (Harker's Kukri knife, Morris's Bowie knife, Seward's lancet, or Van Helsing's stake), represent powerful phallic symbols. Berenice must undergo the symbolic castration that Poe's narrator fears for himself. Bram Stoker unwittingly dealt with *vagina dentata* long before *Dracula*. His short story 'The Squaw' features an Iron Maiden torture device shaped like a woman. 'She' is filled with spikes (teeth) to embrace any man who 'enters' her. In *Dracula*, however, the vampire women's 'assault' on Jonathan Harker provides a classic account of the *vagina dentata* myth. One critic has written:

> The danger of sexuality, the punishment that threatens all who yield, is shown by the manner in which [he] is obsessed by her teeth. And, indeed, in psychoanalysis, many cases of male impotence reveal, though more or less buried in the unconscious the notion of the female vagina being furnished with teeth, and thus a source of danger in being able to bite and castrate ... Mouth and vagina are equated in the unconscious: [he] yields both the yearning for the mother's organ, and to be revenged upon it; since the dangers that hedge it about make him sexually avoid all women as too menacing. His act is therefore a sort of retributive castration inflicted on the mother whom he loves, and yet hates, because obdurate to his sex-love for her in infancy ... The memory, or rather the phantasy of biting the mother's breast must become charged, in the unconscious with past feelings of wickedness [and guilt]. And the child, having learnt by experience what is meant by the law of retaliation when he infringes the code ... begins, in his turn, to fear that the bites he wished to give his mother will be visited on him: namely retaliation for his cannibalism.[20]

This passage actually refers to Poe, but its substance could equally apply to Stoker, and to Harker at the hands of the blonde vampire. It demonstrates the Oedipus complex and *vagina dentata* intertwined. The conflicting emotions of love and hate is another way of recognizing the simultaneous attraction and repulsion of the vampire. As Jones put it: 'All the beliefs about the nightmare in whatever guise proceed from the idea of the sexual assault that is both wished for and dreaded.'[21] This ambivalence is not confined to sexual matters: it surfaces in many forms. On the question of death, for example, desire for oblivion coexists with a yearning for immortality: the wish for our loved ones to rise up clashes with the hope that the dead stay put. Occasionally, those left behind yearn to be reunited with the dead; more often it is the dead who are presumed to seek reunion with the living.

Perhaps, when all is said, the real source of the novel's terror springs neither from Count Dracula nor his vampirellas, but from inside the human mind. The real monster resides within us, the readers. People create for themselves the monsters they fear, stemming from repressed yearnings and anxieties. Because the body is mortal, the twin fears of sexual punishment and of death come into common focus. Sexual repression becomes metamorphosed, transforming itself into visions of frightful beings. Vampires operate as a filter through which the novel can reflect submerged desires. *Dracula* makes bearable to the conscious mind those desires and fears recognized as being unacceptable, and therefore unacknowledged to oneself.[22]

It is arguable that the entire Gothic genre is about the discovery of self-horror. Perhaps readers saw, and see, in *Dracula* echoes of themselves. A bond between two people involves, however tangentially, the taint of vampire exploitation – be it economic, intellectual, emotional, or whatever. Oscar Wilde's was no trite observation 'all men kill the thing they love'. In *Dracula* that over-used phrase is given a savage new twist, for illimitable desire turns love, literally, into possession and an eternity of enslavement.[23]

Two other psychological motifs permeate *Dracula*: the world of dreams and the issue of insanity. Upon finishing the novel the reader may never be entirely convinced that its extraordinary contents are not the product of sleep. Perhaps the whole book should be interpreted as a dream – or nightmare – for Stoker weaves a narrative whereby terror and dream are never easily distinguishable. Harker experiences bad dreams even before he reaches Castle Dracula; his carriage journey is described as dream-like unreality; and he is later tempted to dismiss his entire ordeal as a grotesque nightmare. Dracula had previously warned him that 'there are bad dreams for those who sleep unwisely' (D3:46). Lucy recollects her sleep-walking as weird dreams, and is eventually too terrified to fall asleep for fear of what night may bring. Mina's encounter with the Count is similarly expressed as a surreal dream: 'I thought I was asleep' (D19:308), and her hypnotically induced trances reinforce the view that only the unconscious mind is receptive to Dracula's presence. He is powerless without the consent of the unconscious mind, for his victims have only to wake up to experience a feeling of salvation and a lightening of their mental burden. Throw in Renfield's madness, Van Helsing's graveyard vigils, and the vampires' nocturnal powers, and the whole novel seems pitched in the twilight zone between waking and sleeping.[24] Throughout the novel, actual happenings are phrased in the language and imagery of dreams.[25]

Linked to the fear of dreams is the novel's overpowering obsession with madness, a common enough theme in Victorian fiction. Harker, on many occasions, assumes he has gone mad; Seward entertains similar ideas about himself; and Lucy gives every appearance of derangement ('she makes a curious psychological study' [D5:72]) long before Dracula gets hold of her. Even then, Seward can only diagnose 'it must be something mental' (D9:137). Van Helsing tries to widen his ex-student's horizons by suggesting 'all men are mad in some way or the other' (D10:145), but Seward soon harbours doubts about his mentor, who is so abnormally clever that even he could be 'off his head' (D15:245).

Stoker is offering nothing new in this soul-searching of his characters. Polidori's Aubrey also questioned his own sanity; as did Stevenson's Jekyll. What does depart from Victorian literary convention is that Stoker seems to suggest that madness is nothing to be afraid of. There *are* worse things in life. This notion emerges in an exchange between Seward and the professor: '"Dr Van Helsing, are you mad?" ... "Would I were! ... Madness were easy to bear compared with truth like this"' (D15:233). Stoker shows that whatever terrors lie in store for the insane they are nothing compared to the horrors of everlasting hell as a vampire. Or, rather, he maintains that madness itself is not really at issue: it is the vampire that produces it,[26] just as it is Dracula who gives that extra twist to Renfield's unhappy mind.

Renfield is the focus of madness as explored in *Dracula*. He represents the split personality – a common literary device in Victorian fiction – as well as the 'victim' who must suffer mental torment before being released into the calm waters of sanity. In places, the novel comes close to insisting that Renfield is anything but mad. Seward and company start out believing that only the mad can believe in vampires, yet their prejudices lead to unpalatable conclusions. Dracula *does* exist, demonstrating that Renfield, who knows as much, has clearer perception than the doubters, whose mental faculties cannot comprehend the awful reality. Once the dying Renfield is freed from Dracula's power, and he returns to sanity, he does not dismiss his earlier disturbances as hallucinatory. Renfield when sane is just as sure of Dracula's existence as when insane. The restoration of his mind does not banish his supposed delusions.[27]

Renfield's mortal injury permits Van Helsing to relieve him of his madness in classic fashion. Dracula's murderous attack on his former servant has left Renfield with a depressed fracture of the skull. In order to lighten the pressure on his brain, Van Helsing states 'we must trephine at once or it may be too late' (D21:329). The professor then drills a big hole in the man's head with a cylindrical saw. Stoker must have known that trephination is about the most ancient surgical operation known to man. When illness was thought to be caused by evil spirits, how better to effect cure than to let the spirits out? Renfield's hole-in-the-head permits his madness to escape.

It is fitting that these brief psychoanalytical attempts to fathom *Dracula* conclude with an attempt to fathom his creator. Two scholars have tried to probe Stoker's formative years with Freudian instruments.[28] He was, it will be recalled, sickly for his first seven years, and investigation of that early disability might provide insights into his major fictional work. *Dracula*, mirroring Stoker's illness, is a 'tale of medical detection of puzzling illnesses, of obscure diagnoses, and unusual cures'.[29]

Medical care in Ireland during Stoker's infancy was such that surgery was rare. Many disorders that today would warrant surgery or pharmacy were treated by the practice of blood-letting

– the presumption being that illness was caused by 'bad' blood, an imbalance in the humors. Whether Stoker's malaise was tackled by blood-letting or surgery, it is likely he would have suffered surgically-induced trauma. Anna Freud (Freud's daughter) has written:

> Whenever we have to prepare a child for surgical experience, we find that the greatest difficulty is to keep the event down to its 'real' significance. The extraction of a tooth, the removal of tonsils or of an appendix would not be so frightening in itself. They become horrifying when the child's imagination turns them into amputation, castration, annihilation, etc., i.e. into dangers which existed previously as threats in his conscious or unconscious mind.[30]

The mechanics of hospitals are frightening enough today, for adults as for children. The degree of trauma involved has been vividly described in this account, written in the 1930s:

> Certainly there is nothing in the practice of medicine so barbarous and so fraught with psychological danger as the prevalent custom of taking a child into a strange white room, surrounding him with white garbed strangers exhibiting queer paraphernalia and glittering knives and at the height of his consternation pressing an ether cone over his face and telling him to breathe deeply. The anxiety stimulated by such horrors is probably never surpassed in the child's subsequent life.[31]

According to Shuster, a child's fear of doctors stems from a fantasy that the physician has been defeated in the sexual battles of the primal bedroom. He has become insane, and seeks to alleviate his misery either by castrating the child or by draining his body.[32] The child's response probably accounts for the popularity of the fictional 'mad doctor'. Likewise, doctors play a major role in children's games, such as 'doctors and nurses'. Perhaps some comparable role reversal manifested itself in Stoker when, in later years, he came to write *Dracula*. The Count can be viewed as a reincarnation of the 'cruel' doctors Stoker encountered in childhood, while he himself identifies with the good doctors, Van Helsing and Seward. Nor can Stoker's mother be eliminated from the source of his terror, for she might have taken him, struggling, to the hospital and then 'abandoned' him to whatever horrors lay in store.

This thesis interprets the novel as autobiography at the level of fantasy. Harker's entrapment in the castle re-enacts the fears of a child being abandoned in a nineteenth century medical institution. He tries to escape from his prison, as may the hospitalized child. Dracula plays the part of the wicked doctor fending off his fear of emptiness/death by drinking the blood of children.[33] The Count dressed in black and the doctors in white present stark images of terror. Just as Dracula waits upon Harker hand and foot, to disguise his menace, so the surgeon is all smiles and reassurances prior to picking up his knives. The threat of both is thus displaced, adding to Harker's (Stoker's) terror and confusion. Nightmares are common to both the castle and hospitals. The vampires' injecting teeth correspond to the nurses' injecting needles. The room where Harker lapses into unconsciousness matches the operating chamber. When Harker awakes he finds himself mysteriously transported back to his own room/ward. Harker's lashing out at the Count with a shovel suggests a child bouncing its fists off the surgeon, and his near-miraculous escape might be Stoker's denial that the surgical nightmare ever happened at all.[34]

Harker convalesces in Budapest, where his mother/wife is warned that he will suffer long-term trauma, as may happen after a child leaves hospital. Thereafter doubt assails him until Van Helsing reassures him that his experience was not nightmare, but real. Only with that comfort can Harker/Stoker come to terms with his trauma and lay it to rest.

Traces of possible childhood trauma appear in Stoker's writings long before *Dracula*. They are manifest in his collection of fairy tales *Under the Sunset*. Themes from the anthology reappear in much of his later work, as though he felt compelled to relate them again and again. An attempt has been made to focus on two tales to forge a link between Stoker's childhood and his conception of *Dracula*. They 'help explain the blood sucking, madness, the psychiatrist and the insane asylum, the sleep disturbances of … Dracula'.[35]

Of principal interest is Stoker's cameo 'How 7 Went Mad', a tale that incorporates nightmares, insanity, blood-letting, with not a little wit and humour. A small boy – Tineboy (tiny boy?) – has trouble at school with his arithmetic. He wishes that the troublesome number 7 had never been invented, whereupon his wish comes true in a dream. The Alphabet Doctor, whose job it is to treat sick letters and numbers, uses his instruments, including a horoscope ('horrorscope' to Tineboy), to examine the patient. Poor number 7 complains of being treated badly because he is an orphan: as a prime number he has no relatives, no kith and kin. The tormented digit succumbs to insanity and prompts a passage from Stoker worthy of *Catch 22*: 'You surely are not mad enough to insist on being mad? ... if you are mad enough to insist upon being mad, we must try to cure your madness ... and then you will be unmad enough to wish to be unmad, and we will cure that too.' It is worth noting that the insane digit, who is foaming at the mouth, is restrained by a nurse trying to bleed him – further evidence that this was standard medical treatment at the time.

But why number 7 in particular? Bierman points to the seven Stoker children. Four were younger than Bram and were born while he was disabled. Bierman perceives intense sibling jealousy on Bram's part, identifying death wishes towards his younger brothers. This he supports by noting the instances of infanticide in *Dracula*, and the borrowing of Bram's brothers' names – Tom and George – for minor characters.[36] Bierman reminds us that three of Stoker's brothers entered the medical profession, one of whom, George, became and ear, nose, and throat doctor.

The second story from *Under the Sunset* is 'The Wondrous Child', another tale of sibling rivalry and dreams. Here we find birth expressed in oral terms: to conceive, the girl opens her mouth, into which is poured 'scarlet' milk. The child, who dies and is reborn, is thereafter able to control dragons and snakes.

Common to both short stories and to *Dracula*, according to Bierman, are death wishes towards younger brothers suckling from their mother's breast, and primal scenes expressed in nursing terms. Bierman is impressed by the psychoanalytical concept of the 'oral triad' – the wish to eat, to be eaten, and to sleep.[37] Their interrelationship, in *Dracula* as in the human mind, causes them to be reactivated together: 'Sleep, as expressed in Harker's stupor, would be a first line of defense against being awakened by the primal sounds, but the wishes to eat and be eaten would also arise; and thus the stage would be set for intercourse being seen in terms of sucking and being sucked.'[38] The infant Stoker would have been kept awake by his younger brothers' crying, while also being aroused by their breast-feeding from his mother. Being bed-ridden, he would have been unable to dissipate his aggression through healthy outlets, but would have had to express it orally. 'Killing' his brothers meant eating them (in 'How 7 Went Mad', the raven eats all the number 7s). This in turn triggers the rest of the triad, generating fear of sleep and death. Bierman explains:

> Being bled must have been interpreted by young Stoker as being eaten up. Sucking blood and eating are equated in *Dracula*. After the Count has sucked Mina's blood … Van Helsing remarks, '… last night he banqueted heavily and will sleep late …' Due to the generic linkage of the wish to be eaten and the wish to eat and to sleep, being bled would have become linked to the latter two wishes. Milk would no longer have been white, but blood red.[39]

Is it coincidence, Bierman asks, that the collection of stories *Under the Sunset* were published shortly after the birth of Stoker's son – his new rival in the Oedipal triangle?[40] Having lost his mother's attentions following the birth of his brothers, Stoker now faced the loss of his wife's affections after the birth of Noel.

The application of psychoanalytical techniques to *Dracula* is necessarily speculative and contentious, particularly those that seek a direct correlation between Bram Stoker's life and his fiction. But the questions they raise are nevertheless important: was Stoker reliving his infancy in the form of Jonathan Harker? Was he embodied in the good doctor Van Helsing? Or was he fantasizing as the Count, able to take vicarious sexual pleasure from other men's women? The world of the vampire has been described as a 'twilight borderland where psycho-pathological and religious motives intermingle'.[41] Therefore let us turn to the Christian and moral insights to be gleaned from *Dracula*.

1   Maurice Richardson, 'The Psychoanalysis of Ghost Stories', p.427.

2   Grigore Nandris, 'The Historical Dracula: The Theme of His Legend in the Western and in the Eastern Literatures of Europe,' p.370.

3   Technically, 'castration' refers to the removal of the testicles. Psychoanalytically, its meaning is more flexible, referring to loss of testicles, or penis, or both. Sometimes, too, it is used metaphorically, meaning male loss of control over females.

4   Richardson, p.427.

5   Royce MacGillivray, '"Dracula": Bram Stoker's Spoiled Masterpiece', p.522.

6   Richard Astle, 'Dracula as Totemic Monster: Lacan, Freud, Oedipus and History', p.102.

7   Sigmund Freud, *Totem and Taboo*.

8   Astle, p.100.

9   MacGillivray, pp.522-23.

10   Phyllis A Roth, 'Suddenly Sexual Women in Bram Stoker's Stoker's *Dracula*', p.118.

11   Ornella Volta, *The Vampire*, pp.30, 94.

12   Astle, p.103.

13   Richardson, p.427.

14   Roth, op. cit., p.119.

15   Franco Moretti, *Signs Taken for Wonders: Essays in the Sociology of Literary Forms*, p.104.

16   ibid.

17   Ernest Jones, in Christopher Frayling (ed.), *The Vampyre: Lord Ruthven to Count Dracula*, p.317.

18   ibid., p.314.

19   Penelope Shuttle and Peter Redgrove, *The Wise Wound: Menstruation and Everywoman*, p.262.

20   Marie Bonaparte, *The Life and Works of Edgar Allen Poe: A Psychoanalytical Interpretation*, pp. 209-10.

21   Ernest Jones, in Richardson, p.425.

22   Moretti, p.104.

23   David Punter, *The Literature of Terror*, p.263.

24   Ronald Schleifer, 'The Trap of the Imagination: the Gothic Tradition, Fiction and "The Turn of the Screw",' p.306.

25   Stoker, it will be remembered, had taken rough notes on a theory of dreams. The dreams manifested in *Dracula*, moreover, are psychoanalytically classifiable into recognizable types: 'dental'

and 'anticipatory' dreams on the part of Harker; 'flying' dreams on the part of Lucy. See Thomas Ray Thornburg, 'The Quester and the Castle: the Gothic Novel as Myth, with Special Reference to Bram Stoker's *Dracula*', pp.145-54.

26   Moretti, p.102.

27   See Jean Gattengo, 'Folie, Croyance, et Fantastique dans "Dracula".' In an earlier draft Stoker had Dracula restore sanity to Renfield, thereby hoping to secure his release from the asylum, where he might be of greater use to him.

28   Joseph S Bierman, 'Dracula: Prolonged Childhood Illness and the Oral Triad', and Seymour Shuster, 'Dracula and Surgically Induced Trauma in Children'.

29   Bierman, op. cit., pp.186-87.

30   In Shuster, p.259.

31   K A Menninger, 'Polysurgery and Polysurgical Addiction', in *Psychoanalysis* Q 3 (1934), p.173.

32   Shuster, p.259.

33   ibid., p.264. Shuster concedes that his hypothesis collapses if Stoker's infant disorders were treated at home. Farson insists that the primitive conditions of Irish hospitals at the time would have been a last resort for a respectable middle-class family (Daniel Farson, *The Man Who Wrote Dracula: A Biograpahy of Bram Stoker*, p.160).

34   Shuster, pp.266-67. Shuster's train of thought is speculative, to say the least, for example his attempts to link the name 'Dracula' with the abbreviation for 'Doctor' – both beginning with 'Dr'.

35   Bierman, op. cit., p.189.

36   ibid., p.193. The number 'seven' is regarded as special in Western symbolism. It features prominently in the Bible and classical astrology. Stoker would use the number in connection with Egyptology in *The Jewel of Seven Stars*.

37   See Bertram Lewin, *The Psychoanalysis of Elation*, p.118.

38   Bierman, op. cit., p.195.

39   ibid., p.196. Bierman makes a number of other observations. Regrettably they are dependent on the long-held belief that *Dracula* was conceived in 1895, rather than 1890, as is now known to be the case.

40   ibid., p.197.

41   Nandris, op. cit., pp.392-93.

11

'THE BLOOD IS THE LIFE'

'Now let me guard yourself. On your forehead I touch this piece of
Sacred Wafer in the name of the Father, the Son, and –.'
   There was a fearful scream which almost froze our hearts to hear.
As he placed the Wafer on Mina's forehead, it had seared it – had
burnt into the flesh as though it had been a piece of white-hot metal
… she wailed out: 'Unclean! Unclean! Even the Almighty shuns my
polluted flesh! I must bear this mark of shame upon my forehead
until the Judgment Day.'

Jonathan Harker's Journal,
Dracula 22:353.

It might seem superfluous to claim that *Dracula* is a Christian
parody. Everything that Christ is meant to be Dracula either
inverts or perverts. Christ is Good: Dracula is Evil – an agent of
the devil. Christ was a humble carpenter: Dracula a vainglorious
aristocrat. Christ offers light and hope, and was resurrected at
dawn: Dracula rises at sunset and thrives in darkness. Christ's
death at the 'stake' was the moment of his rebirth: for the vampire
the stake heralds 'death' and oblivion. Christ offered his own life
so that others might live: Dracula takes the lives of many so that
he might live. The blood of Christ is drunk at the Eucharist by the
faithful; Dracula reverses the process and drinks from *them*. Both
preach resurrection and immortality, the one offering spiritual
purity, the other physical excess. The link between Christ and
Dracula is made explicit through the Count's recoiling from
crucifixes, holy wafer, and other symbols of Christianity.
   A basic lesson of the novel was to reaffirm the existence of
God in an age when the weakening hold of Christianity generated
fresh debate about what lay beyond death. The marshalled diary
extracts and letters are themselves endowed with the status of

scripture. Instead of Gospels according to St Matthew and St Mark, we find Gospels according to Mr Harker and Dr Seward. Taken with Van Helsing's concluding remarks, 'We want no proofs' (D27:449), they constitute a 'revelation' of Dracula's existence, as the Bible offers a 'revelation' of Christ's.

In *Dracula*, faith in God is rewarded by incontrovertible evidence of His power, and the means to defeat the evil creature who seeks to usurp it. The book offers an exercise in syllogistic logic: a supposedly immortal fiend is destroyed by the defenders of Christ, armed above all with their faith. The conclusion therefore follows that God exists. What might not be so apparent are the depths to which the biblical allegory reaches. Dracula is replete with Christian imagery, so it is pertinent to commence this chapter by examining those passages that relate in some way to the Bible or to Christian liturgy.

Jonathan Harker dominates the book's opening sequences. His proposed coach journey to Castle Dracula provokes local consternation, particularly fear of the 'evil eye' (the sign of the devil), which must be averted at all costs. The expression has biblical origins: 'The light of the body is in the eye ... But if thine eye be evil, thy whole body shall be full of darkness' (Matthew 6:22-23). Harker's pilgrimage is planned for St George's Eve, acknowledged by the Romanian Orthodox Church at that time as falling on 4 May. According to legend, St George, a mythical 'saint', was as difficult to dispose of as vampires. Several times he was chopped up, buried or incinerated, but each time was resuscitated by God. This early reference in the novel to St George forges at the outset the interconnection between 'Dracul' (dragon) and 'Christian warrior'. Harker's sojourn sparks a Christian crusade against Dracula/the devil. Interestingly, Harker has to *ascend* to Dracula's castle, a reversal of the classical *descents* into hell of such mythical figures as Odysseus, Prosperine, and Orpheus.[1] But once Harker is imprisoned, the Count's vampirellas provide him with a glimpse of licentious heaven – not fire and brimstone, but an eternal dream-like ecstasy.

Dracula is all things to all people. To Lucy he is principally an irresistible lover; to Harker he is a feudal tyrant come to subvert

Britain; to Van Helsing he is in the service of the devil. Dracula might even be the Antichrist. There is some irony in the association: the Count reminds Mina that in his earlier life he campaigned against the Turks on behalf of Christianity (D21:343). The real Vlad Tepes, it will be remembered, actually died for that cause.

There are grounds for supposing Dracula to be cast as the Antichrist. The Antichrist plays a greater role in the Christian faith than its emphasis in the Bible warrants. Only briefly does the term appear explicitly, in the first and second letters of John (1 John 2:18, 22; 4:3; and 2 John 7), though the Antichrist has also been identified with the strange beasts and demons to be found in the Book of Revelation. There we encounter further reminders of the 'dragon-devil' connection: 'And the great dragon was thrown down, that ancient serpent, who is called the Devil and Satan' (Revelation 12:9). Some theologians conceive of the Antichrist not in personal terms, but as an attitude of mind; a collective evil inherent in those who deny the teachings of Christ. Those who believe in a personal Antichrist view him as a being 'who opposes and exalts himself against every so-called god or object of worship, so that he takes his seat in the temple of God, proclaiming himself to be God' (2 Thessalonians 2:4). Count Dracula fits the description.

On the one occasion that Dracula is permitted by Stoker to quote scripture, he alludes to the alienation of an Antichrist. In Transylvania he is a ruler, a boyar, but he would be a nobody in London – 'a stranger in a strange land' (D2:31), the very words of Moses's son, Gershom. There may be a connection here with Stoker's insistence that Dracula can sleep only in consecrated ground. His daily imitation of the true Christian dead may be an indication of his inner torment: he yearns to rest permanently among Christ's believers.[2] Perhaps Stoker is hinting at the powerful proximity between good and evil. Just as a thin line divides love and hate, genius and madness, so 'evil' is intimately allied to 'good'. More likely, Dracula's hotel arrangements are an innovation by Stoker designed to highlight the sense of blasphemy. The Count is not cast out from sacred places, but is a parasite upon them.

The Antichrist is usually depicted as the product of a living woman and a male demon. This focuses attention on young Quincey Harker, who is born thirteen months after Dracula's visits to his mother. Maybe Stoker is alluding to the terrors of the twentieth century when this infant reaches manhood.

If the novel hints at the Antichrist, Renfield emerges as a sort of anti-John the Baptist. Both lunatic and prophet are described as impatient, wild-looking figures, for whom the Messiah is not merely coming – he is here. With regard to Christianity, John the Baptist is 'the operative agent who sets the whole thing in motion'.[3] So it is with Renfield, who prepares the way for Dracula's coming and provides entry into Seward's asylum. The fate of both men is similar: John loses his head, while Renfield also dies of a head wound.

To reinforce his biblical credentials, Renfield is given most of the passages containing Christian symbolism. 'The blood is the life' is his clarion call, but his blood-drinking is a literal interpretation of what is a theological minefield. The Bible contains numerous references to the power of blood,[4] but Renfield overlooks one of their primary purposes as prohibiting the imitation of pagan sacrificial practice. Deuteronomy 12:23, for example, demands 'Be sure that you do not eat the blood; for the blood of the life, and you shall not eat the life with the flesh'.

On other occasions Renfield is less careless as to the context of his scriptural borrowings. He pronounces: 'The bride-maidens rejoice the eyes that wait the coming of the bride; but when the bride draweth nigh, then the maidens shine not to the eyes that are filled' (D8:125). Here he is borrowing John the Baptist's words when witnessing the coming of Christ: 'He that hath the bride is the bridegroom: but the friend of the bridegroom, which standeth and heareth him, rejoiceth because of the bridegroom's voice ...' (John 3:29). There are several explanations behind this reference in *Dracula*. Possibly the Count is the radiant bride, with Renfield the groom, and all his spiders as bride-maidens – made redundant by the coming of the bride.[5] More logically, Dracula is the bridegroom, with Lucy his future bride and Renfield the rejoicing bridesmaid.[6] Whatever the case, the union of two people in marriage in the sight of God is to be violated by Satan.

Renfield is ingenious enough to escape from his asylum, and is discovered whispering through the adjoining chapel wall: 'I am here to do your Bidding, Master. I am Your Slave, and You will reward me, for I shall be faithful. I have worshipped You long and afar off. Now that You are near, I await Your commands, and You will not pass me by will You, dear Master, in Your distribution of good things?' (D8:126). Here Renfield is clearly at prayer, and Stoker's use of capitalizing pronouns when the lunatic is referring to Dracula emphasizes the Count's divine status. When Seward recaptures his patient after a further escape, even he cannot resist reference to a biblical episode: he interprets Renfield's craving for flies and spiders as 'loaves and fishes' – though gathered solely for Renfield's selfish purpose.

When Renfield reflects upon his own relations with his messiah, it is not with John the Baptist that he draws a parallel, but with an Old Testament figure. 'I am, so far as concerns things purely terrestrial, somewhat in the position which Enoch occupied spiritually!' (D20:321). Enoch, the father of Methuselah, was said to have 'walked with God' (Genesis 5:18-24). Renfield expects to be Satan's (Dracula's) minion and to be granted immortality – as God presumably granted Enoch.

Throughout, Renfield is tempted by the devil, as was Christ. The Count, holding up his hands to control the rats, says to Renfield: 'All these will I give you, ay, and many more and greater, through countless ages, if you fall down and worship me!' (D21:333). Here Stoker is repeating Satan's exchange with Christ in the wilderness:

Then was Jesus led up by the Spirit into the wilderness to be tempted by the devil ... Again the devil took him to a very high mountain, and showed him all the kingdoms of the world, and the glory of them, and he said to him: 'All these I will give you, if you will fall down and worship me' (Matthew 4:1-9).

Jesus declined his offer with the rebuff 'Get thee hence, Satan'; Renfield responds: 'Come in, Lord and Master!' But later, angered by Dracula's attacks on Mina, he is prepared for martyrdom. He grapples with the Count, who has slipped into his cell as mist, knowing that lunatics are reputedly endowed with superhuman strength. His efforts here are a dark analogue of Jacob wrestling with the angel of the Lord (Genesis 32:24-25). Jacob's efforts are beneficial both to himself and the children of Israel, and even Renfield attains a spiritual, if not physical, victory from his struggle.[7]

As the principal shaman/priest of the novel, Van Helsing regularly resorts to biblical language. He makes use of the parable of the seed and the sower (D10:145-46; cf. Luke 8:5-8) to explain to Seward that, with regard to Lucy's ghastly malaise, all will be revealed in good time. The parable ends with the words 'He that hath ears to hear, let him hear', and to drive home the message Van Helsing tweaks his friend's ear. Faith, of course, is of the essence to the Dutchman. It is a curious kind of faith, as one might expect from a priest-figure who believes in vampires and the efficacy of pagan antidotes such as garlic. Few modern Christians would accept Van Helsing's definition of faith: 'that which enables us to believe things we know to be untrue' (D14:2332), for it comes close to suggesting that the intellect and the intuition can never act in concert. To Van Helsing, the existence of Dracula is on a par, logically speaking, with that of Christ.

Further indication of Van Helsing's oblique religious views arises with his (mis)use of Catholic relics. His application of certain tools of the Catholic faith is disrespectful at times, futile at others, and on occasions blasphemous.

Especially damaging are the liberties taken with core Catholic precepts. According to Catholic dogma, the sacred wafer is the body of Christ, and cannot be used in any profane manner, no matter what the ulterior motive.[8] The Host, which represents the risen body of Jesus, is intended as food for the faithful – not to be scattered around by the laity for their own purposes. Worse, Van Helsing makes a feeble attempt to legitimize his more extreme acts. Preparatory to the staking of Lucy he claims to have an indulgence (D16:252), to which he refers as if he has received Vatican *carte blanche* to desecrate graves and mutilate corpses. In Catholic theology an indulgence exempts from temporal punishment sins already perpetrated and forgiven. Van Helsing is claiming his indulgence for something he is about to do. Over the centuries fraudulent use of indulgences by Catholic clergy led to their widespread discredit. In any case, their use for the purposes Van Helsing has in mind could not possibly have been sanctioned.

Moreover, in the war against vampires the 'powers' of the crucifix and Communion Host are symbolic only – they serve to remind the faithful of Christ. When used as 'weapons', as if they possessed divine energy in themselves, they are properly objects of magic rather than religion. For that reason Van Helsing acts more like a magician than a scientist/priest.

Lucy's re-entry into the Christian fold does more than highlight Van Helsing's sacrilege. It provides further instance of Stoker linking pagan gods with the Christian God. The act of staking is not described as Christ-like, but as Thor-like (D16:259). The symbolic weapon of Thor, the Norse God of Thunder, happens to be a hammer. From reading Baring-Gould's *A Book of Folklore*, Stoker would have learned of an anecdote linking the Norse gods Thor, Wodin, and Loki, with the Father, the Son, and the Holy Ghost. The devil is nailed to a post with a hammer – the equivalent of staking a vampire.[9]

Evidence that Van Helsing is at heart a more orthodox Catholic than some of his activities suggest, surfaces when the stricken Mina proposes ending her own life. The professor's prohibitions are uncompromising: 'You must not die by any hand; but least of all by your own' (D22:346). He is referring not only to her consequent passage to the world of the un-dead: he is reminding her of the uncompromising Catholic doctrine that suicide is a mortal sin. Nor would he have overlooked the folkloric belief that suicides are candidates for vampirism. Mina would be merely precipitating her own fate.

Mina, herself, is not a Catholic.[10] Yet when she marries Jonathan in a Budapest convent/hospital she wraps his unopened diary and ties it with a blue ribbon as 'an outward and visible sign for us all our lives that we trusted each other' (D9:129-30). These words conform to Catholic symbolism, wherein the sacraments are outward, visible signs instituted by Christ to give grace.[11] Mina is deeply devout, reaching for biblical passages to assist in the expression of the world as she sees it. Early in the novel she prepares the ground for deeper Christian allegory when she notices distant figures on the beach at Whitby. They are described as 'men like trees walking' (D6:93) – the words of a blind man whose sight is restored by Jesus (Mark 8:22-25).

When she is first visited by Dracula she again refers to impaired vision. The Count arrives hidden by mist, prompting her to recall the scriptural phrase 'a pillar of cloud by day and of fire by night' (D19:309; cf. Exodus 40:34-38). The pillar guided the Hebrews across the desert. Mina is unsure of the reality behind her vision. Her brain begins to whirl. Is the spectre beneficent or malevolent? Too late she realizes it is not God who materializes, but the devil.

The graphically described blood exchanges between Dracula and Mina consummates her 'religious' experience. The forcing of her mouth upon his open breast reminds us of the medieval use of the pelican to symbolize Christ's passion; the pelican being fabled for its supposed habit of opening a vein in its breast in order to feed its young. By imbibing the blood of a man-god, Mina is performing a most ritualistic form of cannibalism.

This blood exchange is the second marriage 'ceremony' realized in the novel. First, it was Lucy who took four 'husbands' by receiving their blood; now it is Mina who 'marries' Dracula by receiving his. The Count performs a demonic corruption of the Christian marriage service. Mina has become 'flesh of my flesh; blood of my blood; kin of my kin; my beautiful wine-press for a while; and shall later on be my companion and my helper' (D21:343). He is paraphrasing the words of the Catholic marriage service, taken from Ephesians 5:28, 31.

> So also ought men to love their wives as their own bodies ... for we are members of His body, of His flesh, and of His bones ... For this cause shall a man leave his father and mother, and shall cleave to his wife; and they shall be two in one flesh.

Dracula's words also hint at a re-enactment of Adam and Eve. Deciding that Adam should not live alone, God created a 'helper'; similarly Dracula wants Mina as his 'helper'. When Eve is created out of Adam's ribs it is Adam who says: 'This at last is bone of my bones and flesh of my flesh.' Like Eve before her, Eve has become a 'biological' wife. Furthermore, just as Christ's blood was shed to save humanity, so here Dracula feeds Mina with his own to grant her immortality as a vampire. He performs a devilish communion with the solitary member of his congregation, reversing the process of transubstantiation. Instead of wine being converted into blood, blood is transubstantiated into wine (Mina being his wine-press). By fusing this profane marriage service with Mina's 'baptism of blood', Stoker indicts the Count as an agent of the devil out to pervert all the Christian sacraments.[12]

Mina's torment has an even more terrible sequel. Her anguish is caused less by the fact of her sin than by a visible reminder of it. Christian symbols in *Dracula* are not confined to weapons against the Count, but extend to marks on the body. Not content with stealing Harker's wife, Dracula wishes to settle accounts with the solicitor who inflicted an unsightly scar on his forehead. With that mark, Dracula resembles the 'beast' (Antichrist?) from the Book of Revelation. The beast is sent to earth by the devil, and may be recognized by a mortal head wound which has apparently healed (Revelation 13:3).

When Van Helsing places the sacred wafer upon Mina's forehead it brands her. From now on she is visibly identified with Dracula, and again Stoker seems to have borrowed from Revelation: 'If any one worships the beast and its image, and receives a mark on [her] forehead ... [she] shall drink the wine of God's wrath ... and shall be tormented with fire and brimstone in the presence of the holy angels' (Revelation 14:9-10). The Old Testament offers parallels of its own, for both Dracula and Mina now display the mark of Cain, son of Adam and Eve. Cain killed his brother, Abel, the first act of murder by mankind. Because Cain refused to repent, God decreed he should become a fugitive and wanderer of the earth (undead?). To prevent anyone putting an end to his misery, God placed a distinctive mark upon him (Genesis 4:1-15). That mark is traditionally thought to have been on the forehead.

Mina's desperate cry of 'Unclean, Unclean!' was linked in a previous chapter with menstruation. Now, upon having her flesh seared, she utters the words again, provoking reminders in husband (D22:353) of the biblical leper:

> The leper who has the disease shall wear torn clothes and let the hair on his head hang loose, and he shall cover his upper lip and cry 'Unclean, unclean'. He shall remain unclean as long as he has the disease; he is unclean; he shall dwell alone in a habitation outside the camp. (Leviticus 13:45-46)

This reflects Mina's predicament precisely. She is an outcast from God, and will remain so until such time as the cause of her plight is destroyed. She seems aware of the leper analogy herself: 'Even the Almighty shuns my polluted flesh.' Over the next weeks she comes to feel abandoned and shunned by God: 'As for me, I am not worthy in His sight. Alas! I am unclean to His eyes, and shall be until He may deign to let me stand forth in His sight as one of those who have not incurred His wrath' (D27:430). The modern reader may be puzzled by this. Mina, the walking angel, has done nothing intentionally to incur God's wrath. She takes a severe view of Christianity: perhaps she assumes that because she 'did not want to hinder' Dracula she is culpable of her adulterous union, even though it is manifestly beyond human capacity to resist the vampire: Stoker's notes confirm that Dracula is able to induce evil thoughts in others. As Lucy has discovered previously, in God's eyes innocence is no defence. In the tribunal of heaven, there is no such thing as a plea of honourable intent. The battle now turns to save Mina's soul, and one wonders whether Stoker realized that, spelled backwards, 'Mina' almost replicates the Latin word for 'soul' – 'anima'. (Le Fanu also employed anagrams for Carmilla.[13]) Mina's soul will be saved and the mark will disappear only at the climax of the novel, when Quincey Morris assumes the Christ-like role of dying for her sin.[14]

The battle for Mina's soul is waged with Catholic implements. Stoker might take liberties with the uses to which they are put, but it is nevertheless the Catholic Church which, in the end, is vindicated. The 'open mind' which Van Helsing demands – embracing superstition, science and faith – leads not only to a literal belief in vampires, but also to the demonstrable power of

Catholic relics in exterminating them. The path to God is thereby shown to be not that of Luther, but that of Rome. The question is not asked, let alone answered, but what must this devout Protestant community have believed when all was over? Harker once held crucifixes to be 'idolatrous' (D1:15), and Seward for much of the book refuses to believe anything that cannot be verified by scientific rigour. Yet Harker soon comes to appreciate the gift of a little cross (D3:40), and when in possession of crucifix and holy wafer during a confrontation with the Count, Seward admits to experiencing 'a mighty power fly along my arm' (D23:364). Are Harker and Seward converted to the Catholic faith once they discover its tangible truth? Perhaps it is just as well that Stoker, likewise a confirmed Protestant, chose not to confront the issue.

One other aspect pertaining to the religious inferences of *Dracula* deserves attention. Christianity is predicated on the fact of evil. Dracula is the naked presence of that evil. He is not like the other wicked characters of Victorian fiction: Fagin, for example, is a saint by comparison. Dracula is Evil, and the injunction to destroy him permits, indeed commands, no half-measures. The 'mercy-bearing' staking of Lucy has nothing to do with mercy, but everything to do with expediency. Unless Lucy is staked she will snare more children, maturing as a vampire before targeting her loved-one, Arthur. The Christian faith is evoked not merely to exorcise the threat of the undead; Christianity also rationalizes the 'murder' of the vampires. Van Helsing is the Witch-Finder General returned. The self-assurance is overpowering: Christ *must* be on the side of Dracula's pursuers. Therefore they *must* be right, and have been granted divine licence to perform whatever atrocities they please. A diabolical foe demands diabolical counter-measures. Van Helsing sets out on his quest with the zeal of a nineteenth-century Inquisitor – as he admits (D17:262).

Van Helsing's role as chief Inquisitor ties in neatly with the era of Vlad the Impaler: Vlad had not been dead twenty years when the *Malleus Maleficarum* unleashed the Holy Inquisition. This has the effect of placing *Dracula* simultaneously in two different time scales – the fifteenth and the nineteenth centuries.

At this point let us take a closer look at what Van Helsing interprets as Dracula's malevolence. Stoker's skill lies in creating an aura of evil around his master demon which it is instructive to clarify. It is what Dracula *is*, rather than what he *does*, that strikes terror into the hearts of these representatives of civilized England. Stoker is playing to a gallery culturally conditioned into accepting the sources of its fears. In the opening section of the novel Harker's alarm stems from the realization that he is confronted with an unnatural (he is not yet sure it is 'supernatural') presence. No ordinary man can command wolves, or is eccentric enough to climb face down the castle wall rather than use the stairs. Dracula's appearance might be off-putting, but the solicitor's mounting unease is occasioned by very 'human' observations in his host – such as his volatile, capricious personality. Dracula is all charm and grace, interspersed with spontaneous outbursts of hatred and rage. As already proposed, Harker's real anxiety is instilled by the vampire women: Dracula has no premeditated malice in mind where his guest is concerned.

Paradoxically, Dracula actually *does* very little to merit the vendetta against him. Instances of his cruelty mostly take place in or around his castle, where he is not answerable to the law: he *is* the law. Like Vlad Tepes in life, the fictional vampire-king is lord and master of his native land, and rules with an iron fist. Once in England, moreover, Dracula is the perfect law-abiding citizen, because to be otherwise would make him conspicuous and threaten his purpose. He has laboured to learn British values and customs. His house purchases are meticulously above board. It could almost be said he performs no violence (except in self-defence)[15] or indeed any other offence. His chief crime is to 'seduce' women who are not at all determined to resist him.

Furthermore, once they have turned into vampires, the women he recruits seem not displeased with their new existence, so why the crusade to 'release' them? On the face of it, immortality and perpetually aroused libido do not warrant alarm: quite the contrary. Van Helsing, however, insists that he alone knows what is right and proper: Lucy cannot really want to be a vampire, though a closer reading suggests she might. Although the reader is conditioned to sympathize with a distressed, God-fearing community, from another perspective Dracula is being hunted for what comes naturally to him – as foxes are hunted because their hunting is inimical to the interests of the farmer. Over the years, foxes have come to be associated with negative attributes – slyness, cunning – simply because they compete for the farmers' livestock, keep out of the way of his guns, and undertake their marauding at night. There is something comparable in the circumstances of the 'cunning' Dracula.

In Van Helsing's world view there is no room for 'foxes', or for radical, heretical minority groups as epitomized by Dracula and his acolytes. Would their numbers not enlarge – in the manner of other heretical sects – unless rigorously persecuted? *Dracula* strikes terror because Christian precepts of heaven and hell, good and evil, exist not just in the book: they also exist in its readers. The horror of the former depends for its impact on the preconceptions of the latter. Another age or another culture less imbued with Christian dogma might fail to perceive Dracula's religious challenge. Indeed, his global appeal stems less from the Christian angle and more from the psychological: he symbolizes fear of darkness and of the unknown.

It is to the Christian perception of the 1890s that we now turn. Charles Darwin's *Origin of Species* was published when Stoker was a child. Darwin's theory of natural selection contributed to a widespread crisis of faith in late nineteenth-century Britain. The mechanics of Darwin's thesis were almost a side issue: what was at stake was the previously unquestioned belief in the Bible as the direct word of God. By the 1890s, many educated Protestants had come to accept that a literal interpretation of the Bible was incompatible with the findings of science, though the Catholic Church remained outwardly sceptical of evolutionist principles.

The influence of Darwinian thinking on *Dracula* can be observed at several levels. The Count is nature personified – red in tooth and claw. He does not 'love his neighbour' in the way Christian *agape* is espoused by his pursuers. Later evolutionists, like T H Huxley, believed that all living things were reducible to a basic chemistry. Man is not separate or unique. Trees, plants, insects, birds, animals, and humans all share a common proto-plasm that is the physical basis of earthly life. Any living entity may derive nourishment from consuming any other. Now Renfield's behaviour becomes more comprehensible. Huxley almost prefigures Renfield's insight: 'I used to fancy that life was a perpetual and positive entity, and that by consuming a multitude of living things, no matter how low in the scale of creation, one might indefinitely prolong life' (D18:279-80). Like his patron, Renfield is embarked on an idiosyncratic quest for the survival of the fittest through consuming living creatures. The she-vampires similarly devour living beings. As an aside, Victorian research into protoplasm sought to identify life within primordial ooze; one imaginary species of which was termed 'vampurella'.[16]

Philosophically, Huxley and other evolutionists preached 'materialism'; the belief that everything is reducible to matter. There is no God, nor is there a soul. Materialists denied the existence of free will and immortality, viewing brain activity as nothing more than chemical turbulence, with no detached soul or spirit to direct this activity. Materialism therefore contradicted the essence of Christianity – personal dualism, body and soul. *Dracula* perverts Christian teaching, particularly that of St Paul. The Count dares to offer immortality – not of the soul, but of the body. Even theologians and philosophers express difficulty with the concept of 'soul': no wonder the mind of poor Renfield cannot cope with its implications (D20:320-22). He, imitating Dracula, is preoccupied only with immortality of the body. It is towards that end that his ingestion of protoplasm (flies and spiders) is directed, until its philosophical repercussions leave him bewildered and confused.

Dracula, of course, is an active materialist, for whom all phenomena are simply examples of matter in motion. Like all vampires, the Count is shorn of a soul, physical existence being all that concerns him. Stoker self-evidently does believe in souls, and his novel takes the appearance of a protest – however veiled – against the blasphemies of Darwin and Huxley. But while Stoker would have dismissed with contempt materialism as applied to humans, he is bound to admit it for his vampires. Lacking a soul and operating entirely physically, Dracula – in common with all lower forms of life – can have no free will. Vampire courtship has been likened to that of the amoeba: the victim 'sinks deeper and deeper into the soft unyielding mass, and becomes dissolved, digested and assimilated in order that it may increase the size and restore the energy of its captor.'[17]

Dracula's choice upon death to become a vampire signalled his last act of conscious volition. As a vampire, he is a driven machine, with Satan at the wheel. Though Van Helsing's crusade is directed against conscious evil, according to Stoker's premise Dracula can possess no free will. In the courts of Britain, Count Dracula would escape culpability on the grounds of diminished responsibility. Perhaps it is because Van Helsing knows the futility of legal redress that he feels compelled to take the law into his own hands.

One controversy arising from evolutionary debate was the focus on apes, from whom, it was maintained, man was descended. Apes thus became objects of ridicule. Civilized man was demeaned by the association, for apes were 'characterized primarily by hairiness and horniness'.[18] The myth of the virile ape survives in many cultures – King Kong being an example from our own. What was true of apes, it seemed, was now levelled at humans: 'the male of the species is characterized by cupidity, pugnacity and a simian inclination for the other sex.'[19] For decent folk, it was not merely the claimed biological relationship to apes that appalled, it was disgust at being reminded of their rampant and undisciplined sexuality.

Christian opponents of evolutionism tried to impede the popularizing of science. Zoos became suspect, offering an open window on monkeys perennially playing with themselves – or one another. Darwinism was held responsible for the encouragement of vice and licentiousness. Lust stemmed directly from idleness. No wonder the devil found work for idle hands. Count Dracula, with his ape-like hairy palms and pointed ears, shares with apes their lack of soul and their heightened erotic instincts.

In 1889, the year before Stoker began work on Dracula, a scientific work appeared which proposed a further link between Darwin and the coming Count. The thesis contended that evolution was not necessarily progressive. Retrogressive metamorphosis might occur, leading to the development of parasitic forms. As applied to higher animals:

Any new set of conditions occurring to an animal which render its food and safety very easily attained, seems to lead, as a rule, to Degeneration; just as an active, healthy man sometimes degenerates when he suddenly becomes possessed of a fortune; or as Rome degenerated when possessed of the riches of the ancient world ... It is possible for us [humans] to reject the good gift of reason with which every child is born, and to degenerate into a contented life of material enjoyment accompanied by ignorance and superstition.[20]

Dracula is such a degenerate, 'offering to his followers the power of pleasure, eternal carnal fun, here and now – not as in Christian eschatology, spiritual integration later and somewhere unmapped. In the kingdom of heaven which the Count endeavours to establish there are no disembodied souls strumming on harps, but rather fleshy beings whose business is pleasure'.[21]

Blinderman describes Count Dracula as part Vlad Tepes, part Elizabeth Bathory, part lamia, part werewolf, part bat – and part 'Darwinian Superman'.[22] Carried to its ultimate degree, social Darwinism paved the way for a literal 'superman'. 'Survival of the fittest' might be Dracula's anthem: the strong and the brave prosper, while the weak and cowardly perish. This, it should be noted, was as true of Vlad Dracula as of Count Dracula.

The 'superman' concept is central to the writings of Stoker's contemporary, the German philosopher Nietzsche. The key to Nietzsche's superman is the aristocrat – superior to the masses on account of bloodline, education, and environment. Common people are of no consequence, being like Dracula's 'sheep in a row', and have no purpose other than to nourish the excellence of the élite. Their suffering is of no account if it contributes to the well-being of that élite. 'Trivial people suffer trivially: great men suffer greatly.' Nietzsche espoused the purifying virtues of war, ruthlessness, and aristocratic *noblesse oblige*, while abhorring wishy-washy British liberalism and the celebration of compassion as preached by that 'fatal and seductive lie', Christianity. Human progress is attainable solely by the single-minded 'will to power'. Dracula might almost be Nietzsche's prototype 'superman'.

Professor Van Helsing, Stoker's prototype medico-scientist-philosopher, would have read Nietzsche and Darwin. Part of his long-term fear would have been the prospect of a biological catastrophe. The Count's hoped-for 'family' in England would propagate an incestuous community genetically interrelated through his blood. His immortality and his evil would be disseminated far and wide through a genetically deformed sub-species. Likewise, Van Helsing acknowledges the principle of 'species improvement': when selecting blood donors for Lucy's transfusions, all are intelligent, moneyed, and privileged. Not once does he turn to the parlour-maids to help out by opening their veins. Stoker, too, expresses Darwinian sentiments. Charles Darwin had written: 'There is apparently much truth in the belief that the wonderful progress of the United States, as well as the character of the people, are the results of natural selection.' Stoker would have agreed emphatically, as Seward's evaluation of Quincey Morris confirms: 'If America can go on breeding men like that, she will be a power in the world indeed' (D131:209).

Blinderman sums up the evolutionist angle on *Dracula*. The book 'presents a contest between two evolutionary options: the ameliorative, progressive, Christian congregation, or the Social Darwinian superman in the form of the ultimate parasitic degenerate, Count Dracula'. The novel represents a microcosm of decadent late nineteenth-century England faced with the threat of an evolutionary apocalypse.[23]

---

1   Leonard Wolf, *The Annotated Dracula*, p.14.
2   ibid., p.215.
3   Paul Johnson, *A History of Christianity*, p.20.
4   The 'blood' of Christ is mentioned in the New Testament nearly three times as frequently as the 'Cross', and five times as frequently as the 'death' of Christ. There is theological dispute as to whether the biblical use of 'blood' refers to 'life' or 'death'.
5   Wolf, op. cit., p.100.
6   Raymond T McNally and Radu Florescu, *The Essential Dracula*, p.111.
7   Wolf, op. cit., p.248.
8   See Wolf, op. cit., pp.188-89.
9   Wolf, op. cit., p.194.
10 This is not explicit, but presumed from her marriage to non-Catholic Harker by an Anglican chaplain.

11   Wolf, op. cit., 104.

12   Wolf, op. cit., pp.301, 319.

13   Carmilla also answered to Mircalla and Millarca.

14   See McNally and Florescu, op. cit., p.227.

15   This apology for Dracula requires giving him the benefit of many doubts. It is not clear whether he is responsible for the disappearance of the crew of the *Demeter*, while the death of old Mr Swales at Whitby could be attributable to his blocking access to the grave of a suicide, where Dracula must sleep (D:7.109).

16   C S Blinderman, 'Vampurella: Darwin and Count Dracula', p.418. Much of the remainder of this chapter draws heavily on Blinderman's excellent and original article.

17   G J Allman, in Blinderman, p.418.

18   Blinderman, pp.420-21.

19   Stuart P Sherman, in Blinderman, p.421.

20   E Ray Lankester, *Degeneration: A Chapter in Darwinism*, pp.18-19, 32.

21   Blinderman, p.426.

22   ibid., p.413.

23   ibid., pp.427-28.

12

THE TAROT AND THE GRAIL

> *Dracula* is, like most major Gothics, a book given to symbols and images archetypal in its design. Like the other big Gothics, it is a book of myth, a book which mirrors consistently and insistently in its use of metaphor and in its meaning certain truths of the human spirit ... Most Gothics end happily, and *Dracula* is no exception ... The happiness of [its] ending is that [it] ends in knowledge – thus the happy ending of *Dracula*, of the Fool's Quest in the Tarot, of any story in which the Quester comes home.
>
> Thomas Ray Thornburg,
> 'The Quester and the Castle', pp.167-68.

To present *Dracula*'s religious dimension as simply a series of biblical parodies is to over-simplify. A further aspect of the novel transcends the God-devil, good-evil dichotomy. Thornburg has suggested: 'As a compendium of ancient arcana, *Dracula* knows few rivals in fiction, and as a work of art which demonstrates the properties of world myth and archetype, and the diabolical reversal thereof, the book has no equal'.[1] Through *Dracula*, Bram Stoker delves into the world of the arcane and of myth, illustrating his deep familiarity with its occult and literary expression.

Where better to search for Stoker's hidden symbols than in the mysteries of the Tarot cards?[2] No one is confident about their origins, representations, or meanings. Modern packs probably evolved from various sources and traditions – Christian, gnostic, Islamic, Celtic and Norse – though one school of thought claims that the arcane wisdom of the Tarot originated from ancient Egypt. Bram Stoker's knowledge of Egyptology was expressed in *The Jewel of Seven Stars*, and his wider occult interests remove sensible doubts about his familiarity with the Tarot.

The cards themselves can be put to several uses. Most familiar is their occult reputation as guides for divination. They can, however, also be used for playing games: they are precursors of modern playing cards. A tarot deck comprises seventy-eight cards divided into two series. It is the larger, Minor Arcana, that resembles the familiar modern pack, being arranged into four suits each numbered one to ten, plus Jack, Knight, Queen, and King.

To relate the Tarot to *Dracula*, we turn to the twenty-two cards of the Major Arcana – the Trumps. Occultists hold that these cards embody a systematic key to the mysteries of the universe, and the path to be taken to acquire this knowledge. The Major Arcana lays down a secret language of initiation, whose mysteries the quester after self-knowledge must comprehend. These cards are numbered 1-21, with an extra card – *The Fool* – unnumbered, but usually placed first. The negative aspect of *The Fool* – *The Joker* – survives in the modern pack of cards. The Major Arcana of the Tarot is as follows:

	The Fool	XI	Fortitude
	The Fool	XI	Fortitude
I	The Magician	XII	The Hanged Man
II	The Papess	XIII	Death
III	The Empress	XIV	Temperance
IV	The Emperor	XV	The Devil
V	The Pope	XVI	The Tower
VI	The Lovers	XVII	The Star
VII	The Chariot	XVIII	The Moon
VIII	Justice	XIX	The Sun
IX	The Hermit	XX	The Day of Judgment
X	The Wheel of Fortune	XXI	The World

Taken sequentially, these cards symbolize the classical gnostic quests, of the kind featured in myths and legends around the world – for example, the divinely assisted quest of Jason and the Argonauts for the Golden Fleece. The 'hero' journeys forth, encountering hazards of all kinds, progressing stage by stage on a voyage through life towards the goal of redemption. The cards are capable of multiple interpretation, hence their enduring fascination. It is nevertheless possible to take personalities and themes from *Dracula* and subject them to the symbolism of the Major Arcana. The cards feature an image of a ruined castle, which dominates the novel's opening and conclusion. The cross, too, is represented in the Tarot, as are cutting and thrusting images pertinent to the phenomenon of vampirism.

Let us start with *The Fool*. This depicts a man on the edge of a precipice surrounded by mountains. He is ready to step out into the supreme adventure, accompanied only by his 'Dick Whittington' bag on a stick and a small dog. *The Fool* is Everyman, the ordinary person, faced with the trials of encountering new worlds in his search for the meaning of life. Jonathan Harker is an archetypal example of the questing Fool. He is inexperienced, naïve, yet not without an inner sense of expectation that opens his mind to new experiences, such as travelling alone to the primitive wastes of Transylvania. *The Fool* frequently embarks upon his quest by accident: the undertaking is rarely planned. Sure enough, Harker packs his bags only because gout prevented his employer making the trip himself (D2:27). Likewise, *The Fool* is often given advice or warnings which he either fails to understand or prefers to ignore. Protective figures appear, who provide godly assistance, such as the crucifix pressed upon the solicitor by an old woman. Harker's determination to keep his rendezvous with Dracula, when every instinct tells him to delay or flee, marks him down as a common 'fool', never mind its meaning for the Tarot.

The Fool has a long path to tread in his spiritual journey. He may not even be aware that he is embarked on such a journey. To assist him, he encounters *The Magician* – card No 1 of the Major Arcana. *The Magician* is an adept, a semi-wise man blessed with a degree of understanding. *The Magician* is exceedingly confident, believing that his wishes are those of God. He thinks of himself as the link between God and the creative will of man, and he appears at the appropriate hour, when *The Fool* has most need of him. *The Magician*, brandishing a wand (stake?), is Abraham Van Helsing, 'the scientist-turned-magician'[3] – armed with his faith in the practices of folklore and witchcraft. Only with Van Helsing's support can Harker proceed with his quest.

Later, *The Fool* encounters *The Empress*. This is the blueprint for Mina. *The Empress* is the matronly mother goddess, descendant of other earth goddesses, like *Demeter*. She represents universal fertility, and is a reminder of the multi-fatherhood of Mina's son. The powers of *The Empress* are passive, stereotypically feminine: she has not the active intellect of *The Magician*. She is intuitive, with highly developed values. She is warm, helpful, and stable, gifted at handling people – as Mina is with Renfield.

Further along his questing path, *The Fool* must make the decision of *The Lovers*. In some versions, this card depicts a young man alongside two women, one young and fair, the other older and dark. Possibly he must choose between the 'good' and the 'evil' woman. Possibly, too, he must decide between remaining at home with his mother or departing with his beloved – the classical Oedipal dilemma. It is the moment when the bird flees the nest, leaving comfort and security behind for the excitement of the unknown. In fact, there are many 'lovers' in Dracula, and the card caters both to *Eros* (Lucy, Mina, and their menfolk) and *agape* (brotherly love which binds the whole group together). The card posits a reversal of pleasurable love, hinting at Adam and Eve and the evil which visited them in the Garden of Eden. This might be applied to the anguish of Lucy and Arthur, parted irrevocably from one another.

The next relevant card is No IX. From Stoker's working notes we know Van Helsing was created as a composite figure, combining the talents of scientist, philosopher, detective. Appropriately, *The Hermit* can also be applied to the Dutchman, for both are solitary and austere. *The Hermit* is the ancient looking down from on high, following the flame that burns within him, along the road that leads he knows not where. He seeks answers to the questions that plague him, and like the professor feels driven by duty. His negative side is reflected in stubborn dogmatism. Neither *The Hermit* nor Van Helsing can conceive of answers outside the framework of their thoughts. This sums up the professor: magician, hermit, and bigot.

Thornburg has this to say about the next card: '*The Wheel of Fortune*' is significant for *Dracula*, and for the Gothic generally, in that this card shows the universal balance of things demonic and apocalyptic, diabolic and divine.'[4] The card projects conflicting images – the beast from Revelation – and highlights the cycles of life and death, growth and decay. *The Wheel of Fortune* constitutes a turning point in the ritual of the Tarot. Ahead of *The Fool* (Harker) lie paths of darkness, which he must follow if he seeks enlightenment. The card corresponds to a crossroads in *Dracula*, when Van Helsing assures Harker he experienced neither nightmare nor insanity. His mind is sound. Harker now joins the pack hunting Dracula.

The Hanged Man is one of the most mysterious of the Major Arcana, for the 'victim' – hanging by one foot – wears an expression of contemplation rather than suffering. Thornburg identifies this with the torpor that descends upon Harker after his Transylvanian escape.[5] On another reading, *The Hanged Man* symbolizes bodily death as a prelude to rebirth, a prerequisite of the gnostic quest. *The Hanged Man* may be embarked on self-sacrifice, paving the way to immortality of the spirit. This is the function performed in the novel by Quincey Morris.

Faced with *Death*, the Count's pursuers reach a new understanding of its meaning. The Tarot interpretation of *Death*, however, is less a pronouncement of termination than of transformation. Death, in other words, is at one and the same time a process of destruction and creation – which is exactly how Dracula views it. Some versions of the card portray a skeleton, behind which is a setting sun – the moment of Dracula's expiry.

According to the Tarot, *The Devil* is the purveyor of lust, pride, and ambition; the possessor of unbridled passions and seeker of mastery over earthly things. He symbolizes misused power: he is as savage as nature, a fountain of temptation and the personification of evil. Aside from bat-wings, some versions include hairs on the palms of his hands. He also bears marks upon his flesh, including (like Dracula) an inverted pentagram on his forehead. Further, the card shows a man and a woman, apparently chained one on each side of him. In *Dracula* they are represented by Renfield and Lucy Westenra. It is the function of the card to remind *The Fool* that he must ultimately do battle with *The Devil*. If he wins he will enjoy a special relationship with God.

The concluding five cards of the Major Arcana deserve brief comment. *The Star* illustrates all that is potentially good; the expectancy of a happy future after the encounter with *The Devil*. A young girl on her knees pours water from urns held in each hand. She is Mother Nature, refurbishing the fountain of life. This situation is reversed in *Dracula*, for Harker has not brought 'life' to barren Transylvania. Instead he has set free the powers of darkness that seek to despoil his native England.

The Moon has inferences for Renfield's 'lunacy', for his moods fluctuate with moonrise and sunrise, so that Seward comes to suspect their influence on him (D9:143). Dracula, too, reverses the mythical solar god: it is darkness that lends him strength and the moon that symbolizes his evil. One version of the card offers what looks like a werewolf howling up at the moon, a reminder of the primitive, unconscious fears associated with moonlight.

Next comes *The Sun*, characterized by a naked child riding a white horse bareback under a warm sun. This is the child of Enlightenment. He is rid of the trappings of conventional thought and identifies with the life process of the universe. The child is man: the man is child, reaching out, confident and joyous. He is the reward for earthly love and the symbol of life's renewal. The child is the Harkers' son. (Other versions show two people in an enclosing ring, like the magic circle within which Van Helsing and Mina shelter as they approach Castle Dracula.)

The Day of Judgment depicts floating coffins, out of which a man, a woman, and a divine child rise up with their arms outstretched. An archangel hovers above with his summoning trumpet. This card is associated with renewal; death followed by resurrection. Thornburg takes this to reflect the destruction of the undead and the expression of peace which comes over them at that moment.[6]

The final card of the Major Arcana is *The World*, representing the culmination of *The Fool*'s quest. It denotes release and fulfilment, the attainment of Knowledge and Understanding. The Harker who strides the land following his destruction of Dracula is a different Harker from the one who began his diary on his fateful expedition six months previously. A youthful figure appears within a circular wreath. The figure is androgynous, a veil draped across his/her groin. Its sex is immaterial, its self is unity, a symbol of psychic wholeness. Many exponents of the Tarot interpret the Major Arcana not as a sequence, but as a circle. *The Fool* appears not just at the start, but also at the end, which is another beginning. This time it is young Harker Junior who will one day embark upon the quest for Truth.

This has necessarily been a cursory excursion through the symbolism of the Tarot, yet what is apparent even from this brief reading is that in *Dracula* the ritualistic quest is reversed: it is diabolical rather than divine. The summons that sends Harker off on the journey to open Pandora's Box is issued by the devil, not by God. But as Thornburg notes: 'Although Harker seeks to refuse the diabolical call, the effect upon his psyche is virtually that which is visited upon those who refuse the divine call'.[7] Harker's mind disintegrates once he has released evil upon the world, and the novel pursues its gradual reintegration.

From the perspective of the Tarot, the focus of *Dracula* lies less with the malevolent Count than with a Fool's quest, that of a young solicitor unknowingly directed upon the ultimate spiritual journey. A second, more evident, source for the quest motif in *Dracula* derives from quintessentially British origins. Victorian literature was intoxicated by the great Romantic myths, not least the quest of the Arthurian knights for the Holy Grail. What started out as a legend of gallantry at a time when post-Roman Britain sought a mythical saviour to fend off the Saxon hordes, became endowed over the centuries with ever more complex embellishments. Writers and poets contributed to the skeletal story with tales of jousting, chivalrous knights, the Round Table, courtly romance, and the search for the Holy Grail. No longer did the knights do battle for earthly reward, but for the goal of spiritual truth.

The Holy Grail is identified as the chalice drunk by Christ at the last supper, which was then used to collect his blood at the Crucifixion. Afterwards the chalice disappeared. In romantic fiction it became an object of intense desire for those prepared to search for it. Some versions declare that it gives off light and perfume, that it can heal the wounded, and induce a sense of well-being similar to that of Holy Communion. Sinners can never set eyes upon the Grail; only Arthur's gallant knights may approach it, and they are bound by secrecy. The Grail's mysteries are held to transcend life and death, and its awesome power brings dire misfortune upon anyone who betrays its secret. The Grail manifests the expression of blood worship, and at some stage the legend evidently came into contact with the Tarot. Both represent archetypal quests for the seeker after hidden knowledge. Moreover, the symbols of the Grail all but duplicate the suits of the Minor Arcana. These are cups, batons, swords, and coins in the case of the Tarot; chalice, lance, sword, and platter according to the Grail.

The Grail legend evolved from pagan conceptions of the cauldron of fertility. The theme is enmeshed with primitive preoccupations with life and death, as revealed by the cyclical effects of the seasons. Nature itself is the inspiration behind resurrection following upon death. Vegetation sprouts, withers, dies, then grows again as spring moves through autumn and back to spring. As man is dependent on this cycle for survival, fertility rites came to be performed, with crop-spirits revered and appeased as necessary. As corn was the staple of settled peoples, so corn-gods came to dominate communal religious practice.

Arthurian romance similarly wove itself into the cycle of nature. The Round Table, for example, is emblematic of cyclical death and rebirth. Central to this feature is the introduction of the 'Fisher King'. Some interpretations maintain that the Grail is held in custody in a mysterious castle. The guardian monarch suffers a a spear-thrust through the thigh, a euphemism for castration. The king is unable to govern and his constituency is laid barren and waste (the 'wasteland'). The cycle of rebirth is broken. His kingdom perishes, so the king turns for solace to fishing – the Fisher King. His health and the fertility of his kingdom can be restored only when his wound has been healed by a sinless quester after the Grail. Until that moment, the Grail's powers are suspended. In more recent accounts, the name 'Fisher King' may be loosely applied to any ruler whose virility is linked to the fertility of the land. Any misfortune befalling him – illness, injury, impotence – reflects his own sterility upon his kingdom. Only his restoration may bring verdure back to the 'wasteland'.

Many of these ideas can be discerned in *Dracula*. For one thing, Stoker employs the agricultural calendar, reversing the traditional death and rebirth cycle, so that the novel opens in the spring and concludes in the autumn. Like some malign vegetation, the Count begins to blossom in May and, like the leaves on the trees, returns to dust and is blown away in November. The book's cyclical structure extends even to its geography; opening in Transylvania, blooming in London, and returning to its source for the conclusion. So conscious is Stoker that the beginning should mirror the end that, at the climax, he makes Van Helsing and Mina retrace the precise route traversed by Jonathan Harker six months previously.

Stoker names the ship that carries Dracula to England the *Demeter*. The name was evidently chosen with care.

> Demeter was an earth [corn] goddess and the mother of Persephone; when Persephone was stolen by Hades, Demeter wandered over the earth in search of her, but when Persephone was found Demeter had to strike a bargain with Hades that Persephone stay with him for six months of the year. Thus one has a mythological rendering in the story of Demeter of the origins of the seasons, connected with the king of the underworld. Hades ... Demeter and Persephone, before the Hades incident, lived in a pastoral garden, unspoiled by winter and want. Hades' interference changed the world from a pastoral summer paradise to its present seasonal alternation ... The meaning of Dracula's passage by the *Demeter* underscores the dire threat of Dracula's intention to destroy the pastoral vitality, fertility, and beauty of the West.[8]

Dracula flouts nature through his every essence: 'as an undead he both transcends and subverts the order of natural law, the returning to dust of all mankind according to God's plan. Dracula exists apart from the chain of being:. He might be described as a kind of anti-creation opposing the natural life-to-death cycle of human existence.'[9]

These cyclical dimensions to *Dracula* may be explored by reference to Arthurian grail romance and consideration of what Hennelly terms 'the gnostic quest and the Victorian wasteland'.[10] Gnosticism is a generic term for a range of spiritual beliefs and practices having as their common focus a mystical quest for hidden knowledge of God and the universe; knowledge which cannot be realized through the confines of dogmatic thought. The grail legends similarly reflect the search for psychic growth and spiritual emancipation.

To illustrate, it is constructive to reflect upon the moral decay of late nineteenth-century England, as portrayed in *Dracula*, and Stoker's apparent wish to rehabilitate this Victorian 'wasteland'. Although Transylvania is anaemic in one sense – a 'barren land' (D24:380) drained by Dracula – London in the 1890s is anaemic in another. It presents a *fin de siècle*, smog-bound, decadent culture threatened with moral collapse and in desperate need of redemption before the fresh new century can be born. To Stoker, the Britain of his day was undergoing a profound moral crisis. Van Helsing acts as Stoker's mouthpiece, yearning for a return to pre-sceptical, pre-rationalist times. The traditional values of 'faith' have been eroded, and Hennelly detects in the novel no fewer than six ethical frames of reference: scepticism, transcendentalism, empiricism, criminality, the value of superstitions, and scientific rationalism. As Hennelly explains: 'the small central group of splintered selves is also searching for a new stockpile of communal and personal values.'[11]

Stoker proposes that Transylvania and Victorian London are both 'wastelands',[12] each needing the vitality of the other to heal its own sterility. Irony of ironies, a sceptical community must believe in vampires, with their primitive energies and passions, if the tired, decrepit nineties are to be redeemed. To this end, the novel concludes with a postscript, written seven years after the Count's demise (that is, in the turning year 1900). Stoker's heroes and heroine survey the carnage of the past and look forward with confidence to the hopes of the morrow. These hopes are built around the value of personal faith, not just in vampires, but in the God who provided the means to destroy them. 'Evidence', that accursed accompaniment of modern science, is of no account: 'We want no proofs, we ask none to believe us' (D27:449).

Stoker cultivates an intimate identity between Transylvania and London, between vampirism and Christianity, which cannot be expressed better than in Hennelly's own words:

Dracula's castle is a schizoid dwelling with upper, fashionable apartments and even a Victorian library but also with lower crypts and vaults; while, analogously, Dr Seward's Victorian mansion conceals a lunatic asylum, complete with fledgling vampire, beneath it. Dracula has three lovers; Lucy has three suitors. Dracula hypnotizes; Van Helsing hypnotizes. Dracula sucks blood; Van Helsing transfuses blood; and once, in fact, Seward sucked blood from a gangrenous wound of Van Helsing. Dracula wears Harker's British clothes to steal babies and later in London even wears a 'hat of straw'. Additionally, there is a consistently stressed analogy between vampirism and christianity; and both, given the insights of Frazer ... and Freud's *Totem and Taboo*, seem related to the Oedipal Fisher-King and the wasteland. Thus vampirism deals with 'zoophagy'; christianity with eating the body and drinking of the blood of Christ – the scriptural phrase 'For the blood is the life'. Both employ numerous rituals and complicated liturgy, for example 'the Vampire's baptism of blood'. And lastly, both are locked in a theomachy for control of the world (Crucifix and Host against Demiurge).[13]

Both this Demiurge (Dracula) and his antagonists engage in a climactic quest, journeying to strange lands with strange customs. First to do so is Dracula. In coming to Britain he is engaged upon a quest of his own. The wasteland of Transylvania can offer him no prospects, no battles, no blood. Dracula needs to move with the times. He therefore comes in search of exchanging his 'child-brain' for the 'man-brain' of modern self-awareness.

But his unsavoury activities unleash a counter-quest: the Dracula-hunters embark upon their own journey into the unknown with almost ritualistic secrecy and discipline. On three occasions Van Helsing and his disciples vow to pursue the Count. Their quest formally commences once Lucy has finally been restored to peace. An oath is taken, with everybody in turn taking hold of the professor's hand, whereupon he pronounces: 'And then begins our great quest ... there is a terrible task before us, and once our feet are on the ploughshare, we must not draw back' (D16:261). On a later occasion the inquisitors stand around a table and link hands. They individually swear allegiance in a 'solemn compact' (D18:284-85), suggestive of an initiation ceremony within an occult lodge.

By the time of the third oath, Mina has been 'compromised' by the Count. In this instance all kneel upon the floor, take hands, and swear to be true to one another – all except Mina making a supplementary pledge to raise her veil of sorrow (D22:354). The three oaths, in other words, are made first to Van Helsing, second to the group as a whole, and third by kneeling to God. By this time the Arthurian connections are truly forged. Van Helsing speaks for all: 'We go out as the old knights of the Cross to redeem [Mina's soul] ... we are pledged to set the world free' (D24:381-82). Their quest is not for the grail, but for a spiritual destiny that grants redemptive understanding: 'We shall go to make our search – if I can call it so, for it is not search but knowing [sic]' (D24:374).

The whole novel may be interpreted not as Gothic or Victorian, but as Arthurian and medieval. In *Dracula*, Arthurian chivalry is revealed through the archaic notion of 'comitatus': the retinue of a chieftain bands together and sets forth to fulfil their master's (Van Helsing's) quest.[14] The professor provides a Merlin-like presence. He is alone, without the love and comfort of a family, and buries himself in magic and medicine to offset a life 'barren' of human warmth. King Arthur surfaces as Arthur Holmwood, lending the young aristocrat not only his Christian name but also his wife: both Guinevere and Lucy are expropriated by rivals. The functions of the two Arthurs are also comparable. In earlier days they enjoyed adventures a-plenty; but now the centre of attention has switched to others, of lower social standing – respectively, King Arthur's knights and Holmwood's commoner acquaintances. Good-natured Harker might almost be a reincarnation of Sir Galahad, the purest of the knights and the one who discovers the Grail.

As for Dracula, he is both a corn-god and the Fisher King. The Count direct the elements, just as the ancients supposed their gods could do. He forsakes his own barren land to walk among London's teeming millions, 'like the multitude of standing corn' (D24:380). Like the Fisher King, Dracula has anachronistically outlived himself. Yet he still exudes a primitive life force, of which decadent England, hidebound by its scientific rationalism, is bereft. He must therefore be slain and his energies and vitality

219

re-absorbed if the London wasteland with its swarming population is to be rejuvenated. There is nothing innovative in this concept. Since time immemorial man has slain his gods in order to 'absorb' their powers. And how does Stoker describe the Count's native land after his downfall? 'The castle stood as before, reared high above a waste of desolation' (D27:449).[15] With the withering of Dracula comes the withering of his domain. All traces are wiped away, almost as if they never existed.

Van Helsing appreciates that Dracula's energies are in themselves neutral. They may be used for good or ill: 'For it is not the least of [Dracula's] terrors that this evil thing is rooted deep in all good' (D18:288). The Count's powers may be absorbed and utilized to assist in the creation of a fresh, new century, and one is reminded again that 'there have been from the loins of this very [Dracula] great men' (D18:288). Once again, this focuses attention on Jonathan and Mina's son. Symbolically, the infant will grow to represent twentieth-century manhood, eventually inheriting the renewed wasteland. In Arthurian language he will inherit the mantle of the Fisher King.

Let us reflect on this child's relationship to Dracula. Out of the ashes of one totemic being emerges the conception of another. Young Quincey Harker will certainly be unique, and not just in view of his parents' experiences. Genetically he is alarmingly complex. He is linked to Dracula's adversaries in more than just their names: he also has their blood. Worse, he has that of Dracula flowing through his veins. His mother has sucked the blood of Dracula, who had previously sucked that of Lucy, who had already received transfusions from Seward, Van Helsing, and Holmwood. The only blood *not* in the boy is that of Quincey Morris, his nominal 'father', for Lucy died before she could transmit it to Dracula. Nevertheless, in his matrix of blood-ties, this is no ordinary child, and he will grow into no ordinary man for far more profound reasons than Van Helsing can suspect. This child of the future hints at a demonic parousia.

The diabolical reversal of myth in *Dracula* suggested by the Tarot is reinforced by consideration of the Grail. Fundamental to the Grail myth is the relationship between the vitality of the ailing king and that of his kingdom. The hero must restore the former, and with it the latter. The purpose of Harker's journey to Transylvania, however, is not to heal the Fisher King/Dracula. It is to release the vampire in order that he might drain the living of their blood to regain his youth. Thereafter, the fate of Harker hinges on that of Dracula: the destruction and dissolution of the one is the ecstasy and salvation of the other. In the postscript the reader is introduced to a boy-child. He is not the heir of Jonathan Harker, but a representative of the dark powers at Dracula's command. Here, as elsewhere, Stoker either reverses the classical myth or manipulates it for his own purpose. Either way he acknowledges his debt to the profound mysteries of the Tarot and the Grail.

---

1   Thomas Ray Thornburg, 'The Quester and the Castle: the Gothic Novel as Myth, with Special Reference to Bram Stoker's *Dracula*' pp.108-36.

2   See Thornburg, pp.108-36.

3   Robert Dowse and David Palmer, '"Dracula": the Book of Blood', p.428.

4   Thornburg, p.125.

5   ibid.

6   ibid., p.129.

7   ibid., p.132.

8   Thomas P Walsh, '*Dracula*: Logos and Myth', p.233. Dracula returns to Transylvania on board the *Czarina Catherine*, a vessel named after a woman of legendary sexual appetites.

9   ibid., p.232.

10   Mark M Hennelly Jr, '*Dracula*: the Gnostic Quest and the Victorian Wasteland'.

11   ibid., pp.16-17.

12   *Dracula* was not Stoker's first fictional expression of the 'wasteland'. A threatening wilderness surrounds the kingdom *Under the Sunset*.

13   Hennelly, op. cit., pp.17-18.

14   Brian Murphy, 'The Nightmare of the Dark: the Gothic Legacy of Count Dracula', p.13.

15 Intriguingly, in Stoker's manuscript Dracula's castle disappears
    from sight following a volcanic 'convulsion of the earth'. In the
    published edition, however, the castle is left standing. It is not
    clear why Stoker made this late change. Perhaps he was
    conscious of the similar fate of Poe's *Fall of the House of Usher*.

13

'THE COUNT IS A CRIMINAL'

From the bourgeois point of view, Dracula is ... a manic individualist; from his own point of view ... he is the bearer of the promise of true union, union which transcends death. From the bourgeois point of view, Dracula stands for sexual perversion and sadism; but we also know that what his victims experience at the moment of consummation is joy, unhealthy perhaps but of a power unknown in conventional relationships. Dracula exists and exerts power through right immemorial; Van Helsing and his associates defeat him in the appropriate fashion, through hard work and diligent application, the weapons of a class which derives its existence from labour.

David Punter,
The Literature of Terror, p.260.

In this final perspective on *Dracula*, attention comes back 'down to earth'. The concerns here are not biblical or occult, but social and political. *Dracula* is a valuable period piece, mirroring the ideological strains and tensions that afflicted the Britain of Stoker's middle years. In the following pages class, race, crime, Nazism, Marxism, and the Cold War will be explored. In the process, some understanding will be reached on how the *Dracula* myth has been manipulated for the purposes of twentieth-century propaganda.

As befits the age in which he lived and his own perceived place in the social hierarchy, Bram Stoker was notably class conscious. With the exception of Renfield, the *dramatis personae* of *Dracula* are drawn from the well-to-do, the guardians of the Empire, and the book is shot through with social, class, racial, and sexual prejudices. The novel is unabashedly 'conservative': firstly, death awaits all those who exhibit rebelliousness or independence; secondly, the bourgeois characters at the conclusion revert back to the bliss of the opening – they benefit from no social, as opposed to spiritual, awareness; and thirdly in a more ideological sense. Stoker was writing an ostensibly non-political novel, yet he still creates a work that reinforces the Establishment beliefs of the ruling classes. It has been remarked of Stoker's final fantasy novel *The Lair of the White Worm*: 'the shadow on the edges of bourgeois culture is variously identified as black, mad, primitive, criminal, socially deprived, deviant, crippled, or (when sexually assertive) female'.[1] Likewise in *Dracula*, Stoker's conscious world is rigidly middle class, monogamous, and male dominated – under an all-seeing God. When Renfield is introduced to Morris, Godalming, and Van Helsing he at once recognizes their prized virtues as stemming from, respectively, 'nationality, heredity, and the possession of natural gifts' (D18:292): in other words it helps to be of Anglo-Saxon stock, to possess unearned riches, and to have taken advantage of an élitist (British) education.

Let us glance at some peripheral characters in *Dracula*. Maids and servants scurry about, though the novel is concerned with adventures 'above stairs', not 'below'. Stoker has little patience with those employed in domestic service: he denigrates the ritual of mourning rigidly observed by the 'lower classes' (D12:179); he describes them as untrustworthy and lacking courage when it comes to finding suitable blood-donors (D12:180); and includes among their number a thief – someone who could stoop to stealing a crucifix from a corpse (D13:200).

Stoker's real scorn is reserved for the 'harijans', the untouchables. He seems to flinch every time his demure ladies and gallant gentlemen are forced into social contact with the manual working classes. Their one redeeming feature is their uniform deference to their betters, but each time they are encountered they exhibit the same unspeakable characteristics: uncouthness, illiteracy, peculiar dialects riddled with expletives, excessive drinking, and preparedness to offer favours only for monetary or, better, liquid reward. (In this, their demands are merely parodies of Dracula's: 'First a little refreshment to reward my exertions' (D21:342). His blood is their liquor.) Harker, Stoker's principal alter ego, is of lower social standing than his acquaintances, and he is predictably the most disdainful of those of lower class than himself. He has 'an interview with a surly gatekeeper and a surlier foreman, both of whom were appeased with coin of the realm' (D20:314), and when Harker does encounter a 'good, reliable type of workman' (D20:311) it is only to underline his rarity and obsequiousness.

For their part, the social superiors live according to a kind of cash nexus. 'Money talks' is the dominant unwritten philosophy. Referring to Godalming's funding of their Continental trek, Harker is grateful that 'Judge Moneybags will settle this case, I think!' (D25:397). Mina sighs at the thought of 'the wonderful power of money! What can it do when it is properly applied; and what might it do when basely used' (D26:423). Actually, Mina is not too fussy how it is used. Bribery, for example, is frequently resorted to, and draws no admonition from Stoker. Returning to Transylvania Harker remarks: 'Thank God! this is a country where bribery can do anything, and we are well supplied with money' (D25:397). Ethically, England and Transylvania are on a par: the mere mention of Lord Godalming's title wins him favours from cowering peasants/proletarians in the manner to which Count Dracula has long been accustomed. 'My title will make it all right', his Lordship announces whenever he wishes to break the law or breach confidences (D26:412).

Paradoxically, what might be termed a 'business ethic' surfaces on occasions. On his first arrival in Transylvania, Harker is not deterred by the premonitions of the locals: 'there was *business* to be done, and I could allow nothing to interfere with it' (D1:13). When Seward is acquainted with Harker for the first time, he comments upon his 'quiet, *business*-like' quality (D17:269). Again, when a vow is taken to pursue the Count to the end, Seward notes that the oath was made 'as gravely, and in as *business*-like a way as any other transaction of life' (D18:285; author's italics). Bram Stoker the Lyceum businessman was evidently imbued with the business world's ethos. He was equally favourably disposed to the propriety of inheritance. Harker inherits Mr Hawkins' legal practice, and Godalming, despite his wealth, comes to acquire the Westenra family estate. The unspoken lesson that Stoker teaches is that wealth, and its acquisition, are morally virtuous.

Clearly, too, the novel provides a social lesson. *Dracula* celebrates the middle classes at the expense of the aristocracy. Count Dracula is a fiend incarnate, while Lord Godalming is marginalized, achieving little of note. What he does achieve is to propose marriage to a commoner, Lucy Westenra, as if to reduce his class threat to his bourgeois companions. Godalming has been labelled a 'safe', 'tamed', 'bourgeois', aristocrat.[2]

These archetypal representatives of respectable England implicitly know their place. It would have been as unthinkable for upper-middle-class Lucy to contemplate wedlock with, say, lower-middle-class Harker, as it would have been for schoolma'am Mina to be courted by Holmwood. *Dracula* proscribes socially vertical liaisons – the bedrock of much literary romance. A clear social hierarchy pervades the book. Even in the privacy of their journals, the Harkers persist in respecting their 'betters': they deferentially refer to the socially elevated Lucy Admiration Society as *Dr* Seward, *Mr* Morris, *Lord* Godalming. The questers even speak of their aristocratic foe as 'the Count'. (In this instance Stoker may be alluding to the tradition among occultists of never speaking of malign forces by name for fear of summoning them.)

Yet the novel is not totally static in its hierarchical structure. There is one instance of upward social mobility – Jonathan Harker, and with him his wife. They are 'special' in many ways, not least their shared capacity to survive the attentions of Dracula. Originally a provincial solicitor's clerk, Harker graduates as a fully-fledged solicitor at the commencement of the novel. In time he becomes a partner ('Hawkins & Harker') before inheriting his mentor's legal practice. He also sires the child that represents the light of the twentieth century. Harker, in other words, acquires a fortune beyond his dreams, a wife who is his fairy princess, and a child of the future – pure fairy tale.

Stoker's class prejudices were clearly influenced by the pseudo-sciences of his time, which themselves contributed greatly to the reinforcement of social divisions. In particular, *Dracula* is indebted to the 'science' of physiognomy, which blossomed in the late eighteenth and nineteenth centuries. Pioneered by a Swiss clergyman, John Caspar Lavater, and later modified by Charles

Darwin and many others, physiognomy held that the true character of an individual could be deduced by the structure of the head and body, and from facial expressions and physical gestures. Regarded with disdain nowadays, its practitioners once insisted that the shape and angles of the forehead and the nose, together with the size and contours of the eyes and mouth, constituted reliable guides to the bearer's character. Lavater proposed that a pale face meant susceptibility to sexual pleasures:[3] Dracula complies. As late as 1873, a Dr Joseph Simms, in a quack work entitled *Nature's Revelations of Character*, propagated a distinction between the 'straight' and the 'curly'. Those persons with curly hair, and preferably with rounded features to match, were dismissed as thoughtless and careless, to be avoided at all costs; whereas those blessed with straight hair and straight features were naturally endowed with 'straight' minds.

In *Dracula*, Van Helsing obviously approves of physiognomy (as does Stoker), for the professor comments favourably on Harker's casual deduction of personality from physical features (D14:226). Perhaps Stoker had read Simms, for Dracula has 'curly hair that seemed to curl in its own profusion', and virtually all that is said of the flaccid aristocrat Godalming's appearance is that he is 'curly-haired'. Similarly, the Count's forehead is 'domed', while the good professor's is 'almost straight, then sloping backwards'. Dracula's nose is hooked and curved, 'aquiline', whereas Van Helsing's is 'rather straight'. The Dutchman possesses a 'square chin' to match, and his big, wide-apart eyes are those, according to Simms, of the turtle dove: they signify the morally chaste.

Further instances of Victorian pseudo-science emerge when Van Helsing gives vent to his 'philosophy of crime' (D25:405-6). Criminals, he claims, are all of a type. They are necessarily insane, childish, and incapable of breaking the habits of a lifetime: 'in all countries and at all times' criminals stick to their one practiced criminal art. 'The Count is a criminal and of criminal type', pronounces Mina. Stoker draws upon the theories of contemporary doctors and criminologists to develop his argument. Max Nordau's controversial book *Degeneration* (1893) set out to demonstrate the correlation between genius and moral degeneracy;[4] and Cesare Lombroso, father of modern criminology, had no doubt about the relevance of physiognomy to crime. According to Lombroso, 'born criminals' are physiologically related to their primordial ancestors. In *Criminal Man*, he attributes those of law-breaking predisposition to sensuality, laziness, impulsiveness, and vanity. Referring to the visible hallmarks of the criminal, there is no doubt about the association with Dracula. If Stoker had read Simms, he had certainly assimilated Lombroso:

Harker: '[The Count's] face was ... aquiline, with high bridge of the thin nose and peculiarly arched nostrils.'

Lombroso:'[The criminal's] nose ... is often aquiline like the beak of a bird of prey.'

Harker: 'His eyebrows were very massive, almost meeting over the nose.'

Lombroso:'The eyebrows were bushy and tend to meet across the nose.'

Harker: 'his ears were pale and at the tops extremely pointed.'

Lombroso:'with a protuberance on the upper part of the posterior margin ... a relic of the pointed ear.'[5]

It was a popular Victorian view that societies were afflicted by the criminals they deserved. This implies that as Dracula was the worst possible criminal, England in the 1890s was the worst possible society. Equating vampirism with criminality in this way highlights the virtuousness of those whose lives have been sorely touched by Dracula. Stoker overlooks the fact that most of the book's crimes are performed not by Dracula but by his opponents. This has been expressed succinctly:

Even if Dracula is responsible for all the Evil of which he is accused, he is tried, convicted, and sentenced by men (including two lawyers) who give him no opportunity to explain his actions and who repeatedly violate the laws which they profess to be defending: they avoid an inquest into Lucy's death, break into her tomb and desecrate her body, break into Dracula's houses, frequently resort to bribery and coercion to avoid legal involvement, and openly admit that they are responsible for the deaths of five alleged vampires.[6]

By happy coincidence, the disposal of Dracula and his three consorts is accompanied by their instant dissolution. As Van Helsing cannily explains (D25:398), there is no need to fear prosecution, for without a corpse there is no crime. This is just as well, for the vampires are destroyed outside the law. Dracula and his consorts are the victims of a lynch mob.

None of this invites any moral doubt in the mind of Bram Stoker. His heroes have stooped to imitate Dracula, and have become primitive, violent, and irrational. They play the game he plays, never stopping to reflect upon the probity of their actions. In short, the ethical standards with which Stoker identifies are, upon closer examination, far from comforting.

Stoker's attitudes to race are similarly ambivalent, for there is more than a hint of racial prejudice in *Dracula*. Even the sweeter-than-sweet Lucy is not immune. When she relates to Mina her 'anguish' at receiving three proposals of marriage she recalls *Othello*, and sympathizes with Desdemona having to listen to tales of adventure – 'even by a black man' (D5:74). Gypsies are shown as despicable hirelings of the Count, taking Harker's gold and then betraying him (D4:56); and the one Jewish figure encountered is pure stereotype, down to requisite 'sheep's' nose and a reluctance to impart information except through 'a little bargaining' (D26:415). Furthermore, to Stoker, no country can claim to be civilized if its trains are late, as Transylvania's notably are.

More fundamental to the novel's racial structure is its three foreign imports. None is allowed to speak standard English, which immediately makes them objects of suspicion. The Count, of course, is so malign as totally to deny him the honour of being British. (In none of Stoker's fiction is the villain a true Briton.) Furthermore, Dracula smells! Racism over the centuries frequently harps on the offensive smells supposedly attached to 'foreigners'.

The introduction of a Dutchman and an American seems on the face of it to possess less racial significance, yet Morris's inferiority is persistently demonstrated. Firstly, he is rejected by Lucy in favour of a true-blooded Englishman: secondly, although the provider of raw, frontier courage (itself slightly un-British), the American is dispensed with – cancelled out with the Count – at the climax. Perhaps a trace of nationalism can be detected here: the vulgar Texan is expunged so that the superior English are no longer reminded of America's growing power.

In the case of Van Helsing, Stoker may have felt uncomfortable about permitting an English hero to be of Catholic faith. By pitting a Continental vampire against a Continental vampire-sleuth, Stoker reinforces the alien nature of this demonic invasion. Once Van Helsing has provided enlightenment, he is despatched to the margins of the action, allowing the Anglo-Saxon race the glory of the final scenes.

Throughout, the hard core of Englishness is represented as true grit. Even the insane Renfield is permitted a martyr's death in the cause of saving Mina. Returning to the 'wasteland' theme, the foreign representation in the novel provides the dynamism of which feeble, insular England stands in need.[7] Once that objective has been attained, the foreign intruders can be struck out. Two meet their end, while the third is an old man whose time was the nineteenth century, not the twentieth.

The English axis around which the novel pivots is reinforced by the manner of its telling. None of the foreigners is permitted to keep a diary or supply other written records, save for the odd memorandum of Van Helsing and brief inconsequential letters by Morris. The reader is never made privy to Dracula's thoughts, and is left with his tantalizing statement: 'There is reason that all things are as they are, and did you see with my eyes and know with my knowledge, you would perhaps better understand' (D2:32). Without access to his point of view, the Count is never described 'objectively', but always through the impressionable eyes of others. The same is true of Van Helsing and Morris. This gives rise to a peculiarity in the novel's structure. To give an example: something told to Harker may be passed on to his wife, who might take Van Helsing into her confidence, before he in turn entrusts Seward to record the information on his phonograph. The evidence by then is fifth-hand – and this assumes honest reporting of the most intimate aspects of the diarists' lives, which they know will be read by all. The epistolary framework of the novel, in other words, refracts the testimony of those unable to present their case in their own words. As a result, there is a virtual exclusivity of the English point of view in the provision of primary documentation.

To be precise, there is a virtual exclusivity of the middle-class English point of view, with which Stoker was most able to identify. The bulk of the testimony in *Dracula* is reserved for Harker, Mina, and Seward – solicitor, teacher, and doctor. Stoker can handle the unfamiliar lady of leisure, Lucy, because she is one-dimensional and killed off early. Lord Godalming is effectively neutered. He is allowed to say nothing of importance. As with the three aliens, the reader derives impressions of his Lordship only through the impressions of others. But the case of Renfield is especially curious, for Stoker allows his lunatic the luxury of keeping his own little notebook (D6:88). (The Count has the knack of making all his contacts take up their pencils.) Stoker never allows Seward to divulge the contents of Renfield's scribblings. Irritatingly, Seward will tell only of masses of figures, added up in batches 'as if he were "focusing" some account, as the auditors put it'. What figures? What account? From that moment Renfield's 'diary' is forgotten and does not feature in the accumulating pile of testimony that awaits posterity.

Dracula has been described as reflecting 'alienation', the pathological plight of man in modern industrial society. According to Marxists, alienation results from capitalist exploitation and the division of labour, leading to loss of identity between worker and product. He feels dehumanized, becomes isolated, withdrawn, purposeless, and may end up 'alienated' not only from his work, but also from his fellow men. This may lead to total estrangement from society, and detachment from its prevailing values.

The concept may be borrowed and applied to the Count, who is alienated from everything around him. As a vampire he casts no reflection: metaphysically he has no identity. He is an inversion of man, alienated from mankind. His is an 'epidemic alienation': as in the early, dehumanizing industrial era, he despoils the lives of his victims.[8] Yet when Dracula confides to Harker his longing to walk the streets of London, to be among its whirl and rush of humanity, he alludes to more than just the urge to prey on new victims. In human terms, the Count is lonely. He has no more armies to command, no children to rear; he can no longer 'love', and his castle is surrounded by a wasteland. His loneliness contrasts with the cloying friendships and family sentiments espoused by his pursuers, all of whom would willingly die for each other. Several critics have speculated whether Dracula's quest embraces the hope that he might be defeated and laid to rest in perpetuity. How else, they ask, could such a formidable campaigner be outmanoeuvred by such pathetic opponents?

Renfield, through his incarceration and occasional stints in a 'strait waistcoat', echoes his patron's alienation.[9] Maybe unconscious autobiography lies behind all this. Stoker spent the first thirty years of his life in Dublin, remote from the hub of British artistic and cultural life. He had to contend with the 'alienation' of being a minority Protestant in a Catholic land. Dracula was not alone in coming to teeming London to better himself: Bram Stoker did the same when uprooting from Dublin in 1878. Stoker needed no lessons on the alienating effects of a vast impersonal city. Through handling crates of stage equipment during Irving's many tours, Stoker knew the problems involved in transporting from one country to another Dracula's fifty boxes of earth.

Stoker, we should remember, was no political innocent. His inaugural address to the Trinity Historical Society had been a blueprint for a league of nations of the time. He was a committed supporter of Irish Home Rule and of Gladstonian Liberalism. By and large his fiction steers clear of overt political comment, but there is one notable exception. One of his later thrillers, *The Lady of the Shroud* (1909), opens as another vampire yarn. By the climax, the supernatural has been replaced by the political, for Stoker relates to the ongoing Balkan crisis. Even without any real vampires, *The Lady of the Shroud* resembles *Dracula* in its south-east European setting and in its evocation of Turkish menaces, past or present. The Austro-Hungarian Empire (which embraced Transylvania in the 1890s) was a likely British adversary in any future European war. The Anglo-Dutch-American alliance lined up in *Dracula* against an Austro-Hungarian tyrant provides a dress rehearsal for the First World War.[10]

The Dracula myth has been hailed over the years as justifying all manner of political beliefs. In this, Count Dracula merely emulates Vlad Dracula who, within a century of his death, found his impaling exploits seized upon by Ivan the Terrible in Russia. Vlad had shown himself to be a hero of the Orthodox faith and model of the harsh, autocratic ruler. As such, he was taken to justify Ivan's supposedly divine right to tyranny and sadism.[11]

Marxist critics have alighted on *Dracula* to illustrate the inherent contradictions in capitalism. Through Marxist spectacles the Count presents an extension of feudal *droit de seigneur*, founded on systematic exploitation. He starves the populace and feeds upon them. Back in 1741, the word 'vampire' was employed in English to refer to a tyrant who sucks life from the people.[12] Karl Marx himself was familiar with the vampire metaphor: 'Capital is dead labour that, vampire-like, only lives by sucking living labour, and lives the more, the more labour it sucks.' He also wrote: 'the prolongation of the working day quenches only in a slight degree the vampire thirst for the living blood of labour.'[13]

Seen in this light, the 'vampire' presents a metaphor for capital. Dracula is the archetypal capitalist exploiter, whose objective is the 'possession' of every aspect of his victims' lives. He is not interested in arrangements by 'contract': he demands his slave labour for eternity. Like the vampire, the capitalist's driving force is insatiable and unlimited. Like the vampire, too, the capitalist is unable to break the cycle of continuous exploitation. Neither is propelled so much by the *desire* for blood/wealth as by the *curse* of blood/wealth, and the cycle of endless exploitation. In a striking image, when Harker thrusts a knife at Dracula in Piccadilly, no blood is spilled, but 'a bundle of banknotes and a stream of gold fell out' (D23:364).

As noted previously, Dracula is not a destroyer. He is an accumulator. Moretti describes him as a saver, an ascetic, an upholder of the Protestant ethic.[14] The Count has hoarded his gold for such a plan as now festers in his brain. Armed with his capital he can embark upon his schemes for economic control of the City of London. In this he acts as a perfectly rational entrepreneur. It is noticeable that for several economic groups Dracula presents no conflict of interest. The assorted solicitors, gypsies, seamen, porters, and estate agents with whom he conducts business do very nicely from their client. He pays well, and in cash. In his menial requirements and property deals he is the perfect employer-client. These accomplices have no fear of his sucking their blood: he can buy it.

But Dracula is no common entrepreneur. In his vampiric/ financial dealings he is monopolistic, brooking no competition. 'Like monopoly capital, his ambition is to subjugate the last vestiges of the liberal era and destroy all forms of economic independence.'[15] No wonder he holds such terrors for his complacent, bourgeois competitors. In the name of destroying an agent of the devil, Stoker's heroes are, on a socio-economic reading, ridding themselves of a materializing threat to their bourgeois ideology and prosperity.[16] It is they, representatives of a petty free-trade ethos, whom he is out to subjugate. The vampire/ monopolist permits no independent survival, personal or economic. Unlike Godalming, the 'tamed' aristocrat who accepts the legitimacy of middle-class hegemony, Dracula embodies the anachronistic land-owning class. He seeks to sequestrate the newly-earned privileges of the *nouveaux riches* and reopen the historic struggle between the aristocracy and the bourgeoisie. Feudal monopoly and *laissez faire* capitalism are shown to be irreconcilable, precipitating an economic struggle to the death.

During the 1890s monopolistic capital was more evident in the economies of some of Britain's advanced, industrial competitors. All the more reason why 'monopoly' should appear as a foreign threat and why Van Helsing allies with the British: Holland was a neighbouring sanctuary of free-trade.[17] Yet by the end of the century many economists saw free trade as moribund. The age of the giant, multi-national monopoly was coming. From this angle, the *laissez faire* fanatics seeking to stifle progress are reactionary, attempting to arrest the course of history.[18]

If only for the sake of parity, as Marxism has been read into *Dracula* so has fascism. Elements of Bram Stoker's novel actually found their way into the philosophical underpinnings of Nazi Germany. The late flowering of the Gothic genre unearthed a receptive audience in the German-speaking world. From the depths of her disillusionment following World War One, Germany searched for Teutonic heroes capable of restoring her past glory. Count Dracula offered the perfect model, being of a conquering race and descended from Attila the Hun. Many German authors, among them Hans-Heinz Ewers, were attracted by the potential of the vampire metaphor. The sexual element was exaggerated, and a combination of Nordic myths, Teutonic blood rites, and Wagnerian imagery thrilled the reading public of defeated Germany. Vampires in German literature came to represent superhuman *übermenschen*, whose function was to herald the establishment of a New Order based on blood.[19]

Racist elements of German nationalism were accommodated by German vampire fiction. In the works of Ewers,[20] the undead were depicted not as supermen but as squalid, wandering Jewesses, symbolic of a race seen to be infecting the Continent. Prior to gaining power in 1933, Hitler and the ideologists of the National Socialist Party were happy to utilize any powerful myth for their own ends. Ewers' depiction of sacrilegious blood-lust, and his exultation of pre-Christian, Germanic forms of worship, made him a celebrated author, until he became too much of an embarrassment.[21]

By this time *Dracula* was ripe for a new medium: the screen. The German director F W Mirnau adapted the novel for the silent cinema, resulting in the classic *Nosferatu* (1922). Stoker's widow, however, successfully sued for breach of copyright. All extant copies of the film are pirated.[22]

During World War Two the equation of the Hun-like Dracula with the Hun-like Nazi was gratefully manipulated and exploited by the Allies. The Americans recognized the hate-appeal of Stoker's vampire, who was held to personify German cruelty. American propaganda posters featured a German soldier with canine teeth dripping with blood. To cement the image, free copies of *Dracula* were issued to US forces serving overseas.[23]

With the passing of the years the immortal Count has confirmed his adaptability. After 1945 he proved equally adept at symbolizing the Soviet menace in the Cold War. In the McCarthy era, Dracula switched from representing Nazis to representing Reds. He was no longer the exemplar of capitalism: he was now its staunchest enemy. These turnarounds were assisted by the redrawing of Europe's frontiers. Transylvania was again part of Romania, and conveniently lay behind the Iron Curtain. Dracula was a communist, the bogey-man from the East.

The novel weighs heavily on the distinction between East and West, dark and light, the primitive and the modern. In the book's first paragraph, Harker is aware that beyond 'Buda-Pesth' he is leaving the West and entering the East – that part of Europe indelibly influenced by the Ottoman Empire (and later by the Soviet Union). As his calèche carries him up the Borgo Pass towards Dracula's castle, he notes the dark, rolling clouds overhead, and a heavy, oppressive sense of thunder in the air: 'It seemed as though a mountain range had separated two atmospheres, and that now we had got into the thunderous one' (D1:18). To the cloistered Harker, everything that is civilized and enlightened about the West is being left behind. In the 1890s, no less than today, the upright citizen of the West is alarmed by the concealed terrors of the East.

Dracula as Cold war parable equates the demonic Count with the threat of Soviet expansionism. Both present a material threat to the Western world.[24] Neither intends to further its ends by outright invasion, which carries too many risks. Subversion is the chosen instrument. The complacent defences of the West are not attacked by storm but infiltrated by stealth – though the common aim is the subjugation of the West into East European colonies/ vampires. Furthermore, just as communist subversion focuses on the industrial work-force, so Dracula focuses on women, creating in effect a 'fifth column' to assist his schemes. Dracula is now a Red under the Bed, as well as a vampire hovering above it. His subversive strategy is revealed in his painstaking legal preparations, so as not to arouse suspicion in the British police or legal profession. He ensures he has numerous hideaways. He does not permit any of his unwitting collaborators (solicitors, estate agents, etc.) to know the identities, far less the duties, of the others (D3:43-44). For that reason he employs an Exeter solicitor to purchase a house in London, while he himself arrives at Whitby.

The moral of the Cold War is that constant vigilance must be maintained. If not, the vampire/communist will exploit the complacency that results from the West's rapid scientific and technological progress. The West's smug superiority discounts the possibility of subversion, and is further undermined by British law – the 'innocent until proven guilty' philosophy that hands Dracula a ticket to success. Van Helsing and his clique dare not publicize the danger for fear of ridicule. They are therefore compelled to act as clandestinely on their part as Dracula does on his, and to succeed must operate outside the law.

Van Helsing's hawkishness is manifested in his strictures against Seward's naïve liberalism: 'Do you not think that there are things which you cannot understand, and yet which are; that some people see things that others cannot?' (D14:229). Van Helsing is referring to hidden knowledge shared only with Dracula: he seeks to override 'rational' objection so that he can perform his desecrations without opposition. Dissenters against the McCarthy excesses were swept aside in ways uncomfortably comparable.[25] Importantly, the war against Dracula is spearheaded by a specialist of the mind, well able to manipulate the inarticulate fears of honest citizens for devious ends. An attack on Light-of-the-West Lucy must be avenged by the full weight of Western revenge.

Intruding into this analysis is the twist provided by Quincey Morris, the embodiment of the United States. Perhaps Stoker was challenging America to end her isolationist policies, and to involve herself in world affairs.[26] Renfield articulates this idea when, in a bubble of sanity, he comments on the Monroe Doctrine (D18:291) – an axiom of American foreign policy dating from 1823, but operational for a century thereafter. In essence, the Monroe Doctrine decreed that Europe should stay out of American affairs, and the United States would reciprocate. The effects of this policy hindered Anglo-American understanding and contributed to the mutual ignorance that prompted Stoker to write *A Glimpse of America*. Renfield probably speaks Stoker's thoughts, looking forward optimistically to the day 'when the Pole and the Tropics may hold allegiance to the Stars and Stripes' (D18:291).

Actually, Stoker did not have long to wait. The year of *Dracula*'s publication, 1897, also marked Diamond Jubilee Year, celebrating sixty years of Queen Victoria's reign. The year was awash with imperial pageantry and festival. The British Empire, although actually in decline, had never appeared stronger. But across the Atlantic the American giant was beginning to stir. *Dracula* becomes in retrospect prophetic of the Spanish-American War of 1898, often taken to mark the United States' inauguration into global power-politics. By the end of Stoker's life the United States was poised to supersede Europe's ageing empires, including the Austro-Hungarian which Dracula represents.[27] In the novel Morris provides military aid to the effete Europeans in the form of Winchester rifles (D25:396). America thereby becomes the arms supplier of the free world in fiction not long before she does so in fact.

It might even be said that the Texan declares war on Dracula with the objective of seeking US supremacy over the Old World. American fails in the novel, only to succeed in the real world in the course of the next decades. Some might say America has come to colonize Britain as effectively as Dracula once aspired to do. Morris's spirit has been recycled to flourish militarily and financially over the succeeding generations.[28] America is the land of the future, just as Quincey lends his name to the child of the future.

Ideologically, it is the West's collective resources that must be seen to prevail, the alliance of free men and women. No independent hero (no forerunner of Rambo) will slay Dracula, rather a corporate body in which everybody plays their part in the downfall of the 'solitary' Count. The totalitarian monolith has embarked on an inversed imperialistic quest – 'the primitive trying to colonize the civilized world'[29] He must meet his match in the power of combination, the power that emanates from the democratic, committee-style 'Council of War' (D18:285; 26:420). The Western partners would imperil their security should they break ranks. Disorganized individuals are easy prey to the concentrated energy of the vampire/communism. Only once the alliance is forged, in the second half of the novel, is Dracula confronted by an adversary whose combined strength is superior to that of its constituent elements.

The NATO allies in Dracula (Britain, the United States, and the Netherlands) possess two other decisive advantages over their Eastern adversary. The first is their freedom of thought and action. The Dracula-hunters perceive themselves as having 'self-devotion to a cause and an end to achieve which is not a selfish one' (D18:285). That is, they want to save the world, or so they think, not control it. Even Stoker's mode of address – diaries, letters, journals, etc. – emphasizes the individuality that the vampire threatens to subjugate. These pluralistic perceptions are then collated, and at once the tables start to turn.

The second advantage relates to scientific ingenuity and progress. The East, then as now, is described as lacking sophisticated technological hardware. Transylvania is behind the times, rundown, unable to advance beyond traditional crafts and practices. Britain, however, is portrayed in *Dracula* as a veritable showpiece of efficiency and modern engineering. Mina taps away on her typewriter, Seward goes one better and records his diary on to a phonograph, Harker takes advantage of a telephone, and Morris is an amateur photographer. Throughout, letters and telegrams are delivered with improbable despatch. It comes as no surprise that armed with these weapons – social, political, psychological, technological – ultimate victory for the West is assured.

---

1   Rosemary Jackson, *Fantasy: the Literature of Subversion*, p.121.
2   Burton Hatlen, 'The Return of the Repressed/Oppressed in Bram Stoker's *Dracula*', p.83.
3   Ornella Volta, *The Vampire*, p.145.
4   See the discussion on evolutionary degeneration in Chapter 11.
5   Reproduced in Leonard Wolf, *The Annotated Dracula*, p.300.

6   Carol A Senf, '*Dracula*: the Unseen Face in the Mirror', p.163.

7   Mark M Hennelly Jr, '*Dracula*: the Gnostic Quest and the Victorian Wasteland', p.22.

8   R W Johnson, 'The Myth of the Twentieth Century', p.433.

9   Royce MacGillivray, '"Dracula": Bram Stoker's Spoiled Masterpiece', pp.525-26.

10   Richard Astle, 'Dracula as Totemic Monster: Lacan, Freud, Oedipus and History', p.103.

11   See Gabriel Ronay, *The Dracula Myth*, pp.149-55.

12   Ernest Jones, in Christopher Frayling (ed.), *The Vampyre: Lord Ruthven to Count Dracula*, p.327.

13   Karl Marx, *Das Capital*, Chapter X.

14   Franco Moretti, *Signs Taken for Wonders: Essays in the Sociology of Literary Forms*, p.91.

15   ibid., p.92.

16   Jackson, p.122.

17   See Moretti, p.93.

18   ibid., p.94.

19   Ronay, pp.157-59.

20   For example: *The Sorcerer's Apprentice* (1910), *The Vampire* (1921), *Nightmare* (1922).

21   Ronay, pp.159-60.

22   Harry Ludlam, *A Biography of Bram Stoker: Creator of Dracula*, p.190.

23   Ronay, p.166.

24   See Richard Wasson, 'The Politics of Dracula'.

25   See Ronay, p.169.

26   Wasson, p.26.

27   See Astle, p.103.

28   Moretti, pp.251-52.

29   Senf, op. cit., p.164.

Postscript

'Rubbish Watson, rubbish! What have we to do with walking corpses who can only be held in their graves by stakes driven through their hearts? It's pure lunacy.'

'But surely', said I, 'the vampire was not necessarily a dead man? A living person might have had the habit. I have read, for example, of the old sucking the blood of the young in order to retain their youth.'

'You are right, Watson. It mentions the legend in one of these references. But are we to give serious attention to such things? This agency stands flat footed upon the ground, and there it must remain. The world is big enough for us. No ghosts need apply.'

Sherlock Holmes,
in Sir Arthur Conan Doyle, 'The Adventure of the Sussex Vampire'.

Sherlock Holmes may not have been impressed by vampires, but then he had never met Count Dracula.[1] Bram Stoker's creation has taken hold of the twentieth-century imagination like almost no other fictional being. Dracula belongs with a select group of characters – Frankenstein, Sherlock Holmes himself, Mickey Mouse, Tarzan, James Bond – who have become part of the popular mythology of our age. No fictional detective can compare with Holmes: nor can any dark figure from hell claim to match Dracula in the possession of unbridled wickedness. Yet he is even more universal than his mythical rivals. He can cross language and cultural barriers with ease. The cinema has transported him to all corners of the globe, where he presents a stark image of darkness, of death, of evil.

The previous chapters have attempted to illuminate the sources of Dracula's power; to explore the numerous competing interpretations that can be made of the novel; and thereby seek to substantiate the claim that measured in cultural terms *Dracula* stands as one of the richest of English novels to appear within the last hundred years. The cultural impact of *Dracula* lies all around us. One may buy 'Count Dracula ice lollies': children may watch 'Count Duckula' and 'Bunnicula' on television. And what else is Batman but the Count cleansed of his evil and endowed with a social conscience?

How would one summarize the novel's appeal and its pervasive power and imagery? Some critics have suggested that Dracula reminds us of the dark side of ourselves; that in each of us there exists a hidden, repressed, ferocious quality that we recognize in him. He panders to man's morbid excitement at the prospect of sadistic pleasures. For others, Dracula is a figure to envy. Men yearn for his seductive power; women yearn to be seduced by him. His masculinity is another source of envy: he goes in fear of nobody and is able to command and manipulate people at his imperious whim. In short, he provides a ready model for a society such as ours, eager to exploit corrupt power and sexual titillation, and to celebrate passion at the expense of restraint.

But Dracula does more then this. At a time of increasing secularization in the industrialized world, he serves to unite the world-views of East and West, preaching transmigration, rebirth, and immortality. He also serves to reassure the elderly. In their fantasies they can become young, as he has. In any case, why worry about death if it is as he describes? In death there is no pain, no decay, no hell; rather a world of voluptuous physical excess. More subtly, *Dracula* fascinates because of its irreverence towards clear-cut boundaries. The novel blurs the distinction between the natural and the supernatural, between life and death, good and evil, dream and reality, desire and loathing, love and lust. It blurs the Oedipal configuration, and – in Lucy's case – the question of personal identity. It blurs the demarcation between man and beast: lizards, not humans, can crawl head-first down castle walls.

Dracula is also a vehicle for Stoker's obsessive ambivalence towards women, and their lighter and darker aspects. Punter adds this assessment:

It is hard to summarize *Dracula*, for it is such a wide-ranging book, but in general it is fair to say that its power derives from its dealings with taboo … [which] Dracula blurs … He blurs the line between man and beast … he blurs the line between man and God … and he blurs the line between man and woman by demonstrating the existence of female passion.[2]

Flouting taboos has always presented sources of illicit pleasure in literature, but perhaps nowhere quite so outspokenly and un-ashamedly as in *Dracula*.

---

[1] This deficiency has been remedied in two novels: Fred
    Saberhagen, *The Holmes-Dracula File* (1978); Loren D
    Estleman, *Sherlock Holmes Vs Dracula* (1979).

[2] David Punter, *The Literature of Terror*, pp.262-63.

Select Bibliography

Articles

Norman Adams, 'Bram Stoker', *Leopard*, 2:8, 22 June 1976.

Richard Astle, 'Dracula as Totemic Monster: Lacan, Freud, Oedipus and History', *Sub-Stance* 25, 1980.

C F Bentley, 'The Monster in the Bedroom: Sexual Symbolism in Bram Stoker's *Dracula*', *Literature and Psychology* 22, 1972.

Joseph S Bierman, 'Dracula: Prolonged Childhood Illness, and the Oral Triad', *American Imago* 29, 1972.

—, 'The Genesis and Dating of "Dracula" from Bram Stoker's Working Notes', *Notes and Queries* 24, Jan-Feb 1977.

Charles S Blinderman, 'Vampurella: Darwin and Count Dracula', *Massachusetts Review* 21, Summer 1980.

Wanda Bonewits, 'Dracula, the Black Christ', *Gnostica* 4:7, March-May 1975.

Thomas B Byers, 'Good Men and Monsters: The Defences of *Dracula*', *Literature and Psychology*, 31:4 1981

M M Carlson, 'What Stoker Saw: An Introduction to the History of the Literary Vampire', *Folkore Forum*, 10:2, 1977.

Christopher Craft, '"Kiss Me with Those Red Lips": Gender and Inversion in Bram Stoker's *Dracula*', *Representations*, 8 1984.

Bernard Davies, 'Mountain Greenery', The Dracula Journals, 1:1, Winter 1976-77.

Stephanie Demetrakopoulos, 'Feminism, Sex Role Exchanges, and Other Subliminal Fantasies in Bram Stoker's *Dracula*', *Frontiers: A Journal of Women's Studies*, 2:3, 1977.

Peter Denman, 'Le Fanu and Stoker: A Probable Connection', *Eire-Ireland (Irish American Cultural Institute)* 9, Autumn 1974.

Robert E Dowse and David Palmer, '"Dracula": the Book of Blood', *The Listener*, 7 March 1963.

James Drummond, 'Bram Stoker's Cruden Bay', *Scots Magazine*, April 1976.

—, 'Dracula's Castle', *The Scotsman*, 26 June 1976.

—, 'The Mistletoe and the Oak', *Scots Magazine*, October 1977.

—, 'The Scottish Play', *The Scottish Review*, 23 August 1981.

Paul Dukes, 'Dracula: Fact, Legend and Fiction', *History Today* 32, July 1982.

Ernest Fontana, 'Lombroso's Criminal Man and Stoker's *Dracula*',

Victorian Newsletter, 66, 1984.

Christopher Frayling, 'Vampyres', *London Magazine*, 14:2, June-July 1974.

Carrol L Fry, 'Fictional Conventions and Sexuality in *Dracula*', *Victorian Newsletter* 42, 1972.

Jean Gattegno, 'Folie, Croyance et Fantastique dans "Dracula",' *Littérature* 8, December 1972.

Gail Griffin, '"Your girls that You all Love are Mine": *Dracula* and the Victorian Male Sexual Imagination', *International Journal of Women's Studies*, 3:5 1980.

Burton Hatlen, 'The Return of the Repressed/Oppressed in Bram Stoker's *Dracula*', *The Minnesota Review* 15, 1980.

Mark M Hennelly Jr, '*Dracula*: the Gnostic Quest and the Victorian Wasteland', *English Literature in Transition*, 20:1, 1977.

—, 'Twice Told Tales of Two Counts', *Wilkie Collins Society Journal* 2, 1982.

Gwyneth Hood, 'Sauron and Dracula', *Mythlore*, 52, 1987.

Eric Irvin, 'Dracula's Friends and Forerunners', *Quadrant*, 135, 1978.

Alan Johnson, 'Bent and Broken Necks: Signs of Design in Stoker's *Dracula*', *Victorian Newsletter*, 72, 1987.

—, '"Dual Life": The Status of Women in Stoker's *Dracula*', *Tennessee Studies in Literature*, 27, 1984.

E Randolph Johnson, 'The Victorian Vampire', *Baker St Journal* 18, December 1968.

Roger Johnson, 'The Bloofer Ladies', *The Dracula Journals* 1:4, Summer 1982.

R W Johnson, 'The Myth of the Twentieth Century', *New Society*, 9 December 1982.

Bacil F Kirtley, '*Dracula*, the Monastic Chronicles and Slavic Folklore', *Midwest Folklore* 6:3, 1956.

Royce MacGillivray, '"Dracula": Bram Stoker's Spoiled Masterpiece, *Queen's Quarterly* 79, 1972.

Lionel Milgrom, 'Vampires, Plants, and Crazy Kings', *New Scientist*, 26 April 1984.

Agnes Murgoci, 'The Evil Eye in Roumania, and its Antidotes', *Folklore* 34, 1923.

—, 'The Vampire in Roumania', *Folklore* 37, 1926.

Brian Murphy, 'The Nightmare of the Dark: the Gothic Legacy of Count Dracula', *Odyssey* 1, 1976.

Grigore Nandris, 'A Philological Analysis of *Dracula* and Rumanian Placenames and Masculine Personal Names in -a/-ea', *Slavonic and East European Review* 37, 1959.

—, 'The Historical Dracula: The Theme of His Legend in the Western and in the Eastern Literatures of Europe', *Comparative Literature Studies* 3:4, 1966.

Felix J Oinas, 'Heretics as Vampires and Demons in Russia', *Slavic and East European Journal* 22, Winter 1978.

Robert Phillips, 'The Agony and the Ecstasy: A Jungian Analysis of Two Vampire Novels, Meredith Ann Pierce's *The Darkangel* and Bram Stoker's *Dracula*', *West Virginia University Philological Papers*, 31, 1986.

Christopher Gist Raible, 'Dracula: Christian Heretic', *The Christian Century* 96, 31 January 1979.

Maurice Richardson, 'The Psychoanalysis of Ghost Stories', *Twentieth Century* 166, December 1956.

Phyllis A Roth, 'Suddenly Sexual Women in Bram Stoker's *Dracula*', *Literature and Psychology* 27, 1977.

Ronald Schleifer, 'The Trap of the Imagination; the Gothic Tradition, Fiction, and "The Turn of the Screw",' *Criticism* 22, Autumn 1980.

David Seed, 'The Narrative Method of *Dracula*', *Nineteenth Century Fiction*, 40:1 1985.

Carol A Senf, '*Dracula*: the Unseen face in the Mirror', *Journal of Narrative Technique*, 1979.

—, '"Dracula": Stoker's Response to the New Woman', *Victorian Studies* 26:1, Autumn 1982.

Seymour Shuster, 'Dracula and Surgically Induced Trauma in Children', *British Journal of Medical Psychology* 46, 1973.

Gerard Stein, '"Dracula" ou la Circulation du "Sans",' *Littérature* 8, December 1972.

John Allen Stevenson, 'A Vampire in the Mirror: The Sexuality of *Dracula*', *PMLA*, 103:2, 1988.

Bram Stoker, 'The Censorship of Fiction', *Nineteenth Century*, 64, September 1908.

Philip Temple, 'The Origins of Dracula', *The Times Literary Supplement*, 4 November 1983.

James Twitchell, 'The Vampire Myth', *American Imago* 37, 1980.

Geoffrey Wall, '"Different from Writing": *Dracula* in 1897', *Literature and History*, 10:1, 1984.

Thomas P Walsh, '*Dracula*: Logos and Myth', *Research Studies* 47:4, December 1979.

Richard Wasson, 'The Politics of Dracula', *English Language in Transition* 9:1, 1966.

Judith Weissman, 'Women and Vampires: *Dracula* as a Victorian Novel', *Midwest Quarterly*, 18:4, 1977.

Books

Lory Adler and Richard Dalby, *The Dervish of Windsor Castle: The Life of Arminius Vambery*, Bachman and Turner (London, 1979).

Glen St John Barclay, *Anatomy of Horror: Masters of Occult Fiction*, Weidenfeld & Nicolson (London, 1978).

Austin Brereton, *The Life of Henry Irving*, 2 Vols, Longmans, Green London, 1908).

Margaret Carter (ed.), *Dracula: the Vampire and the Critics*, UMI Research Press (Ann Arbor, Michegan, 1988).

Basil Copper, *The Vampire: In Legend, Fact and Art*, Hale (London, 1973).

Richard Dalby, *Bram Stoker: A Bibliography of First Editions*, Dracula Press (London, 1983).

Hamilton Deane and John Balderston, *Dracula: the Vampire Play in Three Acts*, Samuel French Inc. (New York, 1960).

Daniel Farson, *The Man Who Wrote Dracula: A Biography of Bram Stoker*, Michael Joseph (London, 1975).

Leslie Fielder, *Freaks: Myths and Images of the Secret Self*, Simon and Schuster (New York, 1978).

Radu Florescu and Raymond T McNally, *Dracula: A Bibliography*, Hale (London, 1973).

Christopher Frayling (ed.), *The Vampyre: Lord Ruthven to Count Dracula*, Gollancz (London, 1978).

Nancy Garden, *Vampires*, Lippincott (London, 1973).

Michael Geare and Michael Corby, *Dracula's Diary*, Buchan and Enright (London, 1982).

Donald F Glut, *The Dracula Book*, Scarecrow Press (New York, 1975).

Peter Haining (ed.), *The Dracula Scrapbook*, New English Library (London 1976).

—, *The Leprechaun's Kingdom*, Pictorial Presentations/Souvenir Press (London, 1979).

—, *Shades of Dracula: The Uncollected Stories of Bram Stoker*, William Kimber (London, 1982).

Bernhardt J Hurwood, *Vampires*, Omnibus Press (London, 1981).

Laurence Irving, *Henry Irving: The Actor and his World*, Faber and Faber (London, 1951).

Rosemary Jackson, *Fantasy: The Literature of Subversion*, Methuen (London, 1981).

Clive Leatherdale, *The Origins of Dracula: The Background to Bram*

Stoker's Gothic Masterpiece, William Kimber (London, 1987).

Harry Ludlam, *A Biography of Bram Stoker: Creator of Dracula*, New English Library (London, 1977).

Elizabeth MacAndrew, *The Gothic Tradition in Fiction*, Columbia University Press (New York, 1979).

Andrew MacKenzie, *Dracula Country: Travels and Folk Beliefs in Romania*, Arthur Barker (London, 1977).

—, *Romanian Journey*, Hale (London, 1983).

Raymond T McNally and Radu Florescu, *In Search of Dracula*, New York Graphic Society (Connecticut, 1972).

—, *The Essential Dracula*, Mayflower Books, (New York, 1979).

Raymond T McNally, *Dracula Was a Woman*, Hale (London, 1984).

Anthony Masters, *The Natural History of the Vampire*, Hart-Davis (London, 1972).

Franco Moretti, *Signs Taken for Wonders: Essays in the Sociology of Literary Forms*, New Left Books/Verso (London, 1983).

Charles Osborne (ed,), *The Bram Stoker Bedside Companion*, Quartet (London, 1974).

Sean O'Sullivan, *The Folklore of Ireland*, Batsford (London, 1974).

Barrie Pattison, *The Seal of Dracula*, Lorimer Publishing (London, 1975).

David Pirie, *The Vampire Cinema*, Hamlyn (London, 1977).

John Polidori, *The Vampyre*, Gubblecote Press, (Tring, Herts, 1973).

Mario Praz, *The Romantic Agony*, Oxford University Press (London, 1933).

David Punter, *The Literature of Terror*, Longman (London, 1980).

John R Reed, *Victorian Conventions*, Ohio University Press (Ohio, 1975).

Martin V Riccardo, *Vampires Unearthed: the Complete Multi-Media Vampire and Dracula Bibliography*, Garland Publishing

Gabriel Ronay, *The Dracula Myth*, W H Allen (London, 1972).

Phyllis A Roth, *Bram Stoker*, Twayne Publishers, G K Hall (Boston, 1982).

Raymond Rudorff, *The Dracula Archives*, Sphere (London, 1973).

Penelope Shuttle and Peter Redgrove, *The Wise Wound: Menstruation and Everywoman*, Gollancz (London, 1978).

Jacob Sprenger and Heinrich Kramer, *Malleus Maleficarum* (translated by Montague Summers), Arrow (London, 1971).

Nicolai Stoicescu, *Vlad Tepes: Prince of Walachia*, Academy of the Socialist Republic of Romania (Bucharest, 1978).

Bram Stoker, *The Duties of Clerks of Petty Sessions in Ireland*, Published by Authority (Dublin, 1879).

—, *Under the Sunset*, Sampson Low (London, 1881).

—, *A Glimpse of America*, Sampson Low (London, 1886).

—, *The Snake's Pass*, Sampson Low (London, 1890).

—, *The Watter's Mou'*, Constable (Westminster, 1895).

—, *The Shoulder of Shasta*, Constable (Westminster, 1895).

—, *Dracula*, Constable (Westminster, 1897).

—, *Miss Betty*, Pearson (London, 1898).

—, *The Mystery of the Sea*, Heinemann (London, 1902).

—, *The Jewel of Seven Stars*, Heinemann (London, 1903).

—, *The Man*, Heinemann (London, 1905).

—, *Personal Reminiscences of Henry Irving*, 2 Vols, Heinemann (London, 1906).

—, *Lady Athlyne*, Heinemann (London, 1908).

—, *Snowbound: The Record of a Theatrical Touring Party*, Collier (London, 1908).

—, *The Lady of the Shroud*, Heinemann (London, 1909).

—, *Famous Impostors*, Sidgwick and Jackson (London, 1910).

—, *The Lair of the White Worm*, Rider (London, 1911).

—, *Dracula's Guest – and Other Weird Stories*, Routledge (London, 1914).

Douglas Oliver Street, 'Bram Stoker's "Under the Sunset" with Introductory Biographical and Critical Material (unpublished PhD thesis), University of Nebraska-Lincoln (1977).

Montague Summers, *The Gothic Quest*, The Fortune Press (London, .

—, *The Vampire: His Kith and Kin*, Kegan Paul (London, 1928).

—, *The Vampire in Europe*, Kegan Paul (London, 1929).

Thomas Ray Thornburg, 'The Quester and the Castle: the Gothic Novel as Myth, with Special Reference to Bram Stoker's Dracula' (unpublished PhD thesis), Ball State University (1970).

James B Twitchell, *The Living Dead: A Study of the Vampire in Romantic Literature*, Duke University Press (North Carolina, 1981).

—, *Dreadful Pleasures: An Anatomy of Modern Horror*, Oxford University Press (London, 1985).

Devendra P Varma, *The Gothic Flame*, Arthur Barker (London, 1957).

—, *Introduction to Varney the Vampire; or, the Feast of Blood*, Arno Press (New York, 1970).

Ornella Volta, *The Vampire*, Tandem Books (London, 1965).

Leonard Wolf, *The Annotated Dracula*, New English Library (London, 1975).

—, *A Dream of Dracula*, Little, Brown and Co (Boston, 1972).

Dudley Wright, *Vampires and Vampirism*, Rider (London, 1924).

Bram Stoker's Sources listed in his Working Notes

Rev Sabine Baring-Gould MA, *The Book of Were-Wolves: Being an Account of a Terrible Superstition*, Smith, Elder & Co (London, 1865).

—, *Curious Myths of the Middle Ages*, Rivingtons (London, 1877).

—, *Germany, Present and Past,* (2 Vols), Kegan Paul, Trench (London, 1879).

—, *Curiosities of Olden Times*, John Grant (Edinburgh, 1895).

Fletcher S Bassett (Lieutenant US Navy), *Legends and Superstitions of the Sea and of Sailors – in all Lands and at all Times*, Sampson Low (London, 1885).

Isabella L Bird, *The Golden Chersonese*, John Murray (London, 1883).

Charles Boner, *Transylvania: Its Products and its People*, Longmans, Green, Reader and Dyer (London, 1865).

Sir Thomas Browne, *Religio Medici.*

Andrew F Crosse, *Round About the Carpathians*, Blackwood (London, 1878).

Rushton M Dorman, *The Origin of Primitive Superstitions: And Their Development into the Worship of Spirits and the Doctrine of Spiritual Agency Among the Aborigines of America*, Lippincott & Co (London, 1881).

A Fellow of the Carpathian Society, *'Magyarland': Being the Narrative of our Travels Through the Highlands and Lowlands of Hungary*, (2 Vols), Sampson Low (London, 1881).

Emily Gerard, 'Transylvanian Superstitions' *The Nineteenth Century*, July 1885.

Major E C Johnson MAI, FRHistS, *On the Track of the Crescent: Erratic Notes from the Piraeus to Pesth*, Hurst and Blackett (London, 1885).

John Jones, *The Natural and the Supernatural: Or, Man – Physical, Apparitional and Spiritual*, H Balliere (London, 1861).

William Jones FSA, *Credulities Past and Present*, Chatto and Windus (London, 1880).

—, *History and Mystery of Precious Stones*, Richard Bentley & Son (London, 1880).

Rev W Henry Jones, and Lewis L Kropf, *The Folk-Tales of the Magyars*, Elliot Stock (London, 1889).

Henry Charles Lea, *Superstition and Force – Essays on: The Wager of Law, The Wager of Battle, The Ordeal, and Torture*, H C Lea

(Philadelphia, 1878).

Rev Frederick George Lee DCL, Vicar of All Saints', Lambeth, *The Other World: Or, Glimpses of the Supernatural – Being Facts, Records and Traditions* (2 Vols), Henry S King and Co (London, 1875).

Henry Lee FLS, FGS, FZS, Sometime Naturalist of the Brighton Aquarium, *Sea Fables Explained*, William Clowes and Sons (London, 1883).

—, *Sea Monsters Unmasked*, William Clowes and Sons (London, 1883).

Sarah Lee (sometimes classified under her former name, Mrs Bowdich), *Anecdotes of Habits and Instincts of Birds, Reptiles and Fishes*, Lindsay Blalmston (Philadelphia, 1853).

—, (see also *Anecdotes of Habits and Instincts of Animals*, Lindsay Blalmston, Philadelphia, 1853).

L F Alfred Maury (no titles given, but probably include the following), *Essai sur les Légendes Pieuses du Moyen-Age*, Chez Ladrange (Paris, 1843).

—, *La Magie et L'Astrologie dans L'Antiquité et au Moyen Age: ou, Étude sur les Superstitions Païennes qui sont Perpétuées jusqu'à jours*, Didier et Cie (Paris, 1860).

—, *Le Sommeil et Les Rêves: Études Psychologiques sur ces Phénomènes et les divers États qui s'y Rattachent*, Didier et Cie (Paris, 1865).

Herbert Mayo MD, *On the Truths contained in Popular Superstitions – with an Account of Mesmerism*, William Blackwood and Sons (London 1851).

Thomas Pettigrew FRS, FSA, *On Superstitions connected with the History and Practice of Medicine and Surgery*, John Churchill (London, 1844).

Rev Albert Réville DD, *The Devil: His Origin, Greatness and Decadence*, Williams and Norgate (London, 1871).

F C and J Rivington, *The Theory of Dreams*, (2 Vols), 62 St Paul's Churchyard (London, 1808).

F K Robinson, *A Whitby Glossary*, 1876.

Robert H Scott MA FRS, Secretary of the Meterological Office, *Fishery Barometer Manual*, HMSO (London, 1887).

William Wilkinson, Late British Consul Resident at Bukorest, *An Account of the Principalities of Wallachia and Moldavia: with various Political Observations Relating to Them*, Longman, Hurst (London 1820).

Index